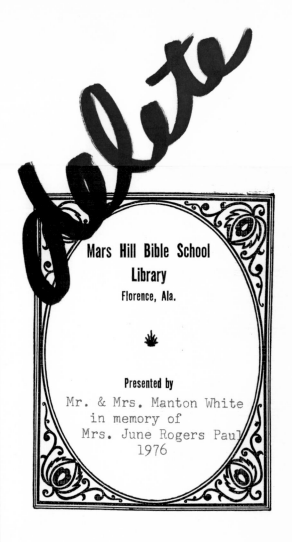

Benton Cordell Goodpasture

The Anchor That Holds

A Biography of
Benton Cordell Goodpasture

by

J. E. CHOATE

Gospel Advocate Company
Nashville, Tennessee
1971

TO:

MARIE

JERRY   TERESA

Contents

Preface

Before the reader begins reading this book, a few words of explanation are necessary. The occasion for this biography is not just to tell the story of the life of B. C. Goodpasture. Large numbers of eminently good and useful men enjoy great success in every generation. The occasion for this study grows out of the crucial need to relate a long chapter in Restoration history among the churches of Christ. B. C. Goodpasture has played a major and key role in the phenomenal growth and worth of the church of Christ in this century. And to accord him a place in the restoration of New Testament Christianity in a major position alongside of Alexander Campbell, Tolbert Fanning, and David Lipscomb does not grow out of the excited admiration and excitement of the author. *The Anchor That Holds* will document this patent fact of church history to any fair minded and informed person.

Since no person is able to work alone, I am constrained to pay some debts of personal appreciation. J. Roy Vaughan has been of inestimable help for his vast store of personal information and in proof reading the manuscript in its formative stages until its completion. H. Clyde Hale has re-lived in memory some of the most significant parts of this study.

I am appreciative to Lewis S. Maiden for reading my manuscript twice and writing the *Introduction* and for his words of encouragement. And to Pat Lutes, our next door neighbor, who is a Nashville school teacher and a summer worker in the Advocate editorial offices, I owe a special debt of thanks for typing chapters of this biography in times of pressing need.

And to a considerable number of people whose names do not appear in this book, who will find their words written in the *Gospel Advocate* and other places, embedded, mirrored, and paraphrased in this study, I only regret that I could not recognize each source of information. I acknowledge my benevolent plagiarism since you would not deny my saying what should be said about our friend.

I am duly appreciative to President Athens Clay Pullias of David Lipscomb College where I have taught for twenty-five years for the complete freedom which I have enjoyed to write and to speak within the security and the high respect which this Christian college enjoys in both high and low places of this nation.

For the never failing source of supplies and countless hours of student help and for his awareness of the time consuming work on my part, I offer thanks to Dean Mack Wayne Craig of the college.

Vice-President Willard Collins, whose recognition and personal encouragement of my writing go back to 1955 at which time I held a copy of my first published book in hand, will be the recipient of my gratitude as long as my memory lasts.

And finally in a personal way, I am grateful to B. C. Goodpasture because he made it possible for me to co-author the biography of H. Leo Boles, to author the life of Marshall Keeble, and now his own biography. For families to open their personal archives to any person is a sacred trust. I appreciate B. C. Goodpasture for another worth and each staff writer will bear me record. The editor of the *Gospel Advocate* expects each *Advocate* writer to think his own thoughts and write his own words. The words of this biography are my own and the editorial comments and interpretations of the facts of this biography are my own. The editor does not re-write the copy of his staff writers. The documentation for this biography is largely cited in the chapters. A major part of the facts is still in the living memory of a large number of people.

I am including a list of bibliography items for the reader who wants to know in a fuller way, what this biography is saying: James Marvin Powell and Mary Nelle Hardeman Powers, *N. B. H.: A Biography of Nicholas Brodie Hardeman*; L. C. Sears, *The Eyes of Jehovah: The Life and Faith of James Alexander Harding*; L. C. Sears, *For Freedom: The Biography of John Nelson Armstrong*; Earl Irvin West, *The Life and Times of David Lipscomb*; Earl Irvin West, *The Search for the Ancient Order*, Vols.

I and II; James R. Wilburn, *The Hazard of the Die: Tolbert Fanning and the Restoration Movement*; Cecil Willis, *W. W. Otey: Contender for the Faith.*

J. E. Choate
Nashville, Tennessee
November 8, 1971

Introduction

LEWIS S. MAIDEN

Benton Cordell Goodpasture stands upon the shoulders of the great leaders of the Restoration Movement. Giants like Thomas and Alexander Campbell, Barton W. Stone, and Walter Scott launched the glorious Restoration. Another line of versatile and gifted men linked hands across the century and were as loyal to the cause: Tolbert Fanning, David Lipscomb, H. Leo Boles, and B. C. Goodpasture. Each steered the *Gospel Advocate* in its proper course, unyielding to error and dedicated to the restoration of New Testament Christianity. The original purpose of the *Gospel Advocate* was to investigate honestly and candidly every issue confronting the church and to test its scriptural validity. None deviated from that principle of Bible interpretation.

The Restoration Movement is the most significant and singular movement in church history which started on the American frontier since the founding of the colonies. Thus B. C. Goodpasture is the beneficiary of a rich heritage. In the latter part of the twentieth century, he has no living contemporary who rivals him in importance in this solid fact of church history; nor has any church leader in this century excelled him among the churches of Christ.

B. C. Goodpasture has steered the *Gospel Advocate* for thirty-two years. It enjoys complete confidence among churches of Christ. It was first called the "Old Reliable" under that stalwart soldier David Lipscomb. B. C. Goodpasture has increased and enhanced this meaning. As the "watchman on the wall," he commands the unbounded respect of the brethren. He is sound in biblical scholarship, is articulate in speech, and has a literary flow in the written language. He soundly and accurately appraises the issues of the brotherhood. The scholarly H. Leo Boles summarized his work, "B. C. has now gone far beyond me."

The author, J. E. Choate, has woven together a splendid presentation of Brother Goodpasture's activities. Detailed information is handled in a scholarly fashion. The story grips the reader's interest and flows smoothly through the book until the end. A significant portrayal of family background enriches the account.

The name Goodpasture denotes European aristocracy. The family moved from Virginia to Tennessee at the close of the eighteenth century. Worn by distinguished men and women through the centuries, the name has flowered in the history of Tennessee and elsewhere in this nation. Its bearers have distinguished themselves in the fields of the military, medicine, law, oratory, and writing.

Overton County, Tennessee, attracted settlers, including the Goodpastures, by its bold features and rugged beauty. It was called the "Mountain Bench" of Tennessee because it comprised the foothills of the Cumberland Mountains. Picturesque coves were walled in by towering hills. Many streams like Caney Fork formed cascades. B. C. Goodpasture grew into young manhood among the fifth generation of Cumberland Mountain people. The folk traditions, language, laws, and social institutions of the Cumberland frontiersmen were indelibly stamped on the land and its inhabitants. One described it as "a hard land that tested the iron in a man's soul." The iron in B. C. Goodpasture's soul has been tested many times and always has stood the test.

B. C. Goodpasture descended from illustrious ancestors and one relative of an earlier time fought with Andrew Jackson at New Orleans as well as against the Creek Indians and later in the Mexican War. The Bible was studied and believed. Only God was feared in their homes, and not man at all. He has a solid link to his heritage in the Restoration Movement. His ancestors were familiar with the movement and more particularly with the work and writings of Barton W. Stone. They subscribed to Stone's *Christian Messenger*.

B. C. worked on the farm, cleared new ground, and developed into an all around Cumberland Mountain boy. He loved nature intensely. He absorbed natural history and was captivated by the wild flowers, birds, and animals that abounded around him. The curious and colorful rock formations caught his interest. His contemporaries said he never played second fiddle in his life. At school he was the best speller and best in arithmetic. At this early age his keen disciplined mind showed its brilliance. In sports he could outjump, outrun, outswim, and outshoot any other student in school. His pioneer ancestors prided themselves on being able to "shoot without a rest." To save their lives, they had to shoot fast. His father, John Jefferson Goodpasture, gave him the advice while preaching "to shoot without rest."

This motto has been his rule in all his preaching career. A glowing tribute to his preaching ability was expressed by his beloved friend Gus Nichols:

> The greatest and best gospel preacher whom I have ever had the privilege of hearing. No living preacher could excel several of his great masterpieces. His presence commands attention. His voice was rich and mellow which at times plucked the heartstrings of those who heard. His delivery was warm and fervent with interest in his audience whom he loved and admired. He always spoke deliberately and with ease,—yes, and without notes. His vocabulary was always ready to lend him the right word, or phrase, or the right quotation, at the right time. His illustrative material makes one think of the parables of Jesus. His power of exhortation and persuasion made his discourse and the invitation almost irresistible. But, as I view B. C. Goodpasture, he cannot be put into the molds and confines of a book. It will take the divine picture of his whole life of loving and sacrificial service in the Kingdom of God, both as a great preacher and editor of the *Gospel Advocate* to portray the greatness of this man whom I love and admire for his work's sake.

This sentiment is shared by thousands of his friends and admirers.

This boy of the Cumberland Mountains showed early his love of learning. Scholarship came to him as easily as his qualities of leadership. An early teacher, B. H. Hunt, one of the best teachers he ever had, explained material so clearly that his students were inspired to achieve. Rocky Mound, his first school, was a primitive log building. There he learned many of life's valuable lessons. The debating society played a vital role in his education. At the age of eleven, he engaged in his first debate. He explained it thusly, "since those early speaking experiences I have felt little, if any, embarrassment standing before an audience." His close friend and co-worker of many years, J. Roy Vaughan, described him much later as he recalled him in debate at the Nashville Bible School:

> He was a handsome young man and walked straight as an arrow. His hair was coal black. His general appearance was very neat. In debate he showed his keen mind and gave straight answers. His response was logical and clear.

B. C. Goodpasture began his walk with God at the age of fourteen. He responded to the gospel invitation and was baptized into Christ by T. C. Fox. Neither the preacher nor the boy could have realized that he would develop into one of the most influential leaders of the church of Christ in the twentieth century. Like water in a thirsty desert, he plunged into his lifelong habit of reading. Like Abe Lincoln he borrowed books and devoured them. From Dr. T. A. Langford he borrowed Johnson's *Notes on the New Testament* and Adam Clarke's *Commentaries*.

The test of every religious, political, or educational system is the man that it forms. Nature was generous with her ingredients when B. C. Goodpasture was formed. At seventeen he entered on his preaching career at Holly Springs church. His second sermon was at Flat Creek, also in Overton County. Until the present time he continues his long, rich, and rewarding work for the Lord. Only eternity will adequately measure his success. But through his long and fruitful life, he has constantly stored his mind with knowledge. He realized he needed the academic discipline of a college background. Thus a new page was written when he decided to enroll in the Nashville Bible School.

Tennyson expressed his ideal fittingly in *Ulysses:*

Thus gray spirit yearning in desire
To follow knowledge like a sinking star,
Beyond the utmost bound of human thought.

In recent times B. C. Goodpasture said about President H. Leo Boles, who was president of the Nashville Bible School, "He knew that I had a struggle to get there and I meant business when I got there." Goodpasture studied four languages at the same time and continued the study of Latin and Greek for five years. Recently he said, "There isn't any source of information quite like a knowledge of the Greek New Testament." He currently studies his

Greek New Testament. During the graduation exercises for the seniors in David Lipscomb College, the "B. C. Goodpasture Award" is made to the preaching student who has made the highest grade point average in Bible. The presentation of a beautiful Bible is made by Vice-President Willard Collins.

The Nashville Bible School became David Lipscomb College after the death of the founder. B. C. Goodpasture began college with $85, and when he graduated in 1918 did not owe a penny. A successful business man today, he could possibly have made a great name in the business world had he desired to do so.

Goodpasture's life was blessed when he fell in love and married Emily Cleveland Cliett, a relative of President Grover Cleveland. Contemporaries describe this charming lady as "ambitious, studious, with high qualities of leadership." Her enthusiasm was noted in work and play. She was strictly honest, self-confident, and full of vitality. She had graduated from David Lipscomb College in 1916 as salutatorian and taught in the primary department until her marriage on September 3, 1918, by S. P. Pittman. J. Roy Vaughan mentions her great influence on her husband: "She was a gracious, intelligent, kind lady. She possessed the charm of a southern lady when the South was in her glory." B. C. Goodpasture suffered a great loss on November 2, 1964, when Cleveland Goodpasture passed away.

In the beautiful "B. C. Goodpasture Collection" room in the Chrisman Memorial Library, the portrait of Cleveland Goodpasture is beside that of her husband. Following her death, the "Mrs. B. C. Goodpasture Memorial Fund" was set up, and her husband gave the initial contribution of one thousand dollars.

Perhaps no other preacher except David Lipscomb has been so honored by his own brethren during his lifetime. A brilliant group of speakers were scheduled at a lectureship at Tracy City, Tennessee, in 1919. These included such celebrities as G. C. Brewer, A. B. Lipscomb, M. C. Kurfees, S. P. Pittman, and the younger Goodpasture. He spoke on the subject "Seed Time and Harvest." M. C. Kurfees noted "some good grazing in the message." G. C. Brewer thought that "he stole the show. Everybody was talking about his lecture." The "prince of preachers," G. C. Brewer asked, "Who is this young preacher B. C. Goodpasture? He just walked away with the preacher's meeting at Tracy City." The able comment of Charles R. Brewer was that:

He never glanced at a note, and his fluent quotations from the Bible, works of scholarship, and classical literature, demonstrated his remarkable memory retention. He hardly ever referred to an author, but the effective way he uttered the quotations impressed his audiences that he knew what he was talking about and he knew more than he was telling.

Saul, the first king of Israel, towered over his brethren. B. C. Goodpasture stood in a similar fashion among the young preachers in 1919.

The Goodpastures moved to Atlanta, Georgia, in 1920. One of the most interesting occurrences was his victory over error. A "Reverend" Shuler, a Seventh-Day Adventist preacher, had preached in Savannah for six weeks. He boldly challenged any and all preachers for a debate on the Sabbath question. Goodpasture went to Savannah to accept the challenge. Bedford Beck met him at the station. "Do you think we ought to go over and see the Adventist preacher?" "No," replied Goodpasture, "we will see him tonight in the presence of his audience so everybody will know what happened."

About six hundred people were in the tent. Shuler rose and invited anybody to make an announcement. Goodpasture stood before the audience, "I would like to make an announcement."

"Does your announcement have any bearing on the literature we are distributing?" asked Shuler.

Goodpasture answered, "Yes, not directly, but indirectly it does."

"Go ahead."

Then addressing the audience, Goodpasture said, "I am ready to expose his false teaching on the Sabbath question tomorrow night. Are you ready, Mr. Shuler?"

"No, I wouldn't debate with any little Dick, Tom, or Harry."

Never at a loss for words, the young preacher replied in a flash, "That's the way Goliath felt about David."

Shuler replied, "I know who you are."

Goodpasture answered, "That may be the reason why you don't want to debate." Then turning to the audience, "This has taken Mr. Shuler rather suddenly, but maybe on second thought he will screw up his courage to the sticking point. I am going to challenge him to defend his teaching on the Sabbath question." To Shuler, "Are you willing to have the debate?" The reply "No,"

Goodpasture continued to the audience, "Now you see that his challenges are nothing but a big bluff. Tomorrow night I'm going to review Shuler's doctrine at the Knight's Hall." Newsboys hit the street yelling, "Shuler backs down." This encounter broke the backbone of Shuler's meeting.

The greatest contribution B. C. Goodpasture has made to the Lord's work has been his editorship of the *Gospel Advocate*. J. C. McQuiddy and F. W. Smith went to Shelbyville in 1919 to bring him back to Nashville as the circulation manager for the *Gospel Advocate,* but he worked only a short time for the paper. He was made a staff writer in 1931 and wrote under the caption of "Pioneer Pulpit." The material was carefully gleaned from Restoration literature. Then in 1939 he assumed the editorship of the *Gospel Advocate* that he has retained until the present time. His versatility and talents have been demonstrated through the years. His older contemporaries that included H. Leo Boles, Batsell Baxter, G. C. Brewer, and N. B. Hardeman have gone to their reward. B. C. Goodpasture has passed through the crucibles of time. The church members with the most detailed knowledge of the Bible and the highest attainments in academic training generously acknowledge his superior character and ability among his peers. Among the "rank and file" of the church, he is implicitly trusted. The venerable N. B. Hardeman stated that "the *Advocate* had been in the forefront for a hundred years. It had more influence in staying the innovations, the hobbies, and the tendencies to depart from the ancient order than any other, perhaps of all other papers combined."

The *Gospel Advocate* has loyally supported every good work. It also has refuted the false charges of the "antis" who opposed Christian colleges, "Herald of Truth," orphans' homes, and cooperative meetings. The editor summarized them all in the perfect answer: "The 'anti-movement' was started by disgruntled preachers who did not get the attention they thought they deserved. They thought they could get attention by riding some hobby they couldn't get by preaching the gospel." He answered one attack made by the *Gospel Guardian* as the Indian's appraisal of the preacher's sermon: "Much Wind! Big Thunder! No Rain!"

His interests and influence have affected widely varying activities. The Hillsboro church, where he preached for many years, gave $100,000 to establish the work in Manhattan in New York

City. He encouraged work among the Negro brethren. Marshall Keeble was ever a close personal friend. The Christian colleges never had a stronger champion for their right and need to exist than B. C. Goodpasture as long as they remained loyal to the Bible, nor have the orphans a more compassionate friend. President Athens Clay Pullias of David Lipscomb College expressed it succinctly,

> For a quarter of a century, Brother Goodpasture has held the helm of the *Gospel Advocate,* holding a steady course amid the rough seas of religious controversy. Raging around him have been the storms, on the radical right the hobby riders, those opposing orphan homes, those opposing Christian colleges and schools and other extremists. —And on the modernist left the destructive forces of modernism, in a hundred different hues. In these troubled waters, unmoved and unshaken, he has steered a steady straight course of loyalty to the Word of God and to principles of New Testament Christianity.

In appreciation for his help, Harding College, George Pepperdine College and Magic Valley Christian College have conferred honorary doctorate degrees upon him. No recipient was more worthy.

Editor Goodpasture expressed the policy of the *Gospel Advocate:*

> The *Gospel Advocate* doesn't give an uncertain sound. It is our purpose that the people know where we stand and what we stand for. We want the *Advocate* to support only what is right and good and oppose only what is evil. We want to maintain its reputation as being the 'Old Reliable.' We want our readers to feel that when we read anything in the *Advocate,* it is true.

Appreciation for Goodpasture's sound judgment and stability was expressed by the scholarly Guy N. Woods:

> B. C. Goodpasture has, through the years, demonstrated his ability to discharge this function in the most widely read periodical as well as the most influential journal among us; he has adhered faithfully to the truth and the best traditions among the people of the Lord, avoiding radicalism and hobbyism on the one hand, and contending for a pure faith and faultless practice in all matters religious on the other hand.

The "antis" launched their attacks in the late 1940's. Not since the "digressive erosions" of the Disciples of Christ at the turn of the century has the church been so sorely tried from within. One of the most subtle dangers has arisen through the liberal theological schools of religion. L. R. Wilson summed up Goodpasture's handling of the matter: "Through the period the editor of the *Gospel Advocate* kept a level head. He adhered to the same principles that have characterized our work since the beginning of the Restoration Movement."

Had Diogenes lived in the twentieth century, he would have stopped with B. C. Goodpasture in his search for a man. The life of the reader will be enriched by reading this biography. Perhaps he himself has best summarized his own accomplishments:

"1. I have been able to encourage and help the preaching of the gospel in all the countries of the English speaking world through the *Advocate*.

2. The editorship has offered me an opportunity to help stabilize a brotherhood torn by hobby riders and factionists.

3. I hope that I have made a major contribution in indoctrinating and strengthening churches wherever the *Advocate* has been read."

At a time when most men are retired or wishing they could be, B. C. Goodpasture is continuing to serve as the editor of the *Advocate* and evangelist with a work schedule that would test the energies of the strongest; and this is being done with the solid approval of the church which admires Goodpasture in no undiminished way.

The churches of Christ are suffering inroads being made into their ranks through the introduction of the "liberal theologies" which produced the "Death of God" dialogue a few years back. H. Leo Boles several years before his death was already running up the "danger signal" that the church was being threatened by a modern "anti-christ" that was even more dangerous than any of all the previous generations. Any concerned person interested in the principles of New Testament Christianity would hardly be called an alarmist because of his fears of "creeping liberalism." The editor of the *Gospel Advocate* has unstintingly used the *Gospel Advocate* to warn the brotherhood with the deepest concern against the determined challenges from the ranks of religious liberals.

A few years back, "schools of preaching" were started in the West to give men the opportunity to study the Bible under highly trained faithful teachers of the Bible to equip them to better preach the gospel more effectively and to be better church leaders and teachers. The schools were planned for men who had not had the opportunity to attend a Christian college. First through the interests of Roy J. Hearn, the Nashville School of Preaching was set up in Nashville, Tennessee. B. C. Goodpasture was made the chairman of the board.

One of the great satisfactions in the life of Goodpasture is centered in the Nashville School of Preaching which has been successfully training good men under the most capable preachers and teachers. The adult students of the Nashville School of Preaching would have otherwise been denied the splendid training they are now receiving.

B. C. Goodpasture married his second wife, Freddie Goetz Goodpasture, November 11, 1965, who has held up the arms of her husband in his demanding work as evangelist and preacher. Freddie Goodpasture has won the admiration of all who have made her acquaintance for her supporting role as the wife of B. C. Goodpasture.

Two editors of the *Gospel Advocate* have schools in Nashville, Tennessee, which are named after them—David Lipscomb College and the B. C. Goodpasture Christian School. There has not been a climax or anti-climax in the life of B. C. Goodpasture. This "mountain man" has found the climbing the mountain trail to his liking and each year finds him in higher country and still climbing because he too is looking for a city "whose builder and maker is God."

The "Old Reliable" stands today at her peak of glory. By linking hands across the years with H. Leo Boles, David Lipscomb, and Tolbert Fanning, B. C. Goodpasture has enjoyed a vital role in its triumph. At the Centennial Celebration, Guy N. Woods eloquently expressed the sentiments of thousands:

> The *Gospel Advocate* is at its zenith in the long and eventful period which characterized its history. For one hundred years it has unswervingly adhered to its calculating course of contending earnestly for the faith once delivered to the saints. From the goal it has turned neither to the right nor to the left, but has pressed steadily onward ever fighting for a pure faith and a faultless practice for the people of God.

B. C. Goodpasture in his career has answered the challenge expressed in the lines:

God give us men.   A time like this demands
Strong minds, great hearts, true faith and ready hands!
Men whom the lust of office does not kill,
Men whom the spoils of office cannot buy,
Men who possess opinions and a will,
Men who love honor, men who cannot lie.

I

Elm Crag

Benton Cordell Goodpasture stands among the giants of the Restoration Movement in church history. Around the turn of the nineteenth century, the tide was running strong for the restoration of Apostolic Christianity free from all human additions that had been growing since the start of the second century A. D. The history of the Restoration Movement has been largely told by the spokesman and apologists for the Disciples of Christ. It was not until 1906 that the United States Religious Census gave the Disciples of Christ and the churches of Christ a separate listing. The work of Tolbert Fanning and David Lipscomb set in motion a chain of circumstances that brought about the separation.

The names of James O'Kelly, Abner Jones, and Elias Smith are familiar to the students of Restoration church history. Such men were calling generally for the agreement to acknowledge that Christ is the head of the church and to accept the name "Christian" to the exclusion of all human names for both the individual members and the corporate church body of Christians and to believe that the Bible is the all sufficient creed for the faith and practice of all Christians.

Two giants among the pioneer restorers were Barton W. Stone and Alexander Campbell. Barton W. Stone moved slowly to accept faith-baptism by immersion and to reject infant baptism as unscriptural. He adopted the name "Christian" for baptized adult believers. When Barton W. Stone and Alexander Campbell met, the two men found themselves in common agreement that the New Testament should be the creed and final authority for Chris-

1

tians. Those associated with Alexander Campbell called themselves "Disciples of Christ." Alexander Campbell insisted upon an exact conformity to the primitive faith and practices of the New Testament. Stone had emphasized the uniting of all men in Christ. Both positions were scriptural, and it was not difficult for them to unite on the two New Testament doctrines.

The enemies labeled the movement—"Reformers," "Campbellites," "New Lights," or "Stoneites." The outstanding personality among the Restoration leaders was Alexander Campbell, a Scotman, trained in the University of Glasgow in Scotland. Step by step Alexander Campbell advanced into the liberty in Christ. He sounded the slogan created by his father, Thomas Campbell, for the restoration of New Testament Christianity: "Where the Scriptures speak, we speak; where the Scriptures are silent, we are silent."

Alexander Campbell was one of the best scholars of his age. He believed in the church of the Bible and had the courage to condemn sects and denominations with their creeds and human devices. He began to call upon the people to worship as the New Testament directed. Many were eager to do this and local congregations were established upon New Testament doctrine. Campbell was a religious debater without peer. He challenged and debated the atheist, Robert Owen. The polemical champions and apologists for the Catholic and Protestant theologians in turn met Campbell in debate and seldom did one call for a return match. The identification of Alexander Campbell with the Restoration Movement was such that the Christians who refused denomination ties were dubbed "Campbellites."

The Restoration Movement that promised so much for Christianity was splintered by Restoration educators and preachers who took divergent views mainly over the missionary society and instrumental music questions. The first divisive issue to split the church was the introduction of the missionary society within the organization of the church. Alexander Campbell took the lead in this divisive movement when he became in 1849 the first president of the American Missionary Society.

Another breed of gospel preachers took up the "Sword of the Spirit" to restore the New Testament order of things and not one deserted the cause. There is a line of those men who joined hands over a century of time—Tolbert Fanning, David Lipscomb, H.

Leo Boles, and Benton Cordell Goodpasture; and each in this order served as editor of the *Gospel Advocate*. Their work has continued in an unbroken line of succession to this day with the same uncompromising purpose to restore New Testament Christianity strictly patterned after the apostolic doctrine as set forth in the New Testament.

The biography of B. C. Goodpasture would be of some interest outside church history as is generally the case of unusually gifted men. But the real meaning of Goodpasture's life is vitally centered in the church and a lifetime spent in building up the church from the pulpit and as editor of the *Gospel Advocate*. Alfred North Whitehead, the British philosopher, remarked that history is a series of footnotes appended to Plato. And the comment was made the reason for this is that Plato stood upon the shoulders of giants. So is the case with B. C. Goodpasture, for he too stands upon the shoulders of unusually gifted leaders of the Restoration. Had it not been for their work, the occasion for this study would not likely exist.

For more than a century, the name of Tolbert Fanning has been pushed around in the "odds and ends" of Restoration history. Church historians have been at loss to know where to place him. In the first place, Tolbert Fanning was overshadowed by his gifted contemporaries such as Alexander Campbell and Isaac Errett. The late A. R. Holton made the first clear statement as to Fanning's rightful position among the Restoration leaders: "Whatever the churches of Christ are, as over against the Christian Church and the Disciples of Christ is due, in the beginning at least, to Tolbert Fanning."

Tolbert Fanning was personally and favorably known to Alexander Campbell who made frequent trips to Nashville to fill preaching appointments. Campbell probably met Fanning in the early 1830's while he was in Nashville to visit his daughter. Campbell commended Fanning about this time.

> The church in Nashville counts about 600 members, and employs Brother Fanning as its evangelist. This devout, ardent and gifted brother is about finishing his studies in the University of Nashville, under the presidency of the justly celebrated Doctor Lindsley.

When Fanning was barely twenty-five, he was invited to accompany Campbell on a preaching tour; and a year later, he accompanied Campbell on a preaching tour that carried them into New England and Canada. Some years later, Campbell complimented Fanning on the initial publication of the *Gospel Advocate* and Fanning's Franklin College. But Alexander Campbell's good wishes were short lived. Later he accused Fanning of pitting the *Gospel Advocate* and Franklin College against the *Millennial Harbinger* and Bethany College. Tolbert Fanning denied the charge.

Actually, the crucial date in Restoration history is 1849. This was the year that the American Missionary Society was organized in Cincinnati, Ohio, with Alexander Campbell chosen as the first president. This was the fateful step that started the Disciples of Christ in the direction of liberalism. Tolbert Fanning distrusted the concept of the missionary society from its inception.

Tolbert Fanning was present for the annual meetings of the American Missionary Society in 1859 with a place on the program to address the assembly. Fanning planned to question the scriptural integrity of the missionary society from the floor. Isaac Errett, the successor of Alexander Campbell as editor of the *Millennial Harbinger* and later the editor of the *Christian Standard,* was Grand Secretary of the Convention. He learned about the intention of Fanning and calculated to neutralize the statements of Fanning before he spoke. Errett read the following statement to the convention: "Resolved that there was no objection, in doing our work through the church, as presented by Brother Fanning, and through other agencies." Errett was successful in his thinly veiled rebuttal of Tolbert Fanning even before he spoke. The convention listened to what Fanning had to say, but did not respond with any display of interest.

The influence of Tolbert Fanning was destined to last through two of his projects. In 1840 Fanning moved to "Elm Crag" five miles east of Nashville, and here he built Franklin College and served as its president until 1861. David Lipscomb College is the direct descendent of Fanning's school. Fanning planned for Franklin College, which was a co-educational institution, to provide both moral and practical instructions for its students. William Lipscomb, the older brother of David Lipscomb, graduated from Franklin College in July of 1848. In July of 1855 Tolbert Fanning and William Lipscomb started publication of the *Gospel Advocate* which was the second the most important venture of Fanning's life in several important respects. It was the misfortune of Tolbert Fanning, in a sense, to live in the day of Alexander Campbell, Robert Milligan, J. W. McGarvey, and other Restoration household names. Fanning espoused the unpopular side of the missionary issue. Fortunately the plaudits for the champions of the hour are short lived. History is generous to recognize her true prophets who are sometimes regarded as dissenters by their contemporaries. The *Gospel Advocate* has long been the most influential of the brotherhood papers, and David Lipscomb College, in many respects, may be regarded as an extension of Tolbert Fanning's educational philosophy as reflected in the efforts of David Lipscomb and James A. Harding.

Granville Lipscomb, the father of William and David, was a great admirer of Tolbert Fanning. David Lipscomb was baptized by Tolbert Fanning at the age of fourteen in a box while Lipscomb was recovering from typhoid fever.

David Lipscomb graduated with an A.B. degree from Franklin College in 1849. Following graduation, David Lipscomb went into business. He managed a large plantation in Georgia for a while. He farmed in Tennessee and was a good money maker. He contracted with the Nashville, St. Louis, and Chattanooga Railway to build and grade a section of the railroad bed.

At the age of twenty-six, David Lipscomb had never given a thought that someday he would preach or edit a religious paper. A brilliant and erratic preacher, Jesse B. Fergusson, was preaching for the church of Christ in Nashville before the Civil War. Fergusson embraced a religious fad of the period, "spiritism," a form of necromancy. He wrecked the church in Nashville. David Lipscomb was disgusted and considered going with the Baptist Church; but after a careful study of Baptist doctrine, he could not.

Instead Lipscomb turned to build up the shattered church in Middle Tennessee. On January 1, 1866, he joined Tolbert Fanning to co-edit the *Gospel Advocate*. In 1868 Lipscomb became the sole editor of the paper. E. G. Sewell joined Lipscomb in 1870 as co-editor and served until his death.

David Lipscomb embodied the thinking of Tolbert Fanning in his resolute opposition to the missionary society concept. The rebirth of the *Gospel Advocate* came at a time when innovations were sweeping the brotherhood. The "music controversy" was being pressed. It was not until 1878 that David Lipscomb was finally convinced that the use of instrumental music was unscriptural, and he opposed the practice as long as he lived. David Lipscomb was slow in making up his mind about a principle; but once he did, he rarely ever changed. And even then, the truth as set forth in the Bible was his sole consultant.

The original purpose of the *Gospel Advocate* was to investigate honestly and candidly every issue brought before the church to test its scriptural validity. David Lipscomb never deviated from that principle of Bible interpretation; and as for this matter, neither has B. C. Goodpasture. Lipscomb was a born leader of men. An aunt once said that when David Lipscomb and William Lipscomb were riding horseback that David "always rode 'point.'" J. M. McCaleb, dean of Christian missionaries to Japan was a close confidant of David Lipscomb and he described the man: "He believed in the correctness of his judgment and rarely ever saw fit to change, but he was not dogmatic; he was willing to allow others to use their own judgment but at the same time willing to cooperate with them." Lipscomb possessed a great intellectual capacity. He exercised sound judgment and always seemed to know what to do in a given case. Lipscomb was always kindly disposed toward those who differed with him exercising a never failing patience.

David Lipscomb was controlled by two strong willed intentions: he meant to build up the church in Middle Tennessee and in other places through the preaching of the gospel from the pulpit and writing in the *Gospel Advocate*. And he was stubbornly determined that all unscriptural innovations should be kept out of the church. The story of David Lipscomb is more fully understood in the work of the men whom he chose to assist him on the *Advocate* staff.

Elisha G. Sewell and David Lipscomb were equal partners in the editing of the *Advocate*. Their names are interwoven in the history of the church for fifty years as preaching and writing yoke-fellows. When Sewell joined Lipscomb as editor of the *Gospel Advocate* in 1870, the paper came to its readers like a messenger from the battle front where the foe contested every inch of the ground. E. G. Sewell had been one of the favorite pupils of Tolbert Fanning. The fact that Lipscomb chose Sewell as his working partner is all that needs to be said in behalf of Sewell.

E. G. Sewell was a gifted preacher. He established seventy churches in his preaching career. Few men in this or the last century baptized more people than E. G. Sewell. He was preeminently a Bible teacher pointing out what the Bible said. When Sewell finished an editorial, there was seldom anything left to be added.

David Lipscomb was joined by two younger men whose names have become synonymous with the *Gospel Advocate,* J. C. McQuiddy and F. D. Srygley. Those four men in time were referred to as the "Old Guard" of the *Advocate.*

It goes without question that the *Gospel Advocate* has wielded an influence far above any other religious journal in more than one hundred and fifty years of Restoration history. And the name of McQuiddy has lasted the longest. In 1885, J. C. McQuiddy became office editor and business manager of the *Gospel Advocate.* David Lipscomb said of McQuiddy that "he was the only man to ever run the *Gospel Advocate* without a loss." One of the great contributions of McQuiddy was to insist upon good Bible school literature for the churches and he moved to supply the need.

"Digression". was enjoying a field day in the church at this time. David Lipscomb and his associates were thought of as reactionaries. Lipscomb was lampooned in the late nineteenth century in a cartoon as an old woman futilely trying to sweep back the incoming ocean tide with a broom. J. S. Lamar who wrote *Memoirs of Isaac Errett* was certain that David Lipscomb and his associates had failed to stop the progress of the church. The Christian Church had swept the region north of the Ohio River and was making good progress in the South. Lamar wrote about his impressions of David Lipscomb in his *Memoirs:* "The David Lipscomb fiasco, which about this time, paraded itself before the civilized world, will not detain us long. And yet it is due to a seriocomic actor, so renouned in the role of lachrymose humor that it should not be passed over in silence." J. S. Lamar proved to be a poor prophet. He wrote this statement on the eve of the revival of the spirit of the Restoration Movement which was brought to fruition by David Lipscomb, his associates, and all who came afterwards. David Lipscomb was then a longtime editor of the *Gospel Advocate,* published in Nashville, Tennessee; and indeed the church of Christ did appear in disarray. There were only five loyal Nashville churches in 1891 standing against "digression." J. S. Lamar made his somewhat prejudicial statements on circumstances he thought were tenable at that time.

F. D. Srygley was the last to join Lipscomb, Sewell, and

McQuiddy on the *Gospel Advocate* as one of the associate editors. Srygley's indecisive stand on the "missionary society" until near the end of his life points up the soul searching that finally led to Srygley's break with the "digressive liberalism" on the need of the "missionary society" as a scriptural method for carrying the gospel into new fields. Srygley's thinking was similar to that of Alexander Campbell, Moses E. Lard, and others; and Srygley was convinced that he was right. Lipscomb first studied the articles of F. D. Srygley. He was not impressed at all and said, "No man could write with profit on a subject he so little understood." Lipscomb, however, answered Srygley's articles lest he labor with the delusion that Lipscomb found his position unanswerable.

Srygley felt keenly the brunt of Lipscomb's pen and went away "to lick his wounds." J. C. McQuiddy was anxious to bring Srygley, his personal friend, to the *Gospel Advocate* as a staff writer. He was confident that Srygley could work with the indomitable Lipscomb. Lipscomb laid down only one ground rule for the *Advocate* staff members. A writer could write on any subject as long as it came from the Bible and was scripturally sound. Srygley consented to come to the *Gospel Advocate* and proved to be one of the great writers for the *Gospel Advocate*. He served as "front page editor" of the *Advocate*. Srygley was just forty-four at the time of his death in 1900.

James A. Harding bore a different relation to David Lipscomb. James A. Harding served with David Lipscomb as assistant editor of the *Gospel Advocate*. After both men were advanced in years, they established the Nashville Bible School. Harding grew up in the Restoration movement and personally knew such men as Moses E. Lard. He was a graduate of Bethany College. James A. Harding scarcely had an equal as a gospel preacher in his day or since. In a forty-year period beginning in 1874, Harding conducted three hundred revivals, started some fifteen churches, and engaged in fifty religious debates.

Perhaps the most eventful occasion in the life of James A. Harding was the religious debate with J. B. Moody in Nashville, Tennessee. The debate was conducted from May 27 through June 13, 1889. Moody in his debates with preachers in the church had maligned some prominent members of the church with some derogatory stories designed to defame their reputations. Such was a part of Moody's "stock and trade" in religious debates. Harding

warned Moody during the debate to leave off his "mud slinging";
and if he did not, Harding told him that the Baptist would not call
on him again to conduct debates for them under the Baptist
Church sponsorship. Moody ignored Harding. Harding had
come prepared with documents to make a complete exposure of
Moody's insults; and Harding presented a completely documented
exposure of Moody's falsehoods. J. B. Moody lost face in this debate and compromised his Baptist supporters. This was the last
major religious debate in Nashville until N. B. Hardeman met Ira
M. Boswell in 1923 on the scriptural adoption of instrumental
music in worship.

James A. Harding made his home with David Lipscomb during
the debate. During those few days, the two men laid their plans to
start the Nashville Bible School which opened its doors in October
of 1891. Lipscomb and Harding knew the worth of a Christian
college and planned to start one of their own knowing that such a
school could be either a great blessing or a great curse. David
Lipscomb and James A. Harding in their day had a formidable adversary in Daniel Sommer and his disciples who fought the Bible
college with everything in their power.

Following his religious debate with J. B. Moody, Harding
started his famed Nashville revival June 19, 1889, in a large tent
that would seat two thousand people. Many came thinking Harding would continue the debate with Moody from the pulpit. But
Harding never once alluded to the debate. In that meeting one
hundred and seventeen persons were baptized. Harding devoted
about six months each year to gospel meetings. The church of
Christ for the first time was brought to the favorable attention of
Nashville through the efforts of James A. Harding in this year of
1889.

David Lipscomb and James A. Harding were unusually remarkable men. Lipscomb was a very plain man in dress and personal bearing. Harding was a handsome man with a ruddy face,
dark hair, and beard. Harding worked with the Nashville Bible
School ten years. But the story of David Lipscomb and James A.
Harding will not be forgotten as long as people are interested in
the ideals of Christian education. Their views of Christian education were embodied in the Nashville Bible School which since has
served as the classic model for establishing similar schools by

members of the church of Christ throughout this nation and in different parts of the world.

David Lipscomb was closely associated with two other men in the closing years of his life—E. A. Elam and H. Leo Boles. Elam was a Tennessean by birth. He graduated from Burritt College in 1879. E. A. Elam was one of the great pulpiteers of his time, and a great many compared his ability with that of James A. Harding and T. B. Larimore. Elam was a powerful writer for the *Gospel Advocate;* he followed F. D. Srygley as "front page editor" in 1900. Eventually he wrote the *Elam Notes,* the annual commentary of Sunday school lessons published by the Gospel Advocate Company. In 1906, Elam was appointed to succeed William Anderson as president of the Nashville Bible School. David Lipscomb chose Elam for the post. Elam resigned as president of the Nashville Bible School in 1913, but he served as a board member of the college for twenty-eight years. He became chairman of the board of directors of the college in 1922 and held that post until his death.

In 1903 H. Leo Boles came under the influence of David Lipscomb while Lipscomb was still vigorous and teaching the Bible daily. H. Leo Boles sat in the Bible classes of David Lipscomb for seven years. Lipscomb suffered a stroke in 1909, and his health gradually deteriorated. When he could no longer teach, H. Leo Boles was appointed by the elderly gentleman to teach his classes. When E. A. Elam resigned the presidency of the Nashville Bible School, David Lipscomb personally chose H. Leo Boles to become president. Boles served in that capacity for sixteen years in two different tenures.

At the beginning of the twenties, Boles served as editor of the *Gospel Advocate* and owned a one-third partnership in the Gospel Advocate Company. No other person connected with the *Advocate* wrote more broadly or served in more capacities on the *Advocate* staff other than David Lipscomb. It would be safe to say that no person knew the history of the church, the *Gospel Advocate,* the Christian colleges, and the problems of the brotherhood better than did H. Leo Boles in his lifetime. B. C. Goodpasture never had a better personal friend in his lifetime than H. Leo Boles.

The mainstream of the Restoration movement as first articulated by Stone and Campbell converged in the efforts of Tolbert Fanning and David Lipscomb and a handful of men who were closely associated with them. B. C. Goodpasture, as heretofore stated, stands in a direct line with David Lipscomb and Tolbert Fanning and H. Leo Boles. Two other great church leaders must take their equal and rightful places with Tolbert Fanning and David Lipscomb. They are Arvey Glenn Freed and N. B. Hardeman. B. C. Goodpasture knew A. G. Freed, but was never closely associated with him. B. C. Goodpasture's long acquaintance and friendship with N. B. Hardeman started in 1920.

Whatever the churches of Christ are today over against the Disciples of Christ is also due in a very great measure to A. G. Freed and N. B. Hardeman. The story of B. C. Goodpasture is inseparable from these two older contemporaries. The influence of Freed-Hardeman College continues to be a powerful force in the brotherhood for preaching the apostolic principles of New Testament Christianity.

The twentieth century is now moving into the final decades. The Restoration Movement initiated by Barton W. Stone and Alexander Campbell is now almost two centuries old. Only in recent years have the names of Tolbert Fanning and David Lipscomb been sounded in a higher key. Their importance in helping restore the principles of New Testament Christianity is now being generally recognized even among the scholars of the Disciples of Christ. And in the roll call of these restorers, the name of A. G. Freed must be placed in the first ranks.

No man stood with a clearer understanding than A. G. Freed about "what divided us" when the differences between the Disciples of Christ and the churches of Christ were sharply crystallizing. If Freed's influence reached no further than the impact he made on N. B. Hardeman, that would be sufficient to immortalize his name. In the same manner that Tolbert Fanning and David Lipscomb met head on the sweep of "digression" into Middle Tennessee, Freed and Hardeman stood their ground in West Tennessee. And they won an equally resounding victory for New Testament Christianity.

Arvey Glenn Freed was born August 3, 1868, to Joseph and Eliza Hayes Freed. His mother was a relative of President Rutherford B. Hayes. Freed attended the Indiana public school system and graduated with honors from Valparaiso University. He became a Christian early in life and soon after he began to preach the gospel. Freed came to Tennessee and first taught in 1889 at Essary Springs, Tennessee. He moved to Henderson, Tennessee, in

1895 to work with the West Tennessee Christian College. Two
years later the name was changed to the Georgia Robertson Christian College. N. B. Hardeman was then a student. A. G. Freed
first met Hardeman in Henderson. The Georgia Robertson College was being dominated by the "missionary society" group. A. G.
Freed left the college in 1905 to teach in Denton, Texas. N. B.
Hardeman had become a member of the Georgia Robertson College faculty and afterwards left to teach in the Chester County
school system.

Freed and Hardeman corresponded while Freed was away
from Henderson and later they decided to start a new school in
Henderson. Freed returned to Henderson in 1907. They started
their new college September 10, 1908, in a new building. The
school was named the National Teacher's Normal Business College, and had an enrollment of five hundred for several years.
However, the outbreak of World War I reduced the school until
its very existence was threatened. In 1919 a board of trustees was
formed to take over the institution, and it was named Freed-
Hardeman College. Both men served in the college until 1923
when A. G. Freed left to become vice-president of David Lipscomb
College and principal of the high school during the second tenure
of H. Leo Boles' presidency. Freed was catalogued in the school
year of 1929-1930 as Dean of the college.

A. G. Freed's loyalty to the Bible as the inspired Word of God
was never questioned by those who knew him. Few men could
stand as quietly and solidly as Freed when the Bible was under attack. He had no taste for religious debates or conflicts; but when
they came, he stood the acid test without flinching.

The contacts that B. C. Goodpasture had with A. G. Freed
were few and widely spaced. He first met Freed in Henderson,
Tennessee, when he was working as circulation manager in 1920
for the *Gospel Advocate*. Goodpasture would occasionally visit
with Freed when he came on the David Lipscomb College campus
after Freed joined the college staff. Their talk was mostly about
the church.

B. C. Goodpasture as a young preacher first met N. B. Hardeman when he came to Henderson, Tennessee, in behalf of the *Gospel Advocate*. Their paths too occasionally crossed over the next
twenty years. N. B. Hardeman invited Goodpasture to teach in
Freed-Hardeman College when Hardeman was preaching in a
meeting at the West End Avenue church. Goodpasture was work-

ing with the church in Atlanta, Georgia, at the time. However, it was not until Goodpasture became editor of the *Gospel Advocate* in 1939 that the two men came to depend mutually upon each other in the work of the church. The cause of the *Gospel Advocate* was fully supported by Hardeman, and he trusted the editorial policy in the hands of his younger contemporary.

N. B. Hardeman was an extraordinary man by whatever biblical or human standard set forth. The stature of his influence in the restoration of New Testament Christianity may now be as carefully and exactly calculated as that of David Lipscomb.

When David Lipscomb laid down his pen and his voice was stilled, no interested person doubted that a basic difference existed between the Disciples of Christ and the church of Christ. N. B. Hardeman was not a "whit behind" the immortal David Lipscomb in articulating the principles of the New Testament as a master preacher, teacher, writer, and debater.

A. G. Freed took N. B. Hardeman and taught him out of the Christian Church. Hardeman was just nineteen at the time. In 1903, Freed and Hardeman invited E. A. Elam to Henderson to help separate the "organ and society" church from the Henderson church.

The religious Census for 1906 which listed the Churches of Christ and the Disciples of Christ separately caused no great alarm among the rank and file membership of the Christian Church. That was to be changed in the early twenties. David Lipscomb was gone, but his influence lived powerfully in the *Gospel Advocate* and the Nashville Bible School A. G. Freed and N. B. Hardeman, and other religious debaters moved around the country leaving in their wake the leading preachers of the Disciples of Christ, Baptist, and the Methodist with little taste to carry on the religious dialogues.

It became crystal clear to the Disciples of Christ by 1920 that they were losing ground from the "Mighty Mississippi River" in the west to the "Smoky Mountains in the East." For twenty-five years the "Disciples" who advocated the "society and the organ" were playing "possum" while they carried on their propaganda privately. They admitted their policy to invade the churches of Christ was a failure and passed resolutions in their conventions "to fight it out from Carter County in the east to Shelby County in the west." They began agitating for a debate.

N. B. Hardeman had risen to great prominence among his

brethren in the 1922 Tabernacle meetings in Nashville, Tennessee. The church was elated that a church of Christ preacher attracted great audiences matching the crowds drawn by Gypsy Smith and Billy Sunday in their heyday.

Following N. B. Hardeman's masterful preaching in Nashville, the Disciples of Christ made their most serious tactical error. A debate was arranged between Ira M. Boswell of Georgetown, Kentucky, and N. B. Hardeman on the "music question." The "Disciples" had no little difficulty in finding a preacher to represent them. William Henry Book, a prominent Christian Church preacher of Columbus, Indiana, told B. C. Goodpasture that church leaders approached him about holding the music debate with Hardeman. Book refused with the comment that he was "more in agreement with Hardeman than with them." The debate was conducted in the Ryman Auditorium from May 31 to June 5, 1923. Large audiences were present for all services. Members of the church were jubilant over the masterly fashion in which Hardeman conducted his side of the debate.

Following the tabernacle meetings and the Boswell-Hardeman debate, the churches of Christ were being generously accepted by the public, and the churches of Christ have been experiencing "mushrooming" growth in the intervening years.

It would be difficult to assess the worth of N. B. Hardeman to the church. He had hardly a comparable peer in the triple role of preacher, educator, and religious debater. During Hardeman's sixty years as a teacher and preacher, more than twenty thousand students passed directly under the teaching influences of Hardeman.

On the evening of May 18, 1959, more than seven hundred and fifty persons from all over the nation gathered in the George Peabody Hotel in Memphis, Tennessee, to honor N. B. Hardeman. Lyndon B. Johnson was among the humble and great who came to honor the Henderson educator. The Memphis *Press Scimitar* described the occasion as "an event without parallel in the memories of those assembled." Lyndon B. Johnson expressed a wish for the volumes of the Hardeman Tabernacle sermons. The request was passed on to B. C. Goodpasture who sent the books to the future president of the United States.

Whatever may be the course of the church in the closing decades of this century, the church historians will have a very long and generous chapter devoted to Nicholas Brodie Hardeman.

N. B. Hardeman and B. C. Goodpasture met in a common cause—preaching the gospel. They formed a team beginning in 1939 when Goodpasture came to the *Advocate* which lasted as long as N. B. Hardeman was active. The members of the church trusted implicitly both men and knew the gospel would not go begging in their hands.

When B. C. Goodpasture became editor of the *Gospel Advocate,* he was the beneficiary of a rich heritage. Goodpasture, while he was a student in the Nashville Bible School, often saw the elderly David Lipscomb sitting on his front porch, but he never had a conversation with the aged man. Goodpasture was present at the funeral of David Lipscomb who died in December of 1917. E. A. Elam and H. Leo Boles had been great working friends with David Lipscomb in the Nashville Bible School in the last years of Lipscomb's life. Goodpasture came under the influence of Boles in 1914; and in time, came to know and count E. A. Elam as a trusted friend in their mutual labors. Now for more than thirty years, B. C. Goodpasture has stood where these men stood and sat where they sat. It is an indisputable fact of history that whatever the church of Christ is today over the Disciples of Christ that credit for this is due to Tolbert Fanning and David Lipscomb and the men who came after them. H. Leo Boles was described in his lifetime as the last of the pioneer preachers. It is not amiss to place B. C. Goodpasture in that line. But in any case Goodpasture is the only leader in the church who can claim an unbroken connection with the Restoration leaders of yesteryears dating back to Tolbert Fanning and Alexander Campbell.

The evaluation has been made that the Restoration Movement on the American frontier is the most significant and singular event that has happened in American church history since the settling of the English colonists on American shores. The churches of Christ now form one of the largest religious bodies on the North American continent. In recent years the impact of the church of Christ, Christian schools, religious papers, and other service media has been felt and nationally recognized. Whatever has been the success of restoring the patterns of Apostolic Christianity in this century, B. C. Goodpasture has no living contemporary who measures with him in equal importance contributing to this solid fact of church history.

B.C. and Cleveland Goodpasture

II

Cumberland Heritage

At the time Benton Cordell Goodpasture was born in Overton County near Livingston, Tennessee, "old timers" who were still living remembered when a large part of the country was a primeval wilderness in isolated sections. The Goodpasture family moved to Tennessee from Virginia in the closing years of the eighteenth century. Nothing is known about the ancestry of the family before their migration from Virginia to Tennessee. The name "pasture" or the French spelling "pasteur" is an old and distinguished European surname worn by an aristocracy of useful men and women over the centuries. It is clear that "Goodpasture" is a hyphenated name "bon-pasteur" in French and "good-pasture" in British and Scot. That both sides of his family came from Britain and Ireland could be logically argued since most of the early settlers in the Cumberland Mountain region were English speaking people with their English, Scot, and Irish traditions.

From such information that is available, the Goodpasture family immigrated to Tennessee from the region of Wolf's Hill in Virginia in the general vicinity of what is now Abingdon, Virginia. The family group moved first to Tennessee, but later most of them moved further on to Kentucky. The scant records now in existence reveal that there were six Virginia brothers and two sisters —James, John, Abraham, Isaac, Cornelius, Solomon, Elizabeth, and Martha. It is of some interest to note that all wore names of biblical origin. A footnote to Virginia history is the fact that one of the Virginia ancestors, Abram Goodpasture, built the first combined courthouse and jail house in Abingdon, Virginia, and was paid eighteen dollars for his labor.

James Goodpasture who was the great-great-grandfather of Benton Cordell Goodpasture was already advanced in years when he settled in Tennessee. He was one of the pioneers of Wolf's Hill, the Abingdon settlement in Virginia where all of his children except the youngest were born. His oldest son had already married and he remained in Virginia where he has many descendants who have taken responsible places in their respective communities.

James Goodpasture first settled at Southwest Point, a federal fort at the junction of the Clinch and Holston rivers on the eastern border of what was then the edge of the Indian reservation. The place was in Knox County about a mile from Kingston, Tennessee, now the county seat of Roane County. One of the last acts of James Goodpasture while he was a citizen of Knox County was to sign a petition for the forming of a new county. This is the only extant paper to which his name is affixed and which has survived. The document reads as follows:

To the General Assembly of the State of Tennessee:

We the subscribers, living in Knox County, below the mouth of Turkey Creek, or North Clinch river, petition that Knox County may be divided, so as to leave the same a constitutional county, and that a new county be formed so as to contain therein a part of the tract of the county lying between the rivers Holston and Clinch, and above Southwest Point, and a part of that tract of country lying north of Clinch, and we, as in duty bound, will ever pray. July 15, 1799.

James and John Goodpasture were among those who signed the document in a fair legible hand.

But in 1880, James Goodpasture moved across the territory which was called the wilderness and made a permanent settlement on Flat Creek located then in Smith County, and later in Overton County when the county was organized. A curious fact is that James Goodpasture signed his name with a final "ture"; and John, his son, changed his name to "Goodpaster." All of the descendants of John Goodpaster adopted their father's orthography. The descendants of Abraham Goodpaster who settled in Bath County, Kentucky, and perhaps other branches of the family, adopted the final "ter" to form the Goodpaster surname which has lasted. All of the descendants of James Goodpasture continue the traditional family spelling. The reason for the change in spelling the surname may have been prompted by the desire to avoid the puns that some people enjoy making about a person's name.

In 1880 when the Goodpastures crossed the wilderness, the Indian Country was considered unsafe for travelers unless they were traveling in fairly large parties. Roving bands of Indians posed a threat and James Goodpasture had encountered such a party of Indians before reaching Overton County. The story of the Goodpastures who were the ancestors of Benton Cordell begins with James Goodpasture, who migrated to the Upper Cumberland country.

In the early 1800's the region was wild and beautiful. A wandering Indian was sometimes seen but posed no threat as such, and a few buffaloes were still to be found here and there. The high country composing Overton County approaches the Cumberland Mountains and is a part of the Cumberland region in Middle Tennessee. The country is rough and uneven. In the early part of the last century, the valleys were covered with cane brakes and the hills were abundantly covered with wild pea vine that would fatten stock running in the woods.

There was no finer timbered region than the country around Hilham, Tennessee, throughout most of the nineteenth century. The earlier settlers avoided the river bottoms because they were considered unhealthy due largely to a vast population of insects and sickness that somehow seemed to plague the settlers living in the bottom lands.

Overton County attracted the early settlers with its beauty and the variety of its bold and rugged topographical features. The towering hills walled in picturesque coves, and the valleys were traversed by impetuous streams often forming magnificent cascades such as the ones on the Caney Fork and Roaring River. This part of the Cumberland Plateau formed a vast wilderness which had been inhabited by Indians until 1805 when the treaty of Tellico opened the mountain region to white settlement. In the next year Overton County was formed.

There are undoubtedly powerful influences stirring in a country where a child grows up that help him to fashion his boyish dreams. A child cannot resist the atmosphere with which he is surrounded. The example and influence of one leading man has affected the character of a whole neighborhood or a nation of people long after he has passed away. What a man becomes is in a large part determined by his heredity and environment.

The people and land that gave Benton Cordell Goodpasture birth and fashioned his character were well suited to that purpose. Overton County is one of the northerly counties of Tennessee, and in the last century was known as the Mountain Bench of Tennessee—a way of saying that the region comprised the foothills of the Cumberland Mountains. The county where B. C. Goodpasture grew up was situated far from the main arteries of communication as late as the first years of this century. Trails and dirt roads crossed the country leading to the farms and settlements. Postal deliveries before and after the Civil War were brought in by a horse drawn hack over the rough, hilly, and muddy roads.

The dry goods, hardware, and groceries were hauled in wagons long distances. Such goods were necessarily costly and money was scarce since settlers faced the same problems in getting the produce to market. The country was new and the settlers possessed little or no material wealth. The men, women, and children worked with their own hands for a livelihood. This was the kind of life that Jefferson Goodpasture, Francis Marion, and the father of B. C. Goodpasture experienced in the Cumberland Mountain region.

Labor was honorable and a necessary labor skill such as the blacksmith was a special badge of honor. The opportunities for securing wealth did not exist. The people were content to live in log houses, to wear homespun clothes, and to live on a plain diet.

There were no factories of any kind; and at first, not even saw mills to cut planks. The houses were built of logs floored with puncheons (planks split out of longs with an axe). The cracks were chinked and daubed with mud. Nails were expensive and roofs of the common houses were weighted down with poles. The chimneys were of wood lined with stone and mortar with large deep fireplaces. The more pretentious houses were built of logs hewed on both sides and nicely notched at the corners. Glass windows were unknown. The windows were openings with board shutters.

The houses were small and the families were large. Many houses had just one room used for all purposes. The better homes were double houses with two rooms, a story and half high with a hallway in between. One room served as a kitchen, dining room, and workroom. In this room were the loom, spinning wheel, and other implements of household labor. And no house was too large or too small to extend hospitality to all comers. The furniture was plain, strong, scant, and made by unskilled hands.

The clothing was home made. Every farmer had a small flock of sheep to furnish wool for family use and a small patch of cotton and flax for the same purpose. All bedclothing was of home manufacturing. The dyeing and coloring were chiefly from the native bark, roots, and herbs of the forest.

The women dressed in cotton clothes in the summer and linsey in winter. The men wore cotton and flax in the summer, and brown jeans in the winter dyed with walnut bark. And the better dressed had a suit of blue for Sunday. And a woman who could make her blue dye "set" well was the envy of her neighbors.

The food was country grown. The mills were small and imperfect in grinding and bolting arrangements. Coffee was a luxury for the sick and for company and special occasions. When times were prosperous, biscuits and coffee were served on Sunday morning. Sugar came from the maple tree; molasses and honey from the hive were the sweetners.

Leather was tanned at home and shoes were made of coarse undressed, unstained red leather. But they were strong. At Christmas, a boy received a pair of these shoes with coarse woolen socks, jeans pants, and coat with a change of underclothes, and a suit of cotton or flax. The clothes were expected to last until the next Christmas.

During the frontier period, houses had to be built, the trees cut down, rolled together and burned for crop land. Rails were split, the new ground grubbed, and the land plowed for planting. When a house was to be raised, logs rolled, or corn shucked, the neighbors came together to do the work. No records were kept and no pay was expected other than to help others as needed.

The recreations of the mountain people were simple. The men hunted game in the wilderness. The ladies had their quilting parties. When the cotton was to be seeded, the young people would meet at the home to help. And there would be a race in the seeding with the boys and girls pairing off according to their preferences. On Sunday evening the young people would meet to practice singing. There were no carriages or buggies. All rode horseback or walked to church. Distances of two and three miles meant nothing.

The people were dependent for news from the outside world, and a traveler was sure of a hospitable night's lodging for the news he would impart. Most everybody attended the monthly religious meetings to talk over the floating news in the neighborhood and about crops and such like until the service started.

Educational opportunities were poor. A few months schooling in the winter was provided when the demand for labor lessened. The teachers were unskilled and often uneducated. To read and figure a little was all that most parents thought was necessary. Later in the century, free public schools would run about three months in the late summer and fall months when there was less need for labor. There were no high schools.

The great-grandfather of Benton Cordell Goodpasture was Jefferson Goodpasture, son of James Goodpasture. The Goodpastures who had come from Virginia were loyal supporters of Thomas Jefferson and were proud for members of their family to wear his name. The names that the Goodpastures gave to their children speak their great pride in American patriots and their faith in the Bible as the Word of God. Jefferson was the only son born to James Goodpasture in Overton County.

Jefferson Goodpasture married Nancy Allen who was the daughter of William Allen. The Allens were Virginia immigrants who settled as had the Goodpastures in Overton County. William Allen and his daughter Nancy were subscribers to Barton W. Stones' *Christian Messenger*. Some of the periodicals are now in the private collection of Benton Cordell Goodpasture. The claims of B. C. Goodpasture to his heritage in the Restoration movement can be traced back to his frontier ancestors.

John S. Allen, a son of William Allen, settled in Missouri. He founded Bethany, Missouri, and established a church there. He was an effective preacher of the gospel and preached forty years in that country. John Allen wrote a chapter in T. P. Haley's *The Dawn of the Reformation*. B. C. Goodpasture's link with the pioneer preachers of the Restoration is a solid fact. In addition to this, however, he is one of the best informed students in Restoration history of all.

Jefferson and Nancy Allen Goodpasture were married in 1827 and nine children were born to them. Their second child, Francis Marion, was born May 10, 1830; and he was the grandfather of Benton Cordell Goodpasture.

Francis Marion Goodpasture

Another son of William Allen was Hiram Allen who served with the McCrory Regiment of the West Tennessee Militia at the Battle of New Orleans in the War of 1812 under General Andrew Jackson. He also saw services in the Mexican War and fought against the Creek Indians in the Battle of the Horse Shoe Bend in Alabama.

The story is handed down through family tradition that Hiram Allen was ambushed by an Indian while he was plowing on the family land in Overton County in the vicinity of the old Goodpasture homeplace on Flat Creek. All of the Indians were gone from the region. Occasionally an Indian would slip furtively through the country taking what he could pick up for his personal needs along the way. Allen was plowing and an arrow fell nearby causing some curiosity on his part. When a second arrow struck the earth near him, he knew that he was being stalked.

It was still a common practice to take a gun to the fields or when traveling. Observing the slant of the arrow, Allen began to stalk the would-be assassin. He learned his lessons in Indian warfare having fought the Creek Indians under General Andrew Jackson in Alabama. He spied the Indian hidden in the dense foliage of a tree and brought him down with a rifle shot. Allen peeled a strip of skin along the Indian's spine for a razor strap and dragged the Indian into the underbrush and went on with his plowing. A tombstone bearing the name of Hiram Allen who served with the McCrory Regiment of West Tennessee Militia is in the old cemetery at Flat Creek. This was the land that Jefferson Goodpasture helped tame and the land where Francis Marion Goodpasture was born, and it was here that Benton Cordell Goodpasture grew to manhood among Cumberland Mountain people of the fifth generation.

Such was the frontier background of Jefferson Goodpasture, and this was the kind of life Francis Marion Goodpasture experienced. It was a hard land that tested the iron in a man's soul. As a young man, Francis Marion left Overton County and went to Bethany, Missouri, to live with his aunt and uncle, John S. Allen, and taught school there two or three years. Then he returned to Overton County where he lived the rest of his life. He married Lydia L. Thomas, July 28, 1868, and five children were born to them. Francis Marion Goodpasture became one of the leading citizens of the county.

He served as Register of Overton County during the Civil War and saved the county records when the courthouse burned. During the Civil War, Livingston was on the border line between the Union and the Confederacy, and the surrounding country side was constantly ravaged by guerilla bands from both the North and South.

Francis Marion was also justice of the peace and had his home built with a front porch. Benches were built up and down on each side of the porch where people could sit while he was holding court.

East Tennessee sided with the Union and Middle Tennessee and West Tennessee had gone with the South. Two infamous guerilla bands roamed that part of Tennessee—Champ Fergusson of the Confederacy and "Tinker" Dave Batey of the Union. "Tinker" Batey occupied Livingston for about two weeks and burned the courthouse down just before pulling out. Prior to this, Francis Marion Goodpasture had carried the court records to a hiding place for safe keeping.

The third child of Francis Marion Goodpasture and Lydia L. Thomas was John Jefferson Goodpasture, the father of Benton Cordell Goodpasture. John Jefferson was born October 12, 1873. He was married January 21, 1894, to Elora Thompson. They made their first home in a log house on the farm of Elora Thompson's father at a place called then Rocky Mound about two miles from Hilham, Tennessee, near the Rocky Mound school which got its name because the log school house was built on a knoll of solid rock. The old farm is now a part of the Standing Stone State Park. The land has been slowly turning back into the wilderness for the past forty years. The first child of John Jefferson and Elora Goodpasture was born at Rocky Mound. They named the child Benton Cordell Goodpasture.

There were five other children born to John and Elora Goodpasture after they moved to Flat Creek. Carrie Velma was born May 16, 1905, Charlie Edward was born July 24, 1907; and Lydia Mae was born September 28, 1909; Jennie Ruth was born November 22, 1912. Helen was born April 9, 1915 and died in 1936.

Life in the rural sections was still far from easy in the early years of this century. The men went out into the fields with their work animals and worked the land from dawn to dusk. The chores on the farm were endless from planting to harvest time.

The livestock were a constant care the year round. Firewood had to be cut and there was no end to the labor. The work of a farm wife was equally demanding. The cooking of food was done over a hot wood stove; the clothes were washed in tin tubs. The clothes were first boiled in a black kettle. The women made their own lye soap. Fruit was dried on the roofs of the farm buildings for winter food. Beans and peas were canned and some were dried. Store bought clothes were available, but dresses for the women and girls were generally made at home. This was the disciplined life Benton Cordell Goodpasture knew as he grew into manhood.

John Goodpasture, Ray, Ethel, Carrie, Elora, B.C.

Rocky Mound home:
B.C.'s birthplace

Goodpasture home on Flat Creek

III

Rocky Mound

The story of a man's life is a tale of two houses. The Good-pastures had been among the early settlers of the Cumberlands. Another family equally well known in the country around Hilham were the maternal ancestors of Benton Cordell Goodpasture, the Thompsons. The Thompsons could trace their ancestry back to Ireland. The first settlers who moved into Tennessee were of Northern European stock and most of them were of British and Irish blood. The language, folk traditions, laws, and social institution of the Cumberland frontiersmen were indelibly stamped on the land. The country from the Cumberland Mountains east to the Appalachian Mountains had remained largely isolated from the outside world until around World War I when road improvement became a necessity for the use of the "gasoline buggy." Telephone lines were lacing the remote communities together thus providing a means of communication with the outside world.

At the time B. C. Goodpasture was growing up, the nearest railroad was eighteen miles from Hilham. Almost every manufactured item used by the people in Overton County came in by wagon freight. The crops and livestock the farmers raised on their farms went out the same way. Some of the freight into Overton County was being hauled in by wagon from the nearest railroad which ran through Algood, Tennessee.

The genealogy of the Thompson family can be directly traced from William Thompson who came to America from the "Emerald Isle." Just how he made his way into the Tennessee frontier is not known. A son was born to William Thompson and his wife

J. C. Thompson and Mary Thompson. Children: Alva, Tina, Anna Mary,
Luther, Martha

Isaiah Thompson, Laura Thompson,
Mrs. Isaiah Thompson

Robert Clemens Hill and
Ann Medlock Hill

whose maiden name is unknown. The child was born September 4, 1829, and named Isaiah S. Thompson. He was married in his young manhood to Margaret Lawson who was born in May of 1828.

Eight children were born to them. The oldest, Martha, was born May 3, 1849, and died November 1, 1928. Elizabeth, the next child, was born November 25, 1850, and died January 16, 1879. All of the remaining children lived well on into this century. Mary was the third child and she was followed by Jesse Calvin whose birthday came on January 17, 1856. Jesse Calvin was the grandfather of B. C. Goodpasture. John William, Bird C., James M., and Laura were born into the Thompson family in this order.

Jesse Calvin Thompson married Tina Hill in 1877. Tina Hill, the maternal grandmother of B. C. Goodpasture, was one fourth Cherokee Indian. Her grandfather was a full blooded Cherokee. He was shot down in cold blood by a white man who was hiding by the roadside. The surname of this Indian family was Medlock. Goodpasture has seen the hat with the bullet hole through the crown that his Cherokee ancestor was wearing at the time of his death. A photograph of his son, Clem Hill, appears in this chapter.

Two children were born to Jesse Calvin and Tina Hill Thompson in their short married life before the death of Tina Thompson. Elora Annis was born January 16, 1878; and Luther A. was born in 1880. Luther who was the second child of Jesse Calvin and Tina Hill Thompson grew up around Hilham. He was married to Addie Sullivan and four children were born to them—Eva, Nellie, Charles, and Shirley. Luther moved his family to Celina, Texas, where they lived several years. Afterwards he moved to California dying there in 1948.

John Jefferson Goodpasture was married to Elora Annis Thompson, the oldest child of Jesse Calvin and Tina Hill Thompson, in 1894. They were the parents of Benton Cordell Goodpasture. The young couple lived first on the farm of her father in the Rocky Mound community. A school house was located just up the road and was built on a solid knoll of limestone rock giving the name "Rocky Mound" to the neighborhood. There were about one hundred acres in the farm.

The home of John and Elora was a log house with large living

room, a hall to the back of the living room, and then a kitchen.
The usual crops were raised on the place—corn and hay for the
livestock, sorghum cane for molasses; and Jesse Calvin raised
chickens, hogs, sheep and cattle on the farm. John Goodpasture
farmed the Rocky Mound farm around eight years before he
moved to Flat Creek about four or five miles between Hilham and
Livingston.

Jesse Calvin was married a second time to Mary Langford.
There were four children born to this union. Tina was born October 14, 1887. She married James Benton Upton. They were the
parents of Ray, Willette, and Clarice. Tina Upton is still living in
the general vicinity where she was born. Annie Mary was born
February 8, 1893, and married Lafe Wheat. Two children, Jesse
and Hester, were born to them. Annie Mary died March 26,
1966. Martha is still living in Hilham, Tennessee. Another child
of Jesse and Mary Thompson, Alva, died at an early age. Both
sets of Jesse Calvin Thompson's children were close to each other;
Jesse Calvin was a Singer Sewing machine salesman for twenty
years of his life. He passed away in 1920.

Benton Cordell Goodpasture was born April 9, 1895, on the
farm of his Grandfather Thompson. John and Elora talked over a
name for their baby boy. He was a goodly child, and the first-
born child on both sides of the house. This caused an additional
interest in the new baby. The credit for naming the child went to
Francis Marion Goodpasture. He suggested that the boy be
named for a promising young lawyer in the high Cumberland
Country, Cordell Hull, now a legend in American history. The
grandfather thought the gifted young man had a promising future.

John Goodpasture wanted to know, "Who is Hull? Nobody
has ever heard of him. He's just a young lawyer."

The grandfather replied, "Well, he's a young man of great
promise and ability. Name the boy after him and some day you'll
be glad you did."

Since the young parents desired to respect the older man's
wishes, they decided to name the boy Cordell for a young man who
had not yet made a mark for himself. They added the name Benton to Cordell. Benton McMillin was a prominent Tennessee political figure. He was then a member of the Congress of the
United States and later was elected governor of Tennessee.

B. C. Goodpasture on several occasions saw Cordell Hull dur-

ing his boyhood years. Cordell Hull was a circuit judge and held
court in Livingston, Tennessee, at regular intervals. Hull was a
very distinguished looking man as Goodpasture remembers him
then. One day on a street in Livingston, the small Goodpasture
boy was walking along with his father when they met Cordell Hull.
Goodpasture said he addressed my father as "Mr. Goodpasture."
That puzzled the boy. He had been taught to address older people
as "Mr. and Mrs." Both men were about the same age and not
old men. He couldn't see any reason why Hull should have addressed his father "Mr. Goodpasture."

B. C. Goodpasture easily remembers his great-grandfather, Isaiah Thompson. He recalls that he was a highly respected man in
the community whose word was his bond. There was a saying in
the Rocky Mound neighborhood that if "Isaiah Thompson said it
was so, it was so." Isaiah Thompson was rather a large man and
his hair was white.

Jesse Calvin Thompson lived until May 31, 1920. He was a
man of medium height and weight. He was rather a distinguished
looking man. The Goodpasture child always looked forward to his
grandfather's visits in their home. There was seldom a time that
he came without bringing the children a toy or something. One of
the earliest memories of B. C. Goodpasture when he was not yet
six years old was seeing his grandfather Goodpasture pulling logs
up from the woods for the fireplace with a yoke of oxen.

One of the stories that has remained in the Goodpasture family
goes back when Goodpasture was three years old. He was out in
the yard eating a sausage and biscuit when a greedy rooster
snatched the food from the child's hand and ran away with it. He
ran frantically after the rooster saying, "Sau, sau!"

One of Goodpasture's earliest memories goes back to a time
when he was not yet five years old. His mother's brother who was
a teenage boy kept talking about volunteering and going to the
Spanish American War. His mother pleaded with her brother not
to go and that made a profound impression in the mind of the
small boy. Along about that time, Goodpasture had a little half-
uncle who was two or three years older than he who died and he
remembers the funeral.

The first school that Benton Cordell Goodpasture attended was
just a few hundred yards down the road from where he was born.
The Rocky Mound school house was a primitive small log build-

ing. The children sat on the smoothed sides of split logs. Holes were bored into the rounded side of the logs and dogwood pegs were fitted into the holes for legs. There were no backs to the log benches which were placed around the room against the wall affording the children some back support. All of the benches were the same height from the floor. The smaller children usually had a hard time since their feet could not touch the floor. The small school house had two windows on the sides and one in the back. A blackboard was fastened on the wall behind the teacher's desk. The blackboard was fashioned from smooth poplar planks painted black.

Rocky Mound was a typical mountain school. Most rural schools had only one teacher. Such schools were not closely graded as we think of it today. The teacher started with the A B C's and worked right on up through the grades. Country schools then were short termed. The schools were in session about ten weeks or three months. The weather and money were the determining factors; limited public funds were the main reason for the short sessions. When winter closed in, the schools were shut down. Rocky Mound was a public supported school; however, other schools were run after the public schools were closed. Such schools were called "subscription schools" because the financial support came from small tuition fees paid by the parents entitling the child to enroll in such schools.

A school day at Rocky Mound was a long day for both the teacher and the students. There was time for play during the two daily recesses and the dinner period. Benton Cordell Goodpasture enrolled in the school in 1902. His first teacher was Fannie Coffman. His special friend and playmate was Burr Maxwell who still lives near the old school site. The two children were born on adjoining farms. Burr Maxwell recalled those early days while walking over the site of the old Rocky Mound school. And he gave the following account:

> In our first year, B. C. and I were buddies. There were several larger boys and one in particular that had a pick at us and would tease and call us names. There was a grove of young hickory saplings real tall and slender. This boy climbed one of those trees and began to tantalize us. We picked up a pile of rocks and began throwing at him, but we could not hit him as he would sway back and forth in the

slender tree. But there was a bunch of boys farther on in the woods. One of the rocks went over and hit one of them. It happened to be a brother of the one we were throwing at. They came leading him up out of the bushes—the blood running down his forehead. They said, 'You boys are ruined now, we are going to tell on you.'

Burr Maxwell said about the incident, "I was sure scared. B. C. will have to answer for himself, but I do remember that we were not punished."

The school house was built on solid bed rock surface and was not the best school ground for their play periods. Here and there were small patches of dirt. The children would run around the school house jumping from one rock surface to another. The point of the game was to jump from rock to rock around the school ground without their feet once touching the ground. Stone bruises were common for the barefooted children as they ran and played over the rocky surface.

Just a short distance from the school a flat ledge of rock jutted from the ground. There was a deep crevice between the two rocks. The girls would play "big meeting time" with singing and praising as some of the children had seen their parents doing in church services. Burr Maxwell recalled a time when the girls were playing "big meeting time." One of the girls was "rejoicing" and fell into the crevice suffering a painful injury. And the teacher stopped the children from playing the game at that place.

Maxwell recalled a severe thunderstorm that came up one day while they were in school. Lightning struck a tree near the house shocking the teacher. The tree was splintered and some of the splinters were driven through the cracks between the logs. The children were terrified.

Two other children were born to John and Elora while they were living at Rocky Mound. Ethel was born January 30, 1897. She was never married, and on June 8, 1923, she passed away. Raymond Casto was born November 7, 1900, and he still lives near the old Goodpasture home on Flat Creek. Ray, as Raymond is called, was married February 14, 1926 to Myrtle Ward, and they have two daughters, Catherine and Dorothy. Ray is still living; and at a time when most men are retired, he works for the forestry service in Standing Stone State Park. Three times each day Ray climbs the fire tower which overlooks the vast timbered reaches of Standing Stone Park that looks much now like the wilderness it was in the frontier days.

The folk humor of a region is indigenous to its people and their life setting. One story Ray tells of the mountain people is about a small boy who carried corn to the water mill to be ground. The water was low, the grinding stone turned slowly, and a trickle of meal ran out, and the boy grew weary. The boy said, "I could eat that meal faster than it comes out."

And the miller said, "For how long?"

And the little boy replied, "Until I starved to death."

And he told the story of a mountain character called by those who knew him as Uncle Bill Masters who was the uncle of Ray's wife. He had a man to dig a well for him. The well rig was powered by a mule which walked around and around the drill. It was said of that well that it was so crooked that Uncle Bill could draw water out of both ends of it.

The Goodpasture family lived at Rocky Mound until 1902 with their three small children. Their home and social life were patterned in the same way as their neighbors'. Burr Maxwell tells another story that gives an insight into the life of the rural people in Overton County around the turn of the century:

> In the community where we lived, folks would help each other with their work, and were never too busy with their own affairs to quit and help their neighbor. I recall one of the neighbors was having a log rolling. B. C.'s parents and mine were there. The entire family went along when they had a log rolling. The men would do the field work and the women did the cooking. They always served a bountiful meal at the noon hour. At this particular time they had the dinner on the table and the men were getting ready to eat. B. C. and I passed around the table, and it was loaded with good things to eat. As we came around, he reached out and got himself a piece of egg custard; but too bad, his mother saw what he did. She took him outside and punished him. My mother was there too. That's the reason I didn't get a piece of pie. I just wasn't as brave as he was.

Another boyhood companion of Benton Cordell Goodpasture was A. R. Hill. The John Goodpasture family lived on one side of the mountain and the George Washington Hill family lived on the other side between 1898 and 1900. A. R. Hill remembers the dates because his father died when A. R. was eight years old and his mother passed away when he was just ten. In 1902 John Goodpasture moved his family from Rocky Mound to Flat Creek, and about the same time A. R. Hill and his brother went to live with their Uncle James Thomas who lived down the road from the home of John Goodpasture. A. R. Hill was twelve years of age then. James Thomas and his wife were already well up in years having grown children of their own. A. R. Hill and B. C. Goodpasture were double cousins. A. R. Hill's mother and John Goodpasture's mother were sisters; the maternal grandmother of B. C. Goodpasture and A. R. Hill's father were brother and sister.

The father of A. R. Hill was one of the elders of the church of Christ in Hilham, Tennessee, located about three miles from Rocky Mound. John Goodpasture was a church going man. The two families attended church at Hilham. The Goodpasture family rode in a four wheel buggy drawn by a white horse. Ethel and Cordell sat on the floor in the back of the buggy while Ray was held in his mother's lap in the front seat. A. R. Hill and B. C. Goodpasture both became preachers and both attended David Lipscomb College. The two Hill boys and the Goodpasture children were inseparable companions during their childhood days on Flat Creek.

John Goodpasture moved from the Rocky Mound community to the Flat Creek neighborhood between Hilham and Livingston after his father's death. Both Francis Marion Goodpasture and his wife Lydia died in the first year of this century. He inherited his share of his father's land and made his home on Flat Creek the rest of his life. The old Goodpasture home place is still intact. Upon the death of his father, B. C. Goodpasture purchased the shares of his brother and his sisters which he has retained to the present time.

IV

A Boy On Flat Creek

After John Jefferson Goodpasture moved from Rocky Mound to Flat Creek, he built a home for his family which is still standing. The house was weather-boarded, sealed, and painted white. The home was heated in the wintertime by a fireplace and a stove. The family first carried water from a spring and later a well was dug. The farm buildings were of the usual kind—a corn crib, smoke house for curing and hanging cured pork, hen house, and a barn for the livestock and storing grain.

There were two hundred acres in John Jefferson's farm. It was described as average land with some creek bottom acreage. When Cordell was growing up, he helped his father clear two or three fields. They cut the timber, rolled the logs, and piled the brush for burning. The father and son grubbed and plowed the new ground as in frontier days.

Each year about sixty acres of row crop were cultivated for harvesting. The main crops were corn, hay, and soybean. A new orchard was set out sometime after John Goodpasture was settled on his land. Cordell helped his father dig the holes and set the fruit trees.

Their farm tools were of the kind commonly used in the South —the Oliver turning plow, double shovel for cultivating the row crops, and a bull tongued plow for "laying off" corn rows and splitting out the middles. At first corn planting was done by dropping the corn a grain at a time in the row. Later John Goodpasture used a one row corn drill. He kept horses on the farm—no mules. Other livestock included milk cows, grazing cattle, sheep, and hogs. B. C. Goodpasture remembers a gray horse they owned called "Old Bob" who lived to be thirty-two years old. "Old Bob" seemed to have instinctive concern for children. Once Cordell fell from the saddle while riding the horse. "Old Bob" stopped as if he had been suddenly frozen to protect the boy.

The neighborhood Cordell grew up in was little more than a generation removed from a pioneer community. The neighbors helped one another out of mutual concern because it was still a necessity of life. A farmer who had a new ground to clear invited his neighbors for a log rolling. The women folk would be preparing dinner, and the children too small for working would be playing. Occasionally there would be a corn shucking or a house raising, and in two or three days a house would be built. If a man was sick, his neighbors planted his crop, or even cultivated and harvested the crops if his sickness lingered on and with no charge to the sick man. In such cases, the man being helped would provide dinner and supper for the workers.

There was one special summer vacation enjoyed by the John Goodpasture family. After the summer crops were laid by and the general farm work slackened, John Goodpasture took his family on an annual visit to the home of his sister, Mrs. Florence Pate, in Jackson County, near Gainesboro, Tennessee. This was a wonderful week for the Goodpasture children. It would be watermelon time, and none grew riper and sweeter than the melons on the Pate farm. The children spent their time fishing, wading, and swimming; and the older folk spent their time catching up with their talking and just visiting.

The most memorable and important years in a person's life are his school days. Benton Cordell Goodpasture had started his first year of school at Rocky Mound in 1902 just a short distance from his home, but he finished the school term that same fall at the Flat Creek school. Jess Fleming was Cordell's second school teacher who was teaching at Flat Creek that fall of 1902. Teachers came and went in the Flat Creek school. One of the teachers was B. H. Hunt. B. C. Goodpasture remembers B. H. Hunt as one of the best teachers he ever had. He was the kind of a teacher who could explain things and made the students see what he had in mind. Hunt was able to inspire students to study and to fire them with ambition to amount to something in life. B. H. Hunt later practiced law in Overton County.

A school day at Flat Creek stretched out over eight hours. Books were taken up at eight o'clock and school was dismissed at four in the afternoon. The children enjoyed a ten or fifteen minute recess in the morning and another around two-thirty p.m.

Front row: Charles, John Goodpasture and Elora Thompson Goodpasture, Jennie, Lydia. *Back row:* B.C., Ethel, Ray, Carrie

Mrs. Florence Pate

The "whirl hole" on Flat Creek. B.C. and Ray Goodpasture

The lunch hour lasted from twelve to one. These periods were spent mostly in playing games in the schoolyard.

Country schools were conducted in much the same fashion in rural regions in the early years of this century. Classes were not closely graded. The children studied their primers, readers, geography, arithmetic, spelling, and physiology. A student advanced through the grades as he was able to master the subject matter. In the Flat Creek school, the smaller children recited their lessons in the morning and prepared their lessons in the afternoons while the older students recited their lessons. Sometimes the boys and girls just day-dreamed their hours away when their classes were not in session. The Goodpasture boy would usually sit and listen to the older students recite their lessons absorbing a great many facts in the process. This was one of the advantages of such a school. A bright student could greatly advance his learning by paying attention to the recitations of older children.

While Cordell was a very small boy attending the Flat Creek school, he spent the night with his best little friend, Barlow Smith. Barlow had a baby brother just a few days old. The mother asked the Goodpasture boy if he would like to see the baby and he said that he would. So he went in and took a look at the baby named William E. who has been a lifelong friend of B. C. Goodpasture. William E. Smith enjoys telling that Cordell was the first non-member of the family to see him. The Smiths were distant relatives of the Goodpastures.

The Flat Creek school house was a small log building with two windows on each side and one in the back of the building. The school was equipped with long benches made out of yellow poplar boards. There were two blackboards in front of the auditorium where the children sat. The blackboard surfaces fashioned from poplar planks were painted black. No writing desks of any kind were in front of the students. The benches at Flat Creek too were of the same height making the day even harder for the small children since they could not reach the floor with their short legs.

The regular school session at Flat Creek started sometime in July or August after the crops were laid by and the children were no longer needed to help with the farm labor. School was usually dismissed a week or two in September for the children to help pull fodder for the winter feeding of the livestock. Then the school would run on for about eight weeks. Public money for the support of the school was limited. The winter months set in and the schools were closed. Some of the books they studied were Stickney's *Readers* and Lee's *Readers,* McGee's *History of Tennessee,* and Hunt's *Speller.*

Benton Cordell Goodpasture never played second fiddle in his life. He has always played the leading role at whatever he set his mind to. He has from childhood stood out in a class to himself. A favorite pastime of students in the "old time" schools was to excel in the spelling bees and rapid calculation contests. Whoever advanced to the head of the spelling class or worked his problem first knew he must beat the Goodpasture boy.

William E. Smith who was the baby that Cordell first saw recalls his childish impression of the larger boys. Cordell was about seven years older than William:

> I can remember that in the little one-teacher school where we attended; he was a big boy as I thought then, and could do anything. When we divided for town ball, cat ball, or spelling matches, the person who got first take always took Cordell. He could out run, out jump, out spell anyone in our school. My eldest brother was the teacher, and Cordell pretending to study geography with a New Testament in his textbook memorized the second chapter of the book of Acts. He could run so fast that none of us could catch him, or escape his speed. He could knock a ball into the woods from our small playground so far that we often lost them. He likes to hunt. He could beat anyone shooting. When he fired, you could well know there was a dead bird, or whatever he was shooting at was hit. None of us dared challenge him on anything. In what was called 'rapid calculation,' his slate was first on the table (paper writing tablets were not used). He had a sister who was his equal in learning. He could out swim a fish and climb equal to a squirrel. There was a paw paw thicket near our school. We smaller boys would get him to climb the trees and get paw paws for us. He would climb the big chestnut trees and shake them. The entire school would pick up the nuts.

Children living out in the country played such games that they could improvise. Their games were seasonal and especially the marble playing when school was in session. One of the marble games was called euchre. A square would be marked on the ground and nine marbles were placed in the square. The players started from a shooting line. The purpose was to knock all the marbles from the square, and the boy who came out with the most marbles was the champion. An expert marble player could often knock out each marble from the square without bouncing his marble out of the square. During the summer months when the boys were not in school and when they could not work in the fields on rainy days, they would gather under the shed of the Goodpasture barn to play marbles.

The boys in the Flat Creek neighborhood liked ball games, and they especially enjoyed playing "town ball." Several boys had to be present to play the game. The bases were run as is in baseball. Two boys chose sides by running their hands alternating up to the small end of the bat until one boy had the last firm grip covering the end of the bat with his clasped hand. If a small portion were exposed, the other boy would grip the exposed end. If he could manage to throw the bat some ten feet, first choice belonged to him.

Another favorite game was "cat ball." Two boys would stand with bats in their hands with a hindcatcher behind each boy. The other boys would be out in the playing field. The ball would be thrown to alternate batters. If a boy caught a fly driven out in his direction, he took his turn at the bat.

Other games the mountain boys played were not conventional, but one was universal. Snowball fights go on wherever the snow falls and it falls in the Cumberlands. Barlow Smith said while they were growing up in the Flat Creek neighborhood, the boys frequently got into snowball fights and that "Cordell could make the hardest snowballs and throw them the straightest and they always seemed to land on his head." About the only way a boy could elude Cordell was to outrun him if he could. And Barlow said, "He would run me down; he was a long-winded rascal like a foxhound."

The old saying goes that "boys will be boys" and Cordell Goodpasture was an all-around Cumberland mountain boy. He was the champion among the boys in the neighborhood. William E. Smith said he was a natural born peacemaker and would umpire the squabbles the children got into. But sometimes an argument took a different turn when a bully thought to take over. Barlow said, "If anyone interferred when we got into a spat, we would quit and both of us would jump on him. We fought each other, but we would fight for each other just as quick."

In front of the Goodpasture home and just across the road,

Flat Creek rushed along between its deeply wooded banks. The neighbor boys enjoyed swimming in the "whirl hole" where the water course took a turn forming a slow moving whirlpool with just enough force to make the swimming exciting without the danger encountered in swift deep water. The boys enjoyed water fighting, swimming, and diving contests. The boys would divide up into teams to compete as teams and as individuals.

There were numerous other diversions for the children. They all enjoyed pitching horse shoes—"the kind that came off of horses." Cordell also wanted to excel in the swimming matches; he was often—but not always—the champion. In the fall the children would gather hickory nuts, hazel nuts, walnuts, and chestnuts for their mothers to make "goodies" to eat. In those days the children worked hard on the farms, but they were encouraged to play childhood games. Money was scarce, but the children nevertheless had their toys and many of them they made for themselves such as the sling shot (the kind the shepherd boy David had—not a rubber-band flipper), bows and arrows, flutes from elder berry stems, cornstalk fiddles, and other homemade devices.

For the more adventuresome boys, there were the caves to explore (it was not called "spelunking" then). The boys explored with fascination the wilds of the Cumberlands. It was not a formal course in natural history as the boys studied the curious and colorful rock formations and the flora and the fauna. They examined the moss growing from the bark on the north side of the trees, and they enjoyed the wild flowers and ferns. They saw the squirrels and the chipmunks in their natural habitat. Sometimes they saw a fox streaking across an open field and occasionally a beautiful doe and her faun. Long before the boys were allowed to hunt with guns, they hunted the wild animals. Rabbits and possums were chased by dogs belonging to small boys. It was great fun for the boys when their dogs treed an animal in his den and they smoked him out. Tarzan would have enjoyed swinging on the grape vines that grew long and stout in the Cumberlands.

Country people in past generations grew their own orchards with trellises for grape vines back of the house. They picked the wild berries that grew in abundance for their jams and jellies. The father of the Smith boys had an apple tree that produced an apple that Cordell especially enjoyed because of its flavor. Barlow said that he and Cordell got into an apple eating contest. He ate twelve apples and Cordell ate thirteen. Barlow came out twice a loser. He got a stomach ache and Cordell did not.

Cordell, Ray, and Ethel Goodpasture remember one game they played they wished they had not. A farmer will not allow the farm animals to be run or abused in any way. Anyhow a boy or a girl can take a wild run by holding on to a calf's tail. The point is to turn the animal loose before his running momentum causes a child to suffer a painful fall. The Goodpasture children were running the calves. Their father saw them and warned them they could expect thrashing if they were again caught running the calves. Cordell saw his father one day slipping along a paling fence while they were running the calves, and Cordell dropped down in a cedar grove to hide. Ray and Ethel got a switching and they told on Cordell. And the father said, "I'll whip him too." But he never got around to it.

Another game they enjoyed was frightening the sheep. Their Grandfather Goodpasture killed hogs and salted them down to take into town later in the year to sell. He had large meat sacks sewn to hold the meat. Cordell would take one of the old sacks and cut a hole in it and stick his head through the hole. He would lie down while the sheep came down the path driven by Ray and Ethel. Cordell would rise up just as the sheep approached him. No matter how high he raised himself, the sheep would make the jump without once touching the boy.

A good practical joke has been a joy of B. C. Goodpasture early and later in life. Once he played a joke on his uncle, Herschel Goodpasture. One rainy day when the boys could not work in the fields, they made one of their frequent visits to their Uncle Herschel's farm. He suggested that the boys crawl under the house to hunt for eggs and he would award them with an egg fry. Cordell volunteered to crawl under the house for the eggs. He also picked up a dozen eggs out of the store house while he was about it. Uncle Herschel was very much surprised at the number of eggs. The boys had really a big egg fry and equally a big laugh, but the uncle was a good sport. The boys enjoyed riding horses and playing games on his farm, and they were always welcome.

Every boy somewhere along the way wants a wagon. Cordell and A. R. Hill made their own. Their Uncle Jim Thomas helped the boys build their wagon by allowing them to use his tools to fashion such iron work that they needed. The wheels were made out of small black gum logs. The wheels were sawed off at the end of the log and rounded. John Goodpasture had given his son a calf that he named "Porter." Cordell fashioned a yoke for the calf and trained him to pull the wagon with the smaller children riding in it.

Cordell was eleven years old before his father allowed him to use a shotgun. The first gun he carried into the woods and fields was a Remington single barrel, twenty-gauge shotgun with a thirty-four inch, full-choke barrel. He used the gun first to hunt squirrels. The first time he left the house with the gun, he shot down a "blue darter" hawk that killed the neighborhood chickens. He did not go any further that day, but carried his trophy home to show to his mother and father. This put him in good standing with the neighborhood women because the numerous hawks posed a constant threat to their growing chickens. That gun is still in his possession.

The first gun he owned was a twenty-two rifle. His Grandfather Thompson bought the rifle for his grandson while he was in Louisville, Kentucky. The boy enjoyed roaming the fields and woods with his gun. Occasionally he would bag a rabbit. In time he became an expert rifleman and his skill would have impressed a Davy Crockett.

Cordell learned the art of trapping fur bearing animals in the Cumberland high country. He made rabbit traps and sold a few rabbits for a nickel each. He trapped other animals for their hides. A good possum hide brought twenty-five or forty cents; a skunk sold for a dollar; and a fox hide brought about the same. The hides first had to be dried and cured. This was done by stretching the hides tautly over a board and allowing them to dry. The hides were carried into town where poultry, eggs, and hides were sold at a produce establishment.

During the years that Benton Cordell Goodpasture was growing to young manhood, he attended schools other than the Rocky Mound and the Flat Creek schools. These schools were called "subscription schools." Such schools were conducted in the winter months after the public schools were closed and did not start again until the following summer. The schools were called "subscription schools" because the parents paid a small tuition fee for their children to attend the winter sessions. The salaries of the teachers and other expenses were paid out of the fees.

Cordell attended his first subscription school at Holly Springs about two miles from their Flat Creek home. In those days the school houses also served as a community gathering place for socials, public meetings, programs for entertainment, debating, and church services. Such meetings were usually held on Friday evenings. The school was widely known around the country for such activities. The Holly Springs school sponsored a debating society and the eleven-year-old Goodpasture boy was one of the members; and at the age of eleven, he engaged in his first public debate. A. R. Hill remembers one of the occasions—it may have been the first debate. When time came for Cordell to speak, all he could do was to address the chair. But later he got up and made an excellent speech. B. C. Goodpasture said that since those early speaking experiences, he has felt little if any embarrassment standing before an audience.

The next "subscription school" Cordell attended was in Hilham, Tennessee. Moses Fisk had established Hilham early in the nineteenth century. He was a well known pioneer educator in the Cumberlands. He established Fisk Academy. Schools of this kind served a critical need before the development of the American public school system. Some of the founders dreamed that someday their schools would grow to be great universities.

Fisk Academy was housed in this period in a large frame building with one room at first, and other additions were built as advanced classes were added to the school curriculum. The school opened first with one teacher and later a second teacher was added. The students paid three or four dollars tuition fee. The Hilham school term was scheduled so there would be no conflict with the Holly Springs school.

A. R. Hill said that Cordell was an exceptionally good student who especially enjoyed reading and studying. His mother encouraged him to work hard and make good grades. The other children thought he was "mamma's pet" trying to get out of doing the chores. His mother did favor him because she knew the boy was trying to learn, and she allowed him to burn "midnight oil" in the old kerosene lamp long after the rest of the family had gone to bed.

A. R. Hill, a double cousin of the Goodpasture children, remembers well a great deal about those early days because he was a part of them. John Goodpasture lived on one side of a mountain, and the George Washington Hill family lived on the other side between 1898 and 1900. A. R. Hill remembers the dates because his mother died just when he was eight years old. His father passed away two years later. A. R. and his brother went to live with their uncle on Flat Creek, a mile up the creek from the Good-pastures. The Goodpastures always extended a warm welcome to the Hill orphans. Elora Goodpasture was a good cook and she mothered the boys. They spent a good part of their spare time with the Goodpasture children.

A. R. Hill recalled that John Goodpasture allowed the children to pick field peas for spending money. They spent many happy hours together at the sorghum mill at molasses making time. The children drank the cane juice and ate the skimmings from the cooking sorghum juice. The boys especially enjoyed heating the cane stalks in the fire until they exploded like firecrackers. These social gatherings attended by the old and young often lasted far into the night.

Benton Cordell Goodpasture cannot remember first going to church because John Goodpasture took his family to worship services. The Goodpastures came from an ancestry who were honored to be known as "God fearing" people. The Goodpasture and Smith children who played and went to school together also attended worship services at the Flat Creek church of Christ which was established around the time of the Civil War. Their fathers were elders in the Flat Creek church.

T. C. Fox was holding a meeting at Flat Creek when Cordell was fourteen years old, and he decided then to become a Christian. Barlow Smith, one of his best friends, also made up his mind to accept the gospel. He was fifteen at the time. They were baptized in the "whirl hole" in Flat Creek just across the road from the Goodpasture home. This marked another period in the life of B. C. Goodpasture. The boy could not have reckoned that one day he would become one of the most influential leaders of the church of Christ in this century. Cordell from that time on became a serious student of the Bible.

As Cordell matured, he delved deeper into the Bible in his home study. There were difficult passages he could not understand. A man who took an early interest in the bright eager boy was a country doctor who had his office in Hilham. Dr. T. A. Langford was the medical doctor. He was not a graduate of a medical school. His knowledge of medicines and the healing arts

were learned under older doctors; Dr. Langford owned a good
medical library. He was held in the highest esteem by all the people around Hilham. Dr. Langford pulled the Goodpasture child
through a critical spell of pneumonia.

Dr. Langford also preached the gospel and conducted weddings
and funerals. Dr. Langford had accumulated a good and useful
religious library containing such books as *Johnson's Notes* and
Adam Clarke's Commentaries. When the Goodpasture boy came to
Hilham, he was welcomed to use the doctor's library and he often
did. Whenever he was bothered by some troublesome Scripture,
he would write it down to work out later in the doctor's library.
He learned early in life to be a good student of the Bible.

It is now clear that B. C. Goodpasture grew up to be a
preacher. Whatever his other accomplishments in life have been,
it is the great preacher that has always stood out in his life and
does so even to this day. While he was growing up, his mother
kept before him the names of David Lipscomb, James A. Harding,
and E. G. Sewell; and she implanted in him the desire to be a
preacher.

Benton Cordell Goodpasture remembers distinctly the first sermon he preached, but he cannot remember when he did not plan to
be a preacher. He preached his first sermon October 18, 1912, in
the Holly Springs school house on a Sunday evening. Cordell
had attended the Holly Springs "subscription schools" and knew
most of the neighborhood people. Several were members of the
church of Christ. The school served as a community center, and
members of the church of Christ conducted worship services each
Lord's day. The seventeen ·year old boy chose this place to start
preaching because he had often spoken there in debates, and the
older people had heard him on those occasions. He thought the
Holly Springs community would be a good place to begin. Holly
Springs was widely known around Hilham because of the debates
and other such activities of community interest that were conducted there. About that first sermon he said in later years:
"Well, I just made up my mind I wanted to begin preaching and
had the brethren to announce it."

His first sermon was on the subject of faith divided into three
parts: The Importance of Faith; How Does Faith Come?; and
What Faith Does. Neither his father nor any other member of his
immediate family was present on that occasion. The other

Goodpasture children were too young to attend without their parents. And it seems that the boy did not tell his parents. The announcement had been made from the pulpit and somehow the news did not get down the road to the Goodpasture home.

Some three weeks later, Cordell preached his second sermon in the Flat Creek church house. His family and all the Flat Creek community came out to hear him. He remembers that he had a difficult time trying to turn to Daniel 2: 44. About all the father said on that occasion was to make some suggestion so that wouldn't happen again.

The Cumberland Mountain people were proud of their heritage and still are. They are mindful they are descended from hardy pioneers who won the land from the wilderness. John Goodpasture grew up in a generation of riflemen who prided themselves in being able "to shoot without a rest." There had been times when a man needed to shoot without a "rest." John Goodpasture advised his boy when he preached "to shoot without rest." B. C. Goodpasture said his father did not have much to say about his desire to become a preacher or his preaching because he was "from Missouri" and had to be shown. At any rate the father did not have a long wait to learn what his manly young son could do.

Over the next two years Cordell preached in small rural churches and school houses at such places as the Concord school near Flat Creek, White's Bend in Jackson County, Hilham, Livingston, and Algood near Cookeville, Tennessee. He conducted his first funeral service in 1912 for a young woman, Martha L. Stockton; he was seventeen at the time. And the following year he preached the funeral service for Leslie E. Eldrige who died April 8, 1913, and was buried in the Mount Gilead Cemetery.

The summer of 1914 was filled with pleasant surprises for the eighteen year old boy. He meant to become a preacher of the gospel. The results of his first sermons had been encouraging. The first gospel meeting that Goodpasture conducted was at a place called Baptist Ridge in Clay County. He sent in an account of that meeting July 18, 1914, to the *Gospel Advocate:*

> I closed a week's meeting at Baptist Ridge today. The meeting began under very unfavorable circumstances. The Baptist and Methodist formed a coalition to keep me away but made a failure. The meeting was much better than we expected. The meeting was well attended throughout.

Baptist Ridge
meetinghouse

B.C. in 1916

Concord
schoolhouse

Nine were added to the Lord—six baptized and three re-
stored. Two or three of the number were Methodist who
had been on the "mourner's bench" the week before. Two
Methodist and one Baptist preacher were present on the
first day of the meeting. They intended to continue their
meeting on into the next week which of course would have
broken into our arrangements; but when I arrived, they
agreed to let me fill my appointment, which they had announced two weeks before. There are a few faithful Christians scattered around Baptist Ridge. I am now on my
way to Pleasant Grove where I am to begin a week's meeting starting next Lord's Day.

The young preacher held other meetings in the late summer
months before he entered the Nashville Bible school. Everybody
who heard him preach was impressed, and his first efforts promised so much for the future.

Cordell conducted his second revival in 1914 at a church called
Willow Grove. The meeting had been planned as a joint endeavor
with an older preacher, Marion Harris. He had taken Cordell
along to assist him with the preaching. As it turned out, the
young man did most of the preaching. The young people were
carried away by his fine speaking ability and personal appearance.
Benton Cordell Goodpasture has been elegantly handsome from his
childhood into the advancing years of his life. In that meeting
seventeen persons were baptized.

The Willow Grove meeting house was located on Obey River
in Clay County. It was one of the best churches in the Cumberland Country. The church was established during the days of the
Sewells. The Sewell family counted among its illustrious sons
Caleb Sewell, and Jesse L. Sewell, and E. G. Sewell. Some of the
Sewells were still attending Willow Grove services in 1914.
Cordell returned for some five or six later meetings. Crowds esti-
mated at two and three thousand attended the later meetings. He
baptized forty-eight persons in one meeting and sixty-eight in another. The little church in the first meeting was so crowded that
the small children sat on the rostrum. The auditorium was lighted
by kerosene lamps with tin pie pans used as reflectors. The old
church site is now covered by the TVA Dale Hollow Lake.

W. H. (Champ) Clark has been a life long friend of B. C.
Goodpasture. The father of Champ Clark, Dr. Edward Clark, and
John Goodpasture were good friends. During the meetings at

Willow Grove, Cordell would sometimes stay in the Clark home. One night when the young preacher was spending the night in the Clark home, the doctor was roused from his bed. About two o'clock in the morning, a neighbor loudly called Dr. Clark: "Doc, are you in bed?" Whoever was asleep was bound to be awakened.

The doctor called back, "Now where would you expect me to be at this hour of the night?" But being a country doctor, this was a normal happening in the Clark home.

Champ who was a small boy at the time remembers the young preacher always brought his rifle along with him. The rifle was a 22 "Hornet." Cordell enjoyed walking in the rugged mountain region, and a large part of it still belonged to the primeval wilderness. The men in the neighborhood would gather on Saturday afternoons on the front porch of the country store to watch the young man shoot targets from the fence posts. He was a superior marksman which excited the admiration of the old timers.

Champ Clark was baptized in 1952 at Celina, Tennessee, by B. C. Goodpasture. He also baptized Rufus (Uncle Rufe) Langford who was approaching his eightieth year. Uncle Rufe was the brother of Dr. T. A. Langford of Hilham, Tennessee. That night when B. C. Goodpasture baptized the two men, he said he felt like he was paying off some debts to his old friends, Dr. Edward Clark and Dr. T. A. Langford.

By chance the young preacher got the opportunity to hold a meeting for the New Providence church in Giles County located on Pigeon Roost Creek. Mason Ball, one of the elders of the church, wrote John Dunn in Cookeville, Tennessee, to recommend a preacher for a meeting. John Dunn sent the names of two preachers and one was that of Cordell Goodpasture; and he said, "I don't know why they selected me. Perhaps it was because of the unusual name that may have attracted attention."

The gospel meeting got under way in September of 1914 on a Sunday evening. A young girl who attended all the services remembers a great many details of that meeting. She was Wilma Wilson, a daughter of John Wilson, an elder of the church. The members of the New Providence church were impressed when the nineteen-year-old Goodpasture walked into the pulpit. He stood straight in the pulpit and almost motionless as he preached. He moved the audience with words he spoke. Although he carried his Bible into the pulpit, he never opened it and never referred to a note. He was "shooting without a rest." When he quoted from the Bible, he called it "the Book."

Cordell never once during the meeting presumed on the ignorance of any member of his audience, nor left the impression that he was not as equally intelligent as he or any other person present. The young preacher assured the audience that they could understand the Bible as he presented his lessons with simplicity and becoming humility.

The first night of the meeting the evangelist announced to the audience that if any person had a Bible question he wanted answered to place the written question on the pulpit each evening. Older preachers made this Bible "question and answer" period a feature of their meetings and the younger preachers usually followed suit. A question was placed on the pulpit stand the following evening by a man who boasted "that he would trap that boy preacher and that would be the end of the meeting." The preacher was not trapped; at least, the audience did not think so. Without opening his Bible, the preacher answered the question to the complete satisfaction of everyone present with the exception of his interrogator. But his somewhat indignant adversary did not give up so easily. On the two following evenings other questions appeared and then they no longer appeared.

A Negro boy who lived nearby expressed a wish to hear the "boy preacher." He was about the same age as the preacher. He came and sat without missing a word. A great deal of excitement attended that first New Providence meeting. At the close of an evening service, Cordell announced that he would speak on the subject of the "Church" the following evening. The older members wondered what a "boy preacher" would do with a subject like that. Most beginning preachers stuck to first principle sermons. The news got around and a large audience awaited him the following evening. Some thought he would be unable "to make his point" as they termed it. At the close of the evening service, Cordell announced he would complete the sermon the following evening. Needless to say that an even larger audience was present. The members of the New Providence church heard him with complete satisfaction. Wilma Wilson said "some of the older members talked about these sermons until they were called from this world." During the New Providence Meeting, the young man would walk about the farm with his twenty-two rifle target practicing. After the evening service, he would return home with the Wilson family where he was staying. He enjoyed eating his supper at that time. One of his favorite dishes was cornbread and milk with the cream skimmed off which had been cooled in the spring house. The family enjoyed sitting around the supper table talking. Cordell returned for later meetings, and the children enjoyed hearing him talk about Nashville and the Old Nashville Bible School which seemed so far away to them.

The night Cordell started the meeting, the wife of John Wilson was away looking after a sick daughter. The following day she came home and attended the service. The young preacher when he met her at the door said, "I don't believe I have seen you here before."

And she replied, "No, but you have spent the night in my home and I have prepared and served three meals for you." The people standing near by had a good laugh over the exchange of words.

On the last night of the meeting, the elders counted up the money and found they could pay Cordell fifty dollars for his efforts. When they told him how much they could give him, he put his hands together and held them over his head with his voice raised in happy excitement exclaimed, "Now I can go to college!" This was a great moment in the life of Benton Cordell Goodpasture. He was now nineteen years old and fired with ambition to make his mark in life. He had been planning to go to the Nashville Bible School for three years. The year before things were shaping up pretty well. But one night a pack of neighborhood dogs got into his sheep and killed thirteen head. That delayed his going to college one year.

Mason Ball purchased his railroad ticket to Nashville, so he would have the fifty dollars when he got to Nashville. When Cordell left home for the New Providence meeting, he had thirty five dollars in his pocket. He was invited to return each year to New Providence for a meeting as long as he was in school. When his train pulled into Union Station in Nashville, Benton Cordell got off the train with eighty-five dollars in his pocket. About his early preaching experience prior to his coming to the Nashville Bible School he thoughtfully said, "It wasn't discouraging. I felt pretty good about it. I already had six years of debating experience behind me." When the young man enrolled in the Nashville Bible School, he didn't try to impress anybody. But then he did not need to because he was as much at home with his books as he had been walking through his beloved Cumberland Mountains.

Cordell found a new friend who would become his greatest friend, H. Leo Boles, the president of the Nashville Bible School who had been personally selected by the venerable David Lipscomb for the position. Both men had been reared in the Cumberland Mountain region that had not been harsh to either of them, but the hard country had put iron in their souls and character in their lives. It is not likely that time will allow either of them to be forgotten. Soon after B. C. Goodpasture entered the Nashville Bible School, A. B. Lipscomb a nephew of David Lipscomb, who was one of the main writers for the *Gospel Advocate* and later president of David Lipscomb College, introduced the student preacher to the *Advocate* readers:

> B. C. Goodpasture, a promising young preacher of three years, would like to make some regular monthly appointments while he is in the Nashville Bible School. He makes his home with John E. Dunn, 2101 Tenth Avenue South, Nashville, Tennessee. I join with Brother Dunn in recommending our worthy young brother.

B. C. Goodpasture excited the admiration of those who knew him as a boy and that admiration has grown throughout the years. If he has since disappointed his brethren with his performance none have come forward to say so.

V

A Young Man
Went Forth

The singular hallmark of Benton Cordell Goodpasture is his love for learning. After mastering the school subjects at Flat Creek and the "subscription schools" around Hilham, Cordell enrolled in Burritt College in Spencer, Tennessee, in the fall of 1913. The doors of Burritt College were first opened to the public February 26, 1849. Some of the South's finest educators served as president of Burritt College. Around the turn of the century, Burritt College had the reputation as being the best college in the Cumberland Mountains. The college was right on top of Spencer Mountain in Van Buren County. Spencer was a small town located in a rather primitive section of Tennessee.

Spencer was particularly isolated from the outside world. As late as 1899, the only approach to Spencer, Tennessee, was a treacherous mountain road. Communication was by horseback and mail came into Spencer three times a week by stage coach. The founders were determined that nothing would interfere with the work of the students. Burritt College was no reform school. The students came by special permission of the faculty for serious study.

Little change had come over Burritt College between the time H. Leo Boles enrolled there in 1898 and the arrival of Benton Cordell Goodpasture in 1913. The buildings were the same red brick buildings. The founders of the school had erected brick kilns on the school ground. The old fashioned bricks were burned from native clay.

Cordell was disappointed with Burritt College and stayed only a short while. The college was nine miles from the Doyle Station which was located on the McMinnville and Manchester Railroad. He had no way to go and come from the railroad. The young man needed Sunday preaching appointments to help pay his way through school.

Cordell had studied the Greek language at home before he entered Burritt College. He arrived at Burritt College about a week or ten days late. He informed his teacher of his desire to study Greek. The teacher told him that the Greek class was now in the second week and that it would be hard for him to catch up. Cordell said he would try which meant that he would. The teacher had been taking about two days on a lesson. She advised the boy to do a lesson each day in order to overtake his class.

The Greek textbook was different from the one he had privately studied. The next day during Greek class, the teacher sent him to the blackboard to write the Greek alphabet in small and capital letters. His knowledge of the Greek alphabet was good as his knowledge of the English alphabet. Cordell put the Greek alphabet on the blackboard without hesitation. The lady teacher, Mary Gillentine, a few weeks later told a colleague, "That fellow Goodpasture can learn Greek easier and faster than anybody I ever saw."

Burritt College's influence can be compared to the early influence of Alexander Campbell's college in Bethany, West Virginia, and Tolbert Fanning's Franklin College in Nashville, Tennessee. The men who operated Burritt College were members of the church of Christ and interested in the church. And some of the Burritt College faculty were among the best preachers of the period. The Bible was taught as one of the elective subjects. Young Goodpasture studied the Bible in Burritt College the brief time he was a student there. Burritt College had an illustrious past and was the first co-educational college in the South where young women and men were taught in the same classes. W. N. Billingsley, one of Tennessee's most illustrious educators, was president from 1899 to 1911. In 1913 W. C. ("Old Sol") Graves was then president of the school. Cordell recognized the unique qualities of Burritt College, but he could not stay for the reason as already given.

Goodpasture transferred to Dixie College in Cookeville, Tennessee, and finished out the school year 1913-1914 the following spring. Dixie College then would now be thought of as a high school with some advanced subjects included in the school curriculum. Goodpasture stayed on the farm with his Aunt Florence Pate while he attended Dixie College. He paid for his keep by doing the usual farm chores about the home and walked the two miles round trip daily to and from school.

Cordell studied first year Latin, first year Greek, high school Algebra, Brook's *Rhetoric,* Bible, and general history. He studied Latin under a graduate of Harvard College. W. B. Boyd was president of Dixie College. His ambition was to start a college of his own. Dixie College was the forerunner of the present Tennessee Technological University, one of Tennessee's major educational institutions. Cordell's Bible teacher was John E. Dunn under whom he studied the book of Genesis. The students were required to write a chapter outline of Genesis at the end of the course. Goodpasture also studied two books in the New Testament during the school term.

The summer was both a memorable and crucial period in the life of young Goodpasture. He had high hopes of entering the Nashville Bible School, beginning in the fall term. This was the summer Goodpasture conducted the Willow Grove and the New Providence meetings. Goodpasture could see only a short distance into the future. Eighty-five dollars in 1914 was a scant amount for a young man hoping to enter college with no assurance of any form of steady income. And he could not expect any substantial help from home. John Goodpasture had a large and growing family. In those days country people lived largely off the land. Money was hard to come by. John Goodpasture explained his problem to his son and was concerned that he was putting the boy on his own. He understood his father's responsibilities and was confident he could make his own way.

In the fall of 1914, Benton Cordell Goodpasture entered the Nashville Bible School. H. Leo Boles was beginning his second year as president of the school. David Lipscomb was still alive, but old and in poor health. B. C. Goodpasture remembered seeing H. Leo Boles, just one time before the fall of 1914. That was in 1904 when J. D. Gunn was holding a meeting at Flat Creek. H. Leo Boles had accompanied his father, Henry Jefferson Boles, to the gospel meeting. It was announced in the service that "young Brother Boles" who was attended by his father would lead the prayer after the scripture reading. When J. D. Gunn had finished reading from the Bible, H. Leo Boles quietly said, "Father, will you lead the prayer?" The Goodpasture boy was just nine and the memory stayed. Years later Boles explained to his friend, "I had not been preaching long and did not feel able to lead the prayer that night." Goodpasture said that was the last time he knew H. Leo Boles to ask to be relieved of a responsibility.

John Goodpasture was a good friend of the preacher, Henry Jefferson Boles. The famed frontier preacher "Raccoon" John Smith was the father of a daughter, Jane, who married Thomas Jefferson Boles. They were the parents of Henry Jefferson Boles. Henry Boles was thought of as a good preacher on the Cumberland plateau. He held meetings in and around Hilham. B. C. Goodpasture was born and reared in the Cumberland plateau where the pioneer preachers started the Restoration Movement.

From the day Goodpasture enrolled in the Nashville Bible School, President Boles knew who he was and gradually brought the young man into his confidence. As B. C. Goodpasture said, "He knew that I had a struggle to get there and I meant business when I got there." H. Leo Boles was kindly disposed toward a student who was on his own, sincere, and determined. Boles, too, had hoed out the long and short rows in the stubborn soil of Jackson County until the job was done. B. C. Goodpasture remembers that Boles was not too easily approached his first year in the Nashville Bible School. As time went on they became more closely attached to each other.

The memory of Benton Cordell Goodpasture lingers in the minds of people who have known him early and late in life. J. Roy Vaughan, a friend of Goodpasture for more than fifty years, recalls the Nashville Bible School days around the time of the first World War. In describing B. C. Goodpasture, Vaughan said:

> He was a handsome young man with coal black hair and walked as straight as an arrow with head erect. His general appearance was very neat and very handsome. And he didn't run around with the other boys playing ball and things like that. He was more of a studious type. He would be reading and studying while the other boys would be out running around, yelling, or playing ball.

Vaughan was a few years younger than the nineteen-year-old Goodpasture and looked up to the older boy. One day the younger boy was talking to him about how tall and straight he was. Goodpasture told him he made it a practice to walk as if his head were touching the ceiling. That made him stand up straight. Vaughan said that when he would be walking on the street with Goodpasture often times people would stop and turn around to look at him because of his unusually striking appearance. Vaughan made the observation that that kind of bearing in military officers became natural to them, and this manner of carrying himself tall and straight became natural to Goodpasture.

Charles R. Brewer who was a young teacher in the Nashville Bible School remembers many things about Benton Cordell Goodpasture. Being a trained school man skilled in personality analysis, his impressions of young Goodpasture are especially significant. Goodpasture impressed everybody as being a boy of great intelligence. He had a fine dignified appearance and was a little bit aloof from the other students. Goodpasture did not participate very much in the recreational activities. The faculty and students associated him with books from the beginning because he was a good student. He had particularly a quick mind to grasp things and the wonderful ability to retain what he read.

Brewer described the young man as being tall and dignified in appearance. In those days men wore high detached collars. Some of them were open in the front and called "buzzard collars." Then men wore collars called "gates ajar." Older preachers wore this type especially those that were beginning to have double chins. The students in the Nashville Bible School were expected to dress in a dignified becoming way. Brewer added that Goodpasture possessed an attractive, intelligent face with clear straightforward eyes. The girls were attracted to him, but he was not so approachable by them.

Brewer brought into focus a facet of the relationship between President Boles and young Goodpasture. He saw the potentials in the student quicker than the other faculty. Another bright student, Roger P. Cuff, was especially outstanding. The faculty had discussions about which of the two boys would go furtherest in the world. H. Leo Boles had no doubt that Goodpasture would be the outstanding one. Some thought Roger would develop into a very fine scholar. Well it turned out that both parties to the discussion were correct. Roger went on to earn a Ph.D. degree from George Peabody College and taught in David Lipscomb College

and later in the University of Michigan.   Charles R. Brewer
added, "B. C. of course went to what we would say to the top so
far as ability and influence are concerned."

He is remembered respectfully by all of his former classmates
in the Nashville Bible School.   He was both friendly and reserved.
He did not spend his time in sports activities such as tennis and
baseball.   There is no doubt he could have become a fine athlete
had he chosen to be.   When he was a young boy, he would trot or
run to school to condition himself to play ball.   He commented in
recent times about his attitude toward sports when he was a boy,
"I could have been a good ball player, but it would have taken too
much time from my studies.   My prime purpose was my study and
my books.   I wanted to get a good education.   I wanted to know
the things I passed over."

When he was about fourteen, a small traveling circus came to
Hilham.   It was called Haag's Mighty Show.   The boy was
thrilled by the acrobats as they turned cartwheels and other such
acrobatics.   One of the circus performers put both of his feet behind his head.   The young boy went home with new skills to learn.
At the place where the sorghum mill had been set up, the crushed
cane had been thrown into a pile making a cushioned pad for the
boys to practice the acrobatics they had enjoyed at the circus.
Goodpasture mastered gymnastics such as turning cartwheels.   J.
Ridley Stroop who was a student in David Lipscomb College with
him said that Goodpasture could put both feet around his head,
and B. C. Goodpasture at seventy-five can still do this.   He has
always recognized the importance of physical conditioning.   As a
student he worked out daily with Indian Clubs and other forms of
calisthenics.

A year of schooling in the Nashville Bible School ran around
two hundred dollars.   This included fees, tuition, and room and
board. There were other expenses such as laundry, streetcar and
train fare, and spending money. The boy's dormitory was named
Lindsay Hall. There were no screens on the windows and no running water in the rooms. The rooms were furnished with two iron
bedsteads, two tables, and two chairs. A water pitcher and bowl
were set on a washstand in the room. The heating plant was located
off some distance from the dormitory. In extremely cold weather,
the pipes would freeze. There would be a day or two in the winter
when the freezing weather would shut off the heat and water in the

dormitory . The old fashioned bell that started the day off was rung at six o'clock in the morning. The boy who did this honor helped pay his way through college with this chore. The neighbors in the Granny White area marked the time of day with the ringing of the school bell.

Breakfast in the Nashville Bible School consisted of oatmeal, grits, eggs, bacon, and loaf bread. The noon meal consisted of the usual vegetables, roast beef about twice a week, pork, and fried chicken. The food was ample. Some of the boys complained about the quality of the food. But Goodpasture said, nevertheless, they all put on weight.

Chapel was conducted daily at 9:30 A.M. in Harding Hall. All students were expected to be there and they were. The men of the faculty sat on the stage. Usually a faculty member spoke and an occasional visitor came in from time to time. Dr. J. S. Ward called the roll. The student body was small, and both faculty and students soon could recognize each other by name and face. A student who missed chapel without a reason received a demerit. Several demerits resulted in a student's being campused.

The boys were allowed to go to downtown Nashville alone on Saturdays. The girls were chaperoned. Girls in the Nashville boarding schools all wore a similar dress. A Nashville Bible School girl could be easily identified by her dress from a Ward Belmont College girl because of slight differences in the patterns. Other trips were made to town by special permission. The general behavior of the students was good. E. Lacy Elrod was in charge of campus demeanor.

The literary societies were going strong when Goodpasture entered the Nashville College. One of the literary societies in Burritt College was the Calliopean Literary Society. When H. Leo Boles came to the Nashville Bible School, only the Babylonian Literary Society existed for the young men. The faculty decided there should be two societies. Dr. J. S. Ward designated John T. Lewis and H. Leo Boles to choose up sides for two new literary societies. As a result the Calliopean Literary Society was organized with H. Leo Boles as the first president. The Caesarian Literary Society (later the Lipscomb Society) was formed with John T. Lewis as the first president. The girls also had their literary societies, the Sapphoneans and Kappa Nus. Their programs consisted of piano playing, singing, readings, and drama skits.

Rivalry among them was just as great as among the boys' societies.

The literary societies presented their programs on Saturday evenings. The young men debated or delivered orations. The programs were designed to give them experience in public speaking. The boys had rooms or halls for their regular meetings. A critic was appointed to watch for grammatical and other mistakes in the speeches. When the school opened in the fall, the older students would be down at Union Station to meet the new students to enroll them in their respective societies. Letters had been previously written to the incoming students.

Goodpasture, as to be expected, was a member of the Calliopean Society and served as president in turn with other students. He engaged in public debates and the delivery of orations. The literary societies put on programs for their own members. And then there were the occasions when the Calliopeans would meet the Lipscomb boys in formal debates. Rivalry was intense. When the question was asked of J. Roy Vaughan to describe Goodpasture in action, he responded:

> He conducted himself in debate just as you would expect him to. He had a keen mind and could give a fellow a straight answer. It was remarkable to me that he thought so clearly in that he would say things in response the average person wouldn't think about. He was so well read and he knew what he was talking about.

The students had few diversions aside from their school activities. When the weather permitted, and this was usually in the fall and spring, a faculty member would take the students on a walk out to Glendale Park near the school. There was a zoo in Glendale Park then. Sometimes they walked out into the countryside accompanied by a teacher.

Every Sunday afternoon between 2:30 and 4:00 P.M., the students experienced the quiet hour in their dormitories. They were supposed to be quiet and they usually kept it pretty much that way. The students studied, wrote letters home, slept, or just idled the time away. There were few disciplinary problems. When President Boles was convinced a student was hurting both himself and the school, he didn't hesitate to send him home.

The boys had their fun and what they enjoyed most was selling some "greenhorn" from far out in the country a wrench to remove the taps from the steam radiator so the ashes could be removed. On one occasion the radiator was making the usual "knocking" noise. The boy was advised "now was the time to remove the ashes." He was in the process of doing so when he was restrained.

Along toward Christmas in the winter of 1914, Goodpasture had run out of money and was feeling pretty blue. He had been barely able to remain in school with the small sums received from his preaching appointments. Just before the Christmas holidays, Goodpasture preached at the Locust Grove church of Christ near Middleton, Kentucky. Joe McInteer, the grandfather of Jim Bill McInteer, gave Goodpasture fifteen dollars for his preaching efforts. This was the largest amount he had received for a Sunday appointment and his happy surprise was apparent to Joe McInteer. The preaching appointment was coupled with baptizing a woman on that Sunday. Goodpasture spent the night in the McInteer home. Early in the morning he heard rocks hitting the roof and rolling off. Next morning at breakfast, he asked Joe McInteer who was throwing rocks at the house. Then he learned that turkeys roosted on the chimney. When a turkey flew off the chimney, he would kick a brick off the chimney that rolled down the roof.

During the holidays, the young man borrowed fifty dollars from his father to return to the Nashville Bible School in January of 1915. He repaid that loan and never borrowed another dime for his schooling. During the Nashville Bible School years, Goodpasture preached for the Antioch church near Murfreesboro, Tennessee, receiving eight dollars; the New Hermon church close to Shelbyville, Tennessee, paid him ten dollars; the Almaville church near Smyrna gave him the Sunday collection which varied with the weather and sickness in the community which determined both the size of the crowd and the collection.

The small churches Goodpasture preached for were in easy traveling distance from Nashville. Travel then was almost entirely by train when distance was involved. The young preacher would arrive at the depot where he would be met and carried by buggy or sometimes an automobile out to the rural community where the church was located. In those days, preachers travelled to their appointments on Saturday afternoons. The Nashville Bible School did not have classes on Monday mornings which gave the preacher boys a day to return to school. Transportation to and from the school to downtown Nashville was by street car.

During the summer of 1915, B. C. Goodpasture conducted gospel meetings following a full year in the Nashville Bible school. The young evangelist started a meeting at Pleasant Grove in Clay County, Tennessee. During the meeting, Benton Cordell Goodpasture suffered the loss of his beloved mother who had been in failing health. She passed away July 13, 1915, and was buried in the Flat Creek cemetery. John and Elora Goodpasture were the parents of eight children. B. C. Goodpasture was the oldest child. After the death of their mother, Carrie said that he took a protective interest in the children ranging from Ray and Ethel who were a little younger than he, to Helen who was about three months old at her mother's death. Carrie wrote, "He has been an inspiration to us children. He kept us together and close to our Lord and in his work." Soon after the death of their mother, he sent Carrie a New Testament with the words penned inside the cover: "Carrie read this every day and it will make of you what your mama and your God would have you to be." After going away to school, he never returned without bringing each of the children a small gift of some kind. Carrie said, "He has always been thoughtful this way and still is. He is close to us all."

During the summer of 1915, he held a meeting at Willow Grove in Clay County. The account appeared in the *Gospel Advocate,* September 16, 1915:

> The meeting in Willow Grove, in Clay County, closed yesterday at the water's edge, after continuing eight days. Seventeen were added—fourteen baptized and three restored. About one half of those baptized were reared under sectarian influences. Baptistic and Methodistic. The congregation in Willow Grove is an old congregation and one of the largest, if not the largest in Clay County. Brother Albert Roberts, the "blind singer" led in the song service. He is an excellent leader. I have promised to be with the brethren next year at Willow Grove. On the third, Lord's Day, I preached at Cookeville, in the morning, and at night. There was one confession, a lady from the Methodists. I shall begin a meeting at New Providence, in Giles County, next Lord's Day, the Lord willing.

Then in the September 23 issue of the *Advocate,* Goodpasture reported: "The meeting at New Providence in Giles County, closed on September 12, after continuing over two Sundays. Seven were baptized. Five of these were from the sects. I am now in school at the Nashville Bible School."

B. C. Goodpasture made only occasional visits home when he was in David Lipscomb College. His father would meet him at the railroad station in Livingston. Jennie Ruth said that she would stand by the window in the family room of their farm home watching for her brother. The window offered an excellent view of the front gate at the end of the lane. The lane led from the winding creek road to their home. Sometimes the children would argue over who would get the coveted spot at the window.

His home coming was always a red letter day for the children. He would bring each of the children a book, a poem, a game, paper dolls, or just candy. He instilled in the children a love for reading good books including such beautiful stories as those by Louisa Alcott.

Jennie Ruth recalled his superb marksmanship with a rifle. He would stick straight pins (dressmaker type) in top of the gate post in the front yard. He would sit on the porch with a rifle and hit the pins and bend them double. Jennie Ruth also said that he has even now remarkable vision and can read a newspaper or thread a needle without glasses.

The children said their brother never forget to do the things he promised. John Goodpasture once said about his son, "It is remarkable how B. C. remembers to do all the things he says he will do, and how he does them so promptly." Goodpasture would promise to send the children a package from Nashville. The children would wait at the mailbox for the mailman. They could see him coming around the bend on the far side of the creek on horseback bringing their package. Every Christmas a big package came from B. C. and Cleveland for the family.

When the young man returned to Flat Creek during his four college years, he would go hunting. But there would be a period of time when he studied his lessons under a big beech tree just beyond the apple orchard in front of the home. The children knew not to come around while he was studying and to wait quietly until he had studied and laid each book aside. Jennie Ruth especially remembers those days because she could go squirrel hunting with him. Being a younger child, she was favored by her big brother. She would watch him pick up a book and finish it and then turn to

another until he finished his lessons. Then they would go down
into the woods. She tagged along closely at his heels. And sometimes she said she would be standing on one foot like a little bird
while he aimed his gun. Jennie Ruth said: "If I made too much
noise I wouldn't be permitted to go next time. Knowing him to be
a man of his word, one who always did exactly what he said he
would do, I would always slip along quietly."

There were times that work awaited Goodpasture's return to
Flat Creek. The frontier setting in the Cumberlands was gradually changing. Better roads were being built. Telephone lines
were being put up when Goodpasture was in David Lipscomb College. During his vacation he helped dig the holes for the telephone
poles from the Flat Creek Community to Hilham. He climbed the
poles and nailed the glass insulators to the poles and fastened the
telephone wire to the glass insulators.

One primitive practice could still be seen in Overton County.
The farmers grew their own wheat for grinding into flour. The
steep hillsides and narrow bottom lands made the using of thresh-
ing machines impractical. The farmers still cradled wheat with
long handled scythes. During one season, Goodpasture was helping his father cradle wheat with a neighbor, Noah Davis. John
Goodpasture was tying the sheaves after his boy and the older
man. Occasionally young Goodpasture would move ahead of
Noah Davis. And he would call out, "Get out of my way, or I'll
cut your heels." At noon they sat down to a chicken dumpling
dinner and Noah did not know when to stop eating and he went to
the field sluggish from over eating. That afternoon the young man
would press Noah Davis with his own words, "Get out of my way,
or I'll cut your heels."

As a matter of fact, Benton Cordell Goodpasture was never
home except for brief visits after he entered the Nashville Bible
School. During the summer months he held meetings; he was in
David Lipscomb College (Nashville Bible School) for four years.
What marked Goodpasture as a student then has been characteris-
tic of him for a lifetime. He stood quietly apart from the other
students, and as a matter of fact, above the other students. As one
of his fellow students said, "He was a little older than the other
students, studious and smart as a whip." And Goodpasture was a
good student at whatever he put his mind to. Mathematics posed

no special problem for him; however, he preferred languages. There were times when he was studying four languages at the same time. He studied Greek and Latin for five years.

During the full four years in the Nashville Bible School, he studied Greek. He studied Greek grammar thoroughly once a year to keep the tenses and grammar in mind. He believes that all young preachers should study the language and commented: "There isn't any source of information quite like a knowledge of the Greek New Testament."

John Goodpasture taught his son independence, industry, and honesty with the idea that what a person could do for himself, he ought to, and for him not to do so was degrading if not disgraceful. His father often told him, "Never let anybody do for you what you can do and should do for yourself." The impossible for some people meant it only took a little longer for B. C. Goodpasture.

One year Goodpasture resolved he would ask for no outside help with his college homework. Long hours were spent in Wentworth's *College Algebra,* Homer's *Iliad,* and Virgil's *Aeneid* just to gain a greater self-reliance and independence of thought. Goodpasture later in life reflected, "I suppose I learned my lessons of concentration. I was the older of eight children. I used to read with one child in my lap, and sometimes with one on my knee, and two or three on my feet; and in that way I learned to concentrate."

The curriculum of David Lipscomb College weighed heavily in the direction of the classics, and Goodpasture excelled in the classical disciplines. David Lipscomb and James A. Harding founded the Nashville Bible School to teach daily the Bible to each student. Goodpasture came primarily to the Nashville Bible School to study the Bible. He studied the *Evidences of Christianity* under H. Leo Boles and other such subjects that were of special interest. His first English teacher was E. E. Sewell, and later Charles R. Brewer under whom he studied the plays of Shakespeare. Although he excelled in mathematics, he quit after algebra and solid geometry.

Although Goodpasture understands the rudiments of music, he never led singing in worship services. He quoted Alexander Campbell in this connection: "If the Lord expected him to lead singing in heaven, He'd have to give him something up there he didn't have down here."

Goodpasture returned for another of his Willow Grove meetings in July of 1917. The account was dated Livingston, July 31, 1917, which appeared in the *Advocate:*

> Yesterday I closed an eight day meeting at Willow Grove, Clay County. There were forty-seven additions—thirty-eight baptized and nine restored. About fifteen were reared under Baptist and Methodist influences. This was my fourth meeting in Willow Grove, and I have consented to labor with them in a meeting next year.

Large audiences numbering two and three thousands attended the Willow Grove meeting. Those were exciting times for the young preacher. Other meetings that he conducted were not attended by such excitement and great interest, but they were good meetings and encouraging to the young man.

Benton Cordell Goodpasture finished four years of college with the highest academic average of any student to attend the college while H. Leo Boles was president. He was the valedictorian of his graduating class and delivered an oration of his own composition. J. S. Batey, father of Irma Lee Batey, a classmate of Goodpasture and a long time teacher in David Lipscomb College, delivered the commencement address. It was the custom to invite a preacher to deliver the commencement sermon who had a son or daughter in school.

Such opportunities that came to the young man were mostly created by him. B. C. Goodpasture has enjoyed the unqualified confidence of all who have known him over a life time. W. E. Willis met Goodpasture in 1915 and roomed with him for a year commented: "I learned to love him and admire his ability, and I am sure I can safely say, he was the most brilliant person I ever met." When Willis was stationed at Camp Gordon just out of Atlanta, Georgia, a few years later he used several of his passes to go into Atlanta to hear his friend preach.

Another lifelong friend of B. C. Goodpasture, Dr. S. Comer Sadler, looked back some fifty years and more ago when he came to the Nashville Bible School as a thirteen year old boy from Jackson County. The fact that H. Leo Boles came from Jackson County interested several in that county to enter the Nashville Bible school. The Sadler family was a large one, and twelve of the Sadler children enrolled in the Nashville Bible School.

Dr. Sadler, a highly respected Nashville dentist, described his

impressions of the young Goodpasture at the time he came to
Nashville, "I was a little chap and scared, and B. C. would talk to
you. He was a person you liked. He had time to be a good
friend." The acquaintance has continued and Dr. Sadler added,
"There hasn't been a time in his life that he hasn't been a gentleman. You gain something by knowing him. He's not the pious,
long-faced preacher type; he's a lot of fun to be with, and a likea-
ble fellow, broadminded with a ready wit, and a sense of appropriateness."

"The Child is the Father of the Man" so Wordsworth wrote.
What the Goodpasture boy promised has been realized in the man.
B. H. Hunt, a lawyer in Livingston, Tennessee, who taught Goodpasture when he was a boy said in recent years: "It was manifest
to me when Brother Goodpasture was a boy that he had a wonderful future. He possessed a brilliant mind, and as he grew in stature, he also grew mentally and developed into one of the best informed men it has been my good fortune to know."

The four years in David Lipscomb College were good years.
During the summer months, B. C. conducted meetings and
preached regularly every Sunday during the regular school year.
He was able to entirely finance his way through college. When he
graduated from David Lipscomb College in 1918, he did not owe a
penny for his education.

VI

The Clietts of Childersburg

The story of Benton Cordell Goodpasture is inseparable from the family of the Clietts of Alabama. The Goodpasture family settled in the Cumberlands when the vast wilderness was changing into a settled farming region. Some frontier practices lingered on when Goodpasture was growing up. The Clietts on the other hand lived in a part of Alabama that greatly benefited from a long settled community dating a good way back into the *ante bellum* South.

The Clietts trace their ancestral lineage back to Columbia County, Georgia, to Miner Jonathan Cliett and Sarah Ann Smith. They were married around 1835 in Columbia County. Miner Jonathan Cliett had three or four brothers; however, nothing is known about them other than the fact they came to Alabama from Georgia together at the same time. The name of the mother of Sarah Ann Smith is known. She was Sarah Ann Skinner Smith. Her family consisted of two brothers, Henry and Jack Skinner, both were doctors; and two sisters whose names were Susan and Emily.

Miner Jonathan Cliett and Sarah Ann had lived in Augusta, Georgia, and in other parts of Georgia. The children born to them in Georgia were Henry Johnston, Susan Amelia, Sarah Jane (who moved to Texas as an adult), Benjamin Franklin, Jesse Edwards (died at sixteen), and Emma Tallulah. The family moved from Georgia to Talladega, County, and settled in a farming region where Childersburg is located. The Southern Railroad was then building through that part of Alabama. But it was called upon its completion the Selma, Rome and Dalton Railroad. The depot was first located at a road crossing and later was moved to Childersburg. Miner Jonathan Cliett was the first train agent and post-master in Childersburg. He was assisted by his daughter, Sarah Jane.

Other children were born to Jonathan Cliett and Sarah Ann. Walter Joseph, who died when he was sixteen, and Alice Eugenia were among those. There were fourteen children in all. Some died in their infancy. Six of the fourteen children lived to man-hood and womanhood.

Miner Jonathan Cliett engaged in farming and the mercantile business. There was little else to be done for a living that was not somehow associated with farming. The local saw mills, cotton gins, and the traveling salesmen supplied the necessary goods for the people. The oldest son of Miner Jonathan and Sarah was Henry Johnston Cliett who joined his father in business after he returned from the Civil War. The name of their mercantile busi-ness was M. J. Cliett and Son.

When Miner Jonathan died, his oldest son assumed the respon-sibility to become the head of the family. Henry Johnston married Emily Wynn and four children were born to them. Their oldest child Minnie Cliett Ricks was the mother of six children—Cliett, Charlotte, Lillian, Elvin, Robert, and James.

Their next child, Miner James Cliett, is of primary interest be-cause he was the father of Emily Cleveland Cliett Goodpasture, his oldest child. Miner James married Willie Pauline Montgomery. They were also the parents of Agnes, William Henry, and Mildred.

The third child of Henry Johnston and Emily was Ada who never married. She died in Birmingham, Alabama. Their last child was Nina who was first married to Omar Alford and later to T. B. Russell. She lived in the family home until her death. She had no children.

As stated before, Henry Johnston became the head of the fam-ily following the death of his father. He served in the army of the Confederacy and was captured and imprisoned by the Union Army. His harsh experiences and privations suffered in prison served to make him a highly disciplined person. He became a very economical and successful businessman and a good practical farmer. His health gradually deteriorated due to the prison hard-ships. Henry Johnston died in 1885 leaving his young son, Miner James, who had not yet finished high school, to shoulder the re-

William Henry Montgomery

Sarah Cleveland Montgomery

Henry Johnston Cliett

Emily Wynn Cliett

sponsibilities of the family and to help manage the many activities
he had begun. The boy just thirteen years old assumed his tasks
with manly courage.

After the death of her husband, Emily Cliett ran a hotel in
Childersburg to help out with the household expenses. She owned
a large house and rooms were rented and family meals were served
to the hotel guests. The travelers who got off the train in Childersburg included itinerant preachers and salesmen who regularly
called on the town merchants. The Clietts then were of the Baptist Church persuasion. Miner James would meet the trains and
bring in the luggage of the hotel guests and whatever "flunky jobs"
that came along. One of his chores was blacking the boots of a
Baptist preacher who paid for the shoe shine with a "thank you."
Miner James promised himself then that whenever he had a house
of his own that no paying guest would ever spend the night there.

After growing to young manhood, Miner James married Willie
Pauline Montgomery who was born December 11, 1876. She was
the daughter of William Henry and Sarah Montgomery. The
Montgomerys were regarded as being one of the "first families" in
that section of Alabama. William Henry Montgomery was originally from McMinnville, Tennessee. He was a good farmer for
those early days. He loved and raised horses. The father of
Sarah Montgomery was a close relative of President Grover Cleveland. This is how the wife of B. C. Goodpasture, Emily Cleveland, came by her given name Cleveland that she wore for a lifetime.

Miner James Cliett followed in the business footsteps of his
father and grandfather. In his early life he was engaged in the
saw mill business and later was successfully involved in farming,
cotton ginning, mercantile, and warehouse business. Before his
saw mill experiences, he entered into an unsuccessful business with
two partners and had to take bankruptcy. He insured himself to
cover the total amount of his indebtedness and that of his two partners and asked his wife to pay the debts in case of his death.
Miner James paid back every penny of the loss to his creditors.
He became a good business man. He was proud of his community and they were proud of him.

Pauline Montgomery was a worthy wife of Miner James and
mother of his children. She was regarded as being well educated.
Pauline was the sister to the wife of J. M. Barnes, a well known

pioneer educator and gospel preacher in Alabama. Pauline finished the equivalent of a grammar school education in Childersburg and afterwards enrolled in the school founded by J. M. Barnes. Since the Clietts were of the Baptist faith persuasion, the influence of the church of Christ came into the family through Pauline Montgomery.

The school founded by J. M. Barnes was called the Highland Home College. Barnes was born in 1836 and reared in the South on his father's plantation. His constant boyhood companions were the children of slave parents. At the age of seventeen, he went to Alexander Campbell's school, Bethany College, in West Virginia and graduated in 1856. When he first left home, his mother gave him a page of paper with these words written on it: "Be kind and courteous to everyone. Be polite and respectful to those older than yourself. Treat others as you would have them treat you. Trust God and serve him, and he will take care of you." He tacked the page on the inside of his trunk lid where it stayed until his home was destroyed by fire in 1883.

Due to his father's request, he started a school in a log house on his father's plantation in Strata, Alabama, September 8, 1856, with thirteen pupils. The school prospered from the day of its founding and became a highly respected school and greatly appreciated in that part of Alabama. Boarding students who came from all parts of the country enrolled in the school. In 1881 the school was moved to Highland Home. J. M. Barnes was an effective preacher for the church and contributed articles to the *Gospel Advocate*. Willie Pauline attended the school after it was moved to Highland Home. The school was named after the town. The Highland Home School was one of the early Bible schools. Many good preachers were trained there.

Agnes Cliett and Mildred Cliett Powell remember their mother with pride and respect. She taught her children good principles and expected them to live by them. She was a matter of fact person and very exacting of everyone who came under her influence. The mother did beautiful sewing and every stitch had to be perfectly straight and evenly spaced. Agnes Cliett said her mother studied art when she was a girl. And she said her drawings reflected her mother's character. Her art work was exactly and precisely drawn. When the local PTA was organized at the beginning of each school year, Willie Pauline was always appointed the chairman of the "ways and means committee." She was always busy with her home responsibilities which extended to the school and church.

Willie Pauline Montgomery was equally well married in Miner James Cliett. He was a good business man and the kind of a person who impressed his neighbors with his good common sense. His formal education was provided by the public school in Childersburg; and for a period of six months, he attended the Marion Military Institute in Marion, Alabama, where the school is still operating. At one time or another Miner James operated a general store, a John Deere Farm Equipment dealership, a cotton gin, a cotton warehouse, and a thousand acre plantation.

He was a "well informed man" as the saying goes. He read the best current literature. One of his favorite periodicals was the *Literary Digest* that fell into disgrace when its poll predicted the victory of Herbert Hoover over Franklin D. Roosevelt. Almost every night after working in the store and before retiring for the night, he would read an hour or so.

Childersburg was a small community when Miner James and Willie Pauline were rearing their children. Agnes Cliett said to be exact that the official census was 416 while the children were growing up. In this period before World War I, the Southern Railroad and the Central Georgia Railroad ran through Childersburg. Each railroad had its own station and several trains passed through the town daily.

Miner James Cliett enjoyed the complete confidence of the people in the Childersburg area. He served on the school board and was elected mayor of the town. Among his many interests, Miner James was also a cotton buyer.

At the time Miner James and Willie Pauline were married, he was a member of the Baptist Church. There was no church of Christ in Childersburg at the time. Pauline Cliett conducted a Bible study in her home on Sunday afternoons. Soon she had the assistance of J. M. Barnes and John T. Lewis to help her; and through their preaching in Childersburg, the church was established in the town—the church gradually grew in the community since the Clietts saw to it that the best preachers came that way. And they made their home with the Clietts while they preached there. Miner James was not easily brought into the church. Agnes Cliett said her mother and others had a time convincing him: "Poppa didn't take things on 'say so.' You had to convince him that you were right. But when he was convinced, he would take right up with you."

Emily Cleveland was the oldest of the Cliett children, and she was followed by Agnes Erie, William Henry, and Mildred Montgomery. Agnes and Mildred remember their father as being pretty strict with his children. But they added, "He would

Seated: M. J. Cliett, Cordell Goodpasture, Pauline Cliett, Mildred Cliett. *Standing:* B. C. Goodpasture, Cleveland Goodpasture, Agnes Cliett, William Henry.

Cliett homeplace

Henry Cliett, Cleveland Cliett, Agnes Cliett

really help you if you needed it. We stepped when he came around."

Pauline Cliett had been reared in easy circumstances, but Miner James had known both good and bad times after he became the head of his family at the age of thirteen. Agnes compared their parents: "Mother would help a person who would help himself, but Poppa had more compassion."

Miner James became a member of the church after it was started in Childersburg by his wife, J. M. Barnes, and John T Lewis. He was a good church member and taught the adult Bible class. The mother taught the younger children. She was the treasurer of the church when the little bank failed in Childersburg during the "Depression" in the 1930's. Agnes Cliett said, "It took Mama a long time to pay back the money to the church. But she felt responsible. It was her sense of fairness."

The church in Childersburg grew as the town prospered. During World War II, Dupont set up a powder plant in the town, and the population increased to between four and five thousand. Some of the population who came to Childersburg were from Old Hickory, Tennessee. Several were members of the church of Christ, and they stayed on after the war when a paper plant replaced the munitions factory.

Emily Cleveland Cliett was born May 12, 1897, and was named after her two grandmothers. Her grandmother's name on the mother's side was Sarah Cleveland, a relative of President Cleveland. She was married to William Montgomery. Her paternal grandmother was Emily Wynn. She attended church services from babyhood. One of the earliest memories about the child resulted from her being taken from the church because she was disturbing worship. On the way out in her mother's arms, she called back, "Bye, bye, preacher, baby going home." Another incident grew out of her being warned not to eat grapes with the seed in them that it might kill her, and she said, "I'll be dead then."

Cleveland Cliett attended grammar school in Childersburg and three years of high school; a fourth year was not yet added. The memories of Emily Cleveland add up to the fact that she was an unusually gifted person and she planned to be so. Lillian Ricks, a first cousin, who grew up with Emily Cleveland described her friend:

Cleveland was extremely ambitious, very studious. She was a good student and made good grades. She displayed qualities of leadership at an early age. Cleveland was enthusiastic in her work and play. She was always keenly alive, possessing self confidence and vitality. She had a high sense of values, strictly truthful and honest. We enjoyed playing ball, hop-scotch, and jumping rope. Those were happy days and Cleveland did her part to make them so.

Agnes Cliett and Mildred Powell are the only two surviving children. They recall their older sister while they were children. Emily Cleveland possessed a strong feeling of responsibility to help look out for the younger children, and she saw to it that they discharged their responsibilities. "She was real fair and she meant for the rest of us to measure up. She was just a little bit bossy," Agnes said.

Cleveland Cliett was as good as the best at whatever she did. She was at the top of her class in Childersburg because she was ambitious and wanted to be at the head. This was likewise true of Agnes and Mildred, but not so about William Henry. The girls came up in classes that were ambitious and they wanted to be at the head and they pretty well managed to stay there.

Their only brother, William Henry, saw it differently. The sisters explained that "William Henry came up in a class that didn't have too much ambition. And he would just get around and get along." When time came for home study, the mother would have Henry to get his books down. He would look at one book for about three minutes and lay it down and take up another one. It would take him about fifteen minutes to go over all of them.

His mother would ask, "Have you got your lessons?"
Henry would answer, "Yes mam."

Then she would tell him, "Bring me that spelling book." And he could not spell all the words. And his mother would say, "Go back and start over and learn your words."

But his sisters said he was smart and had a good mind with a good business head. He finished school in Childersburg and attended David Lipscomb College for a while. Miner James sent his son to a Memphis cotton grading school. As a result Henry had a technical knowledge for grading and recognizing cotton that his father did not have. Agnes Cliett described how her father and brother worked together as business partners. The father would raise cotton and he would send Henry out to sell it, saying, "Henry, you are a better trader than I am. I haven't got the heart to trade as hard as you do." And his sister added, "Henry was that kind. He would pull it to the last notch."

Miner James and Pauline Cliett reared their children and lived to see them grow into adulthood. Mildred Cliett married J. M. Powell, a well known preacher and leader in the church. In addition to his preaching, he has been a staff writer for the *Gospel Advocate* and has served as president of Ohio Valley Christian College.

Emily Cleveland entered the Nashville Bible school when she was just sixteen. She was born to be a leader. A long time friend, James D. Groves wrote that she belonged to that rare royalty of natural aristocracy, and that she was born to her ladyship. Her qualities were not learned in any school. There was a kindness and gentleness about her when she came into another's home. She was tolerant in conversation with an incisive and discerning mind.

Cleveland entered the Nashville Bible School two years ahead of B. C. Goodpasture. She graduated as the salutatorian of her class (1915-1916). She was the fourth young woman to graduate with a bachelor of science degree. The girls of the Nashville Bible School usually majored in music, literature, or home economics. The B.S. degree required more work in such subjects as the natural sciences, mathematics, and physics. After her graduation, she taught in the primary department of the Nashville Bible School (David Lipscomb College) from 1917 until she married B. C. Goodpasture. It was a practice for all the teachers to sign the diplomas of students graduating from the college. So her signature appeared on the diploma of Benton Cordell Goodpasture in the graduating class of 1917-1918.

Benton Cordell Goodpasture was too busy with his school work to court the girls when he came to Nashville to enter school. He was friendly with all alike. Goodpasture was aware of the presence of Cleveland Cliett since they had classes together. Goodpasture ate at a table in the dining room with S. P. Pittman who was a friend of the Cliett family. He would commend the Cliett girl in their line of general conversation. Cleveland was plainly a faculty favorite. Goodpasture enjoyed with H. Leo Boles a close student-faculty relationship and he approved the match. Dr. J. S. Ward acted as a marriage broker since he thought the young people were ideally suited. The young people were unaware of the maneuvering that was going on. Dr. Ward learned of Emily Cleveland's interest in the young man through an aunt of the girl with whom she had confided. The news was passed along the grape vine to E. Lacy Elrod and he informed Goodpasture.

Goodpasture was attracted to Emily Cleveland because she was an outstanding student. Social contacts between the boys and girls were seldom and closely chaperoned. A boy walking down Granny White Pike by Avalon Home, the girl's dormitory, dare not wave at one of the fair damsels who might be on the campus near the road. The boy would smooth down his hair and get in a wave at the same time. The students enjoyed a period each Saturday evening after one of the literary societies had presented a program called the "After Meeting." The boys and girls would pair off according to their preference and talk. Many a romance blossomed on those occasions. The "After Meeting" lasted as long as it suited President Boles which was determined by how sleepy he was or his work schedule for the following day. Anyhow, B. C. and Cleveland began seeing each other in those meetings. There were special occasions when the students enjoyed a special treat. On one occasion B. C. took Cleveland with the other students to hear the Irish tenor, John McCormack.

Their courtship blossomed, and during the school year of 1917-1918, the two young people became engaged. Cleveland told Agnes who was a student in David Lipscomb College that she and Goodpasture were engaged to be married. The young girl was happily excited over the prospect of the handsome young man becoming her brother-in-law. The friends started teasing the couple saying that B. C. was enrolled in the primary and senior departments at the same time. After graduation, Goodpasture told Cleveland that "since she had signed his diploma she couldn't go back on it."

At Christmas time, Benton Cordell Goodpasture went down to Childersburg to visit the Cliett family for the first time. He said, "I was putting up the best front I could." The Clietts lived in a stylish "gingerbread house" for that period. During his stay, the older girls and their mother were busy with the holiday preparations. Mildred who was just a small child was left to entertain the young man. And she gave him some advice. "You can go into all the rooms except the kitchen. We got all the rooms cleaned up but the kitchen before you got here." Shortly afterwards Mildred was called to another part of the house. She volunteered no other such information that day.

On another day, Mildred was entertaining B. C. on the front porch. She looked up at him and said, "B. C." He did not answer her. Then she addressed him again and finally got his attention.

Mildred asked him, "Do you know how come Cleveland picked you up?"

B. C. answered her, "No, Mildred, why did she?"

Mildred informed him, "Because she thinks you are pretty boy!"

Goodpasture upon entering the college resolved not to become involved in any courtship with a Nashville Bible School girl and he gave his reason: "I just set my mind that I wouldn't become involved in any love affair until my last year in school. I would devote my time to my books and in the meantime be looking around. That's the way I did. The last year I was in school I began seeing her more often." When B. C. and Cleveland were courting and talking about marrying, she was very conscientious. She had her misgivings about being a preacher's wife. What she did not then understand was that a young man planning to preach is filled with apprehensions of his own.

The young people had planned their future wedding at the close of the regular school year. Goodpasture had already made his plans to begin preaching June 1, 1918, for the Shelbyville church of Christ. He devoted the summer to holding meetings and the Shelbyville pulpit. The wedding date was set in early December.

The wedding of Benton Cordell Goodpasture and Emily Cleveland Cliett was performed September 3, 1918, by S. P. Pittman. The wedding ceremony took place on the front porch of the Cliett home in Childersburg. Cleveland's best school friend, Christine Ward Hale, played the piano for the wedding. She was one of the lovely daughters of Dr. J. S. Ward who for a while served as president *pro tem* of the Nashville Bible School. Christine entered the school at the same time Goodpasture did two years behind Cleveland. Christine and Cleveland became friends through their associations in the Sapphonean Literary Society. She remembers Cleveland then as being "very sweet, easy to talk to, and a good student."

After the wedding ceremony Cleveland and Cordell went to Shelbyville, Tennessee, where her husband had begun his work as a preacher for the Shelbyville church. Benton Cordell Goodpasture was loved and appreciated by the Cliett family and he returned the affection. William Henry Cliett and B. C. Goodpasture grew close as brothers and entered into a business partnership that lasted to the death of Henry Cliett.

Goodpasture first met the Clietts at Christmas time. Every Christmas afterward he carried Cleveland and their children to Childersburg. All of the Cliett family would be home for the holidays. Agnes Cliett said about their being in Childersburg for the holidays, "I believe that Poppa would have had a spasm if they hadn't come."

J. Roy Vaughan, a school mate of Cordell and Cleveland, described her from the vantage point over the years to the time of her passing:

> I would say that her influence in B. C.'s success was incalculable. She was a most wonderful character and she influenced B. C. so much for good. She knew him well and she knew how to work with him. She was one of the most gracious ladies I ever knew; intelligent, kind, good, and gentle. I have often thought she was a perfect example in manners and charm of the southern lady when the South was in her glory, before the Civil War. She could entertain in her home forty people with as much ease as the average wife entertains three or four people. She was the perfect minister's wife. Whenever someone needed looking after, or there was church work to be done, Cleveland was there. She was as great in her field as a mother, a Christian, and a preacher's wife, as Goodpasture was a gospel preacher.

Whatever reservations Cleveland Cliett felt about being the wife of B. C. Goodpasture were dispelled. Intelligence is a condition for both recognition and appreciation of another's worth. Cleveland knew how to evaluate her husband's qualities and her good fortune in being his wife. She fully understood her husband perhaps as no other person has been able to. She knew his burdens and how to help carry them. She knew the scope of his knowledge and how to live on the same plane with him. Her background and training were similar to his. B. C. Goodpasture's disposition and singular genius did not escape her perceptive mind.

The children of B. C. and Cleveland Goodpasture are appreciative of their parents. Their daughter remembers her mother as a happy person who laughed a lot. She loved the beautiful in life and felt an intense love for her family. Eleanor said, "It was a sun filled home." Cleveland was a good mother. She exercised firm discipline and there was never a trace of nagging the children. The mother said what she meant and the children knew she meant what she said.

The children had to abide by one standing rule which was to have their Sunday school lesson prepared before they could leave on Saturday evenings with their dates. Eleanor remembered they had been especially busy one Saturday working in the home and she was unprepared with her Bible lesson. The boy was standing at the front door.

The mother asked, "Sister, did you get your Sunday school lesson?" Well, she had not; and while the boy waited in the living room, she went off in another part of the house to study.

Their daughter remembers her father pretty much as Jennie Ruth, his youngest sister, did when she was a child. B. C. was firm with his children. When he spoke, they moved. On the other hand, he was gentle with his children and especially when they were ill or hurt. If one of them expressed a wish for a bicycle at Christmas or on a birthday, he would go out and buy the best one he could afford.

The oldest son, Cordell, married Nell McQuiddy on September 20, 1943. Two children were born to them, B. C. III and Sherry Anna. B. C. III was married to Angela Odum and they have three children—B.C. IV, Angela, and Ginger. Sherry Anna is married to Alvin Goins and they have one child named Shawn.

Eleanor Pauline was married August 13, 1945, to Myron Lyzon King who is a leading art dealer in Nashville, Tennessee. They have two children—Emily Catherine and Myron Lyzon, Jr. Myron King has an especially adventurous chapter in his life. He was a pilot on a "flying fortress" during World War II. His plane was forced to land in Europe and then he flew into Russia where he hoped to find help. He spent the last months of the war living just off Red Square in Moscow.

J. Cliett Goodpasture, the youngest child, was married June 29,

1956, to Sarah Lou Traughber. They have three daughters—Sara Gay, Amy Lou, and Nancy Lynn.

At the present time, Cordell Goodpasture is living in Memphis, Tennessee, and working as an accountant for a Memphis firm. Cliett Goodpasture is a member of the Bible faculty of David Lipscomb College and minister of the Ashland City, Tennessee church of Christ.

Emily Cleveland Goodpasture became ill in the early months of 1964. Her health gradually worsened; and on November 2, 1964, she passed away. B. C. and Cleveland had lived together almost forty-six years. The funeral services were conducted in the Hillsboro church of Christ with J. Roy Vaughan, Batsell Barrett Baxter, and Athens Clay Pullias officiating. She was laid to rest in the Woodlawn Cemetery in Nashville, Tennessee.

VII

What of the Morning

Saul, first King of Israel, towered above every man in all the land from Dan to Beersheba. B. C. Goodpasture stood in a similar fashion among the young men aspiring to preach the gospel in the springtime of 1918. H. Leo Boles, president of David Lipscomb College, liked to tell that B. C. Goodpasture graduated with the highest point average of any student in the history of the college. Boles stayed on as president of the college, with the exception of a brief interval, until 1932. He resigned in 1934 his teaching responsibilities with the college severing the last of his official connections with the school.

In 1954 David Lipscomb College became an accredited senior college and joined the Southern Association of Colleges and Universities. Not since the Nashville Bible School started in 1891 by David Lipscomb and James A. Harding has another student from David Lipscomb College equalled the stature and influence of B. C. Goodpasture among the churches of Christ until the present day. Perhaps no other famed preacher among the churches of Christ in this century has been less spectacular and at the same time more pleasing to his audiences than B. C. Goodpasture. He has never sought the limelight of the center of the stage, but there has not been a time since Goodpasture came to the Nashville Bible School that he has not played the leading role. The quiet presence of the man, as he picked up a pen to write or mounted the podium to speak, has inspired his brethren with confidence and admiration. Perhaps only David Lipscomb was honored in such a manner during his lifetime. David Lipscomb was a plain man and people listened to him because he had something to say. B. C. Goodpasture is no plain man, but audiences hear him too because he has something to say.

On June 1, 1918, the young evangelist started preaching for the church of Christ in Shelbyville, Tennessee. He was the first regular preacher to work for the Shelbyville church of Christ. The small church had a membership that numbered about seventy-five persons. The church in Shelbyville had earlier gone into digression. A small group had remained loyal to the New Testament pattern of Christianity. At the time Goodpasture came to Shelbyville, the church had built the first unit of a brick meetinghouse named the Main Street church.

Goodpasture had preached on several occasions for the Shelbyville church while he preached at New Hermon out from Shelbyville. Then they were meeting in the courthouse since they did not have a meetinghouse. The Christian Church had taken over the church property when "digression" was sweeping the South. During the four years he attended David Lipscomb College, Goodpasture preached for New Hermon church which was a rural church near Shelbyville in Bedford County.

The meeting work of Goodpasture was limited to three meetings in the summer of 1918. At the closing of the school in May, Cleveland Cliett returned to her home in Childersburg, Alabama. They saw each other only one time before their marriage in September. B. C. Goodpasture made a train trip during the summer months to Childersburg for that purpose.

During the first two weeks in August, he conducted a meeting in Portland, Tennessee. The weather was so hot that services were held only in the evenings outside the building in a tent. In the August 29, 1918 issue of the *Advocate,* B. C. Goodpasture wrote about the three meetings he conducted that summer:

> Beginning on the first Sunday in August I preached two weeks in Portland. Eight were baptized. I am now in the midst of a meeting at New Hermon, in Bedford County. Six have been baptized thus far. On the second Sunday in September the Lord willing, I shall begin a meeting in Shelbyville. Congregations within reach of Shelbyville are requested to announce the meeting and all are cordially invited to attend every service.

B. C. Goodpasture was joined by Cleveland Cliett Goodpasture after their wedding in early September. Whatever apprehensions may have troubled her about the responsibilities of being a preacher's wife were soon dispelled. Their first home in Shelbyville was with Mrs. Charles Wiggins. They ate their meals with the family. The young preacher and his wife worked hard for the church. Such traveling they needed to do about Shelbyville was in a buggy owned by Dr. Lonnie Reagor. The buggy sat in the doctor's yard with a standing invitation for the preacher to use it whenever he needed it.

The outstanding experience of Goodpasture while he lived in Shelbyville grew out of a preachers' meeting in Tracy City, Tennessee, near Monteagle in the Upper Cumberland Mountains. Meetings of this kind were the forerunners of the college and church lectureships that became so popular in the late 1920's. The meeting started the third Sunday in March, 1919, and ran eight days. Some of the speakers were outstanding preachers of the time including such men as G. C. Brewer, A. B. Lipscomb, M. C. Kurfees, and S. P. Pittman. Some of the preachers spoke on assigned subjects and others used sermons of their own choosing. There were eighteen addresses on a wide variety of subjects delivered in much the same way as in a protracted meeting. The meetings were attended by large numbers of people. The visiting preachers were invited into the homes for their meals and lodging. And each speaker went home with a check in his pocket to cover expenses. There were eight baptisms and two restorations in the meeting.

B. C. stayed in the home of George Thorogood in the eight day meeting. He spoke on the subject "Seed Time and Harvest." The "Goodpasture" surname creates a measure of curiosity. One of the outstanding preachers of the church and a member of the *Gospel Advocate* staff was M. C. Kurfees from Louisville, Kentucky. The thinking and the good judgment of M. C. Kurfees were based upon a broad background of biblical scholarship. Kurfees highly commended the message of the young minister and remarked that we have had some good "grazing in the message."

It would be an understatement to say the visiting preachers were impressed with his performance—they were startled. They expected the usual kind of sermon from a young preacher. Charles R. Brewer knew first hand about the Tracy City meeting including the impressions of his brother, G. C. Brewer. Goodpasture was the youngest preacher present. Somebody knew enough about him to recommend him, and he was called to have a place on the lectureship. And Charles R. Brewer said a short while before his death, reminiscing, "I think he stole the show. Everybody was talking about his lecture."

G. C. Brewer came to his brother after the meeting because Charles Brewer had known Goodpasture since 1914, and said, "Who is this young preacher, B. C. Goodpasture? He just walked away with the preachers' meeting in Tracy City." Charles described the reactions of his older brother: "There was a little tone of envy when he spoke about him."

Charles Brewer answered, "Well that's not the last you are going to hear about B. C. because he was an outstanding student in David Lipscomb College, and he's making good wherever he goes as a preacher." Charles R. Brewer described the young man even then as having a fine command of the language and beginning to show the singular characteristics that would mark him through the years. Brewer remembered that Goodpasture never glanced at a note and his fluent quotations from the Bible, works of scholarship, and classical literature demonstrated his remarkable memory retention. He hardly ever referred to an author, but the effective way he uttered quotations impressed his audiences "that he knew what he was talking about and he knew more than he was telling."

B. C. Goodpasture has not in his life suffered with a "swelled head" because of accomplishments as so often men with small minds are disposed to be. While he was in Shelbyville, an invitation came from the principal of Fayette, Alabama High School to deliver the commencement sermon. When Goodpasture walked into the high school office, the principal could hardly conceal his apprehension about the ability of the young man who had come with such good recommendation and proper credentials. Later the schoolman said that he had serious misgivings that so young a man could satisfy the demands of the occasion; but he commented: "He measured not only up to the standards demanded of commencement speakers, but has set a new standard for them."

Marshall Keeble used an expression for the staff writer of the *Gospel Advocate*. The *Advocate* office was located downtown Nashville and Keeble would go in to purchase church supplies. He called them the "Men of the *Advocate*." David Lipscomb and E. G. Sewell were running the *Gospel Advocate* in the early years of this century. After B. C. entered the Nashville Bible School in

1914, he made visits to the *Advocate* office to make purchases. He, too, saw at a distance the men who ran the *Advocate*. The last three years of David Lipscomb were spent in his home on the Nashville Bible School campus. He sat on the front porch of his home on the Nashville Bible School campus with his Bible held in his lap.

J. C. McQuiddy, the last of the "Old Guard," as David Lipscomb, E. G. Sewell, F. D. Syrgley, and J. C. McQuiddy were called, became the dominant personality connected with the *Gospel Advocate*. B. C. Goodpasture made the acquaintance of J. C. McQuiddy during the time he attended college. J. C. McQuiddy and F. W. Smith made a special trip to Shelbyville in 1919 to interest Goodpasture in becoming circulation manager for the *Gospel Advocate*. They reached an agreement with Goodpasture to begin work with the *Advocate* on January 1, 1920.

The talents of J. C. McQuiddy as a major leader in the church of Christ have not been adequately evaluated. David Lipscomb had a head for business, but making money was not his primary interest in life. But he realized the importance of keeping the "till." Once he took the management of the *Advocate* away from McQuiddy and soon the paper was in debt. He turned the financial management back to McQuiddy and never bothered him about it again. The story was told about the men of the *Advocate* that when a visiting preacher dropped in for a chat, David Lipscomb would ask the question, "Did you preach the gospel?"; E. G. Sewell wanted to know, "How many did you baptize?"; J. C. McQuiddy would ask, "How much did they pay you?" J. C. McQuiddy knew that sound fiscal policy was the lubricant that made the wheels of business go around, and many times preachers were not paid enough. David Lipscomb said that J. C. McQuiddy was one of the most generous men he knew. McQuiddy would sometimes financially help a preacher who had been poorly supported.

The influence of the *Gospel Advocate* had grown since David Lipscomb joined Tolbert Fanning as co-editor of the *Gospel Advocate* in 1866. McQuiddy was sensitive to the growing influence of the paper. He saw the potentials of Goodpasture working for the *Gospel Advocate* to encourage new subscribers to the religious journal. In this his judgment was good.

McQuiddy's commendation of the young man carried in the

Advocate simply meant they trusted him and this was a passport which was honored by church members wherever the *Advocate* went. McQuiddy wrote in the December 18, 1919 issue of the *Gospel Advocate:*

> On account of the growing influence and increasing useful-
> ness of the *Gospel Advocate,* it becomes necessary to in-
> crease our force of workers. Definite arrangements have
> been made with Brother B. C. Goodpasture, one of our
> most promising young preachers, to become circulation
> manager of the *Gospel Advocate,* beginning next January.
> He will devote considerable time in the field, preaching and
> laboring among the churches, and any encouragement given
> him will be appreciated by the entire force of the *Advocate.*

J. C. McQuiddy made a prophetic statement about B. C. Goodpasture :

> Brother Goodpasture is held in very high esteem by the en-
> tire church of Shelbyville. He comes to the *Advocate* with
> the intention of making journalism his life's work. He feels
> that in journalism his field of usefulness will be much
> broader and that he can accomplish much greater good for
> the Master than by simply confining his efforts to preach-
> ing. He will write regularly for the *Gospel Advocate* and
> will devise ways and means of increasing its usefulness.
> He will spend some of his time in the office.

B. C. Goodpasture stayed with the *Gospel Advocate* just six
months. But the association with the *Gospel Advocate* staff was a
part of his good fortune. He had been tutored by H. Leo Boles
and for awhile had the opportunity to spend some time in the company of such men as F. B. Srygley, J. C. McQuiddy, and F. W.
Smith, and others. In 1939 when B. C. Goodpasture assumed the
helm of the *Advocate,* he was no stranger to the surroundings.

B. C. and Cleveland lived in the home of Miss May Kirkpatrick,
an aunt of J. Roy Vaughan, after coming to Nashville. In the
January 22, 1920 issue of the *Advocate,* Goodpasture wrote about
his new work :

> I began my work as circulation manager of the *Gospel Ad-
> vocate* on January 1. This is not unexpected to our read-
> ers, since Brother McQuiddy recently announced my com-
> ing. Although I am intensely interested in the editorial
> work of the *Gospel Advocate,* it is my purpose, primarily,
> to extend its circulation. In order to do this as effectively as
> possible, I am planning to make a number of trips out

among the churches; in fact I have already visited a few congregations, and have obtained results even beyond my expectations. The brethren where I have gone have been free to express their approval of the present management of the *Advocate* and have predicted for it a future of unusual activity and usefulness. The outlook is inviting. The circulation of the paper can easily be doubled through the co-operation of its readers. I believe they will help in this good work. The campaign for new subscribers has been launched and must be, and will be, carried on to a successful conclusion. To this I am now giving my best efforts.

In the six months Goodpasture worked for the *Advocate,* he traveled among the churches. Most of his time was spent among the churches in Middle Tennessee. Sometimes he would get the directory of the congregations where he was visiting and visit every member in the interest of the *Gospel Advocate*.

Goodpasture and his wife made one long trip out of Tennessee into East Texas by train. Only the steel rails spanned the rivers and crossed the swamps in the early years of this century. Their first stop was in Dallas, Texas, where he met A. O. Colley who was preaching for the church at Pearl and Bryan Street. He accompanied them to visit a relative of Cleveland.

Their next stop was Sherman, Texas, where B. C. and his wife

Mount Pleasant Preachers' Meeting: *Seated:* B. C. Goodpasture, F. B. Syrgley, James E. Scobey, F. W. Smith, R. E. L. Taylor, J. Paul Slayden, John C. Graham. *Standing:* C. E. Coleman, E. Gaston Collins, Claud Woodruff, H. M. Phillips, J. Petty Ezell, unidentified, P. S. Austin

made the acquaintance of L. S. White who preached for the church in Sherman. L. S. White was one of the outstanding church leaders a generation or so ago. The couple traveled to a small town, Celina, Texas, as Goodpasture said "was filled with Tennesseans who are always glad to see one from the 'old country.' "

Celina is the name for one of the towns in the Cumberland Mountains in Tennessee. The Texas trip was cut short because of a severe flu epidemic. A traveler from the East to the American West is not prepared for the vast reaches of the level land stretching as far as the eyes can see, and B. C. shared a similar amazement.

The remaining months that B. C. traveled for the *Advocate* were in Middle Tennessee. He wrote up his church visits for the paper under the caption "Journeyings Often." From time to time vignettes of church history cropped up in the travel accounts. He visited the church in McMinnville, Tennessee, and spent the night in the home of H. T. King. The church in McMinnville had been established more than a century before at the time when Alexander Campbell and other famed frontier preachers were preaching. A preacher by the name of Sandy Jones first preached in the courthouse at McMinnville. And David Lipscomb, Jesse L. Sewell, and T. B. Larimore and other well known ministers had preached there. H. T. King and Miss Nettie Drake gave B. C. the names of church members to visit and he was successful in getting a long list of subscribers. Goodpasture inserted a revealing comment about the McMinnville congregation saying that the church there had sent contributions to David Lipscomb College, Tennessee Orphan Home, mission meetings, and community charities.

He wrote an informative account of the history of the church at Sparta, Tennessee. No church records had been kept until after the Civil War. However, a small group of Christians were meeting in Sparta before 1840. The church worshipped in an old brick school house until 1893 at which time a new meetinghouse was built. The church numbered two hundred in 1920, and Goodpasture attributed this to the fact that the Sparta church had not been troubled by the "society and music" folks who were dividing churches in the period following the Civil War and early years of this century.

B. C. Goodpasture made one of his last trips to Henderson,

Tennessee, hunting for new subscribers. He arrived in Henderson, Tennessee, and spoke for the church during the evening service. The arrangement had been previously arranged through the *Advocate* office. A. G. Freed happened to be present for the worship service. This was the first time for B. C. to meet Arvey Glenn Freed, one of the co-founders of Freed-Hardeman College.

Freed introduced the young preacher to the Henderson church telling them that he was traveling in the interest of the *Gospel Advocate* and urged them to subscribe to the paper. A. G. Freed supplied him with the names of thirty-five prospects. Carrie Neal Hardeman, the small daughter of N. B. Hardeman, went with B. C. to show him the homes. He counted the trip a success since thirty-three of the thirty-five prospects signed up for the *Advocate*.

Goodpasture also had the good fortune to meet N. B. Hardeman the following day. Hardeman came into Henderson on Monday by train and did not stay in town long until he took another train out. That chance meeting developed into a great friendship between the two men. Goodpasture does not recall that Hardeman spoke to the student body of David Lipscomb College while he was there. The rivalry between David Lipscomb College and Freed-Hardeman, College was very pronounced then. The Lipscomb people thought Freed-Hardeman College was too polemic and the Freed-Hardeman people thought that David Lipscomb College did not emphasize the Bible enough.

This kind of work after awhile did not appeal to Goodpasture because it involved more traveling than he was interested in and he was away from home more than he liked. S. H. Hall contacted Goodpasture about going to Atlanta, Georgia, to preach for the West End Avenue church.

While S. H. Hall was away, Goodpasture preached a trial sermon in the summer of 1920. This gave both the preacher and the congregation time to meet each other. The elders of the West End Avenue church reached an agreement with Goodpasture to come to Atlanta. The work appealed to him to such an extent that he was willing to give up his work as circulation manager for the *Gospel Advocate*.

S. H. Hall wrote a special recommendation for his successor which was published in the *Advocate:*

The West End Avenue brethren, of Atlanta, are to be con-
gratulated on securing the services of Brother B. C. Goodpasture for twelve months, beginning the first Lord's day in
August. Brother Goodpasture, without any doubt, is one
of the best preachers the church of Christ has. He is a
graduate of the David Lipscomb College, and, though, a
young man, has had a number of years' experience in the
work since his graduation. It was my pleasure to assist
him in a revival in the fall of last year while he was at Shelbyville, Tenn. I found the people there devoted to him, and
every indication that he is a man who keeps himself fully
alive to every need of the work. His loyalty to our Lord
and devotion to God's truth stands unquestioned, and we
are expecting the very best for the work because of his able
assistance.

B. C. and Cleveland left Nashville on a Thursday for Atlanta,
Georgia, to take up their new work. They made their first home
at 98 South Asby Street in Atlanta. The West End Avenue meetinghouse was far from pretentious. It was a small framed building
located in a section of town where mostly the working class of people lived. The "men of the *Advocate*" sent him on his way with
their blessings saying: "He is a good preacher and we hate to lose
him from Tennessee, but we commend him to the brethren of
Georgia in the belief he will accomplish a good work there." But
Goodpasture did not forget the *Advocate*. He continued to enroll
subscribers and to sell books published by the Gospel Advocate
Company.

VIII

Euraquilo

In the Spring of 1920, B. C. Goodpasture was free to do what he could do best—preach the gospel. He had done his work well as circulation manager for the *Gospel Advocate*. During the summer of 1920, the youthful minister preached in evangelistic meetings in Alabama and Tennessee. S. H. Hall was making his move to leave his work with the West End Avenue church in Atlanta, Georgia. S. H. Hall had been largely instrumental in establishing the church in the Atlanta area. He was naturally interested in his successor who would "water where he had planted." Hall had been in a meeting with the Shelbyville church in the late fall of 1919 while Goodpasture was there. He learned first hand about him. He learned more about the young man from his old friends, H. Leo Boles, J. C. McQuiddy, and others. H. Leo Boles assured S. H. Hall that he could not make a better choice. It would be difficult to locate another preacher among the churches of Christ who promised so much in his early years and fulfilled so well the confidence and expectations of his older contemporaries.

The name of B. C. Goodpasture was first brought to the attention of the *Gospel Advocate* reading audience in October of 1914 when A. B. Lipscomb recommended the young man for preaching appointments at the request of John E. Dunn. After moving to Atlanta, Goodpasture continued his promotion of the *Advocate*. The state of Georgia and Atlanta were regarded as a mission field in the 1920's; and for eighteen years, the name of B. C. Goodpasture was associated with the Georgia work. After moving to Atlanta to work with West End Avenue church, he began writing generally about the work in one of the best known states of the Old South under the heading—"From Georgia and the Far Southern Fields." S. H. Hall had previously contributed similar information for the *Advocate*.

B. C. Goodpasture and Cleveland Goodpasture moved from Shelbyville, Tennessee, to Atlanta to begin their new work. The first meetinghouse of the church was a plain frame building with two classrooms back of the pulpit. The membership numbered about four hundred when he went there. The church was organized in 1905. The congregation grew out of a tent meeting held in May of that same year by F. W. Smith. O. D. Bearden and his family were among the first members. Through the support of the Green Street, Russell Street, and Charlotte Avenue churches in Nashville, F. W. Smith helped the young church to get off to a good start.

The first meeting place of the church was a tent pitched on Norcross Street. The church worshipped in the tent from May 1905 until November 1905 awaiting the completion of their meetinghouse. A. P. McCrory gave the lot and loaned the church $1500 for the erection of the building. The first gospel meeting in the meetinghouse was conducted in June of 1906 by James A. Harding. As a consequence of those early efforts, the West End Avenue church became the mother congregation in the Atlanta area. Through the encouragement of F. W. Smith, S. H. Hall started regular work the first of January in 1907. The thirteen years that S. H. Hall stayed in Atlanta is an epic story which he relates in his autobiography, *Sixty-Five Years in the Pulpit*. The church prospered with S. H. Hall preaching in Atlanta; and two other churches, the South Pryor and East Point congregations in Atlanta resulted from Hall's efforts. In the first forty years of the West End Avenue church, S. H. Hall, B. C. Goodpasture, and H. Clyde Hale were the only located preachers who served the congregation.

B. C. Goodpasture preached his first sermon as the regular minister of the Atlanta church the second Sunday in August. His work prospered from the first; and a month later, all previous records for Sunday school attendance were broken. Goodpasture began a practice of holding tent meetings in the general Atlanta area. His first tent meeting was at the corner of Cooper and

Glenn Streets. The churches of Christ in Atlanta dismissed their
evening services to attend the meetings. He conducted an average
of five or six tent meetings a summer while he was with the West
End church. These meetings were usually held in the suburbs of
Atlanta, and at other times in towns near Atlanta where the gospel
had not been preached.

The young evangelist went immediately to work in the Georgia
mission field. He took an early interest in Savannah, Georgia, a
city with a population of one hundred thousand. A small group of
Christians were meeting in the Knights of Columbus Hall. J. B.
Beck and J. N. Copeland were pushing the work in Savannah. J.
B. Beck was giving full time preaching. Goodpasture announced
that the meetinghouse of the Christian Scientists could be bought
for about $9,000, and he set to work to encourage *Advocate* read-
ers to help raise the money.

Goodpasture almost had a religious debate soon after coming
to Atlanta; the occasion came up in Savannah in the fall of 1920.
A Seventh Day Adventist preacher, "Reverend Shuler" had been
preaching about six weeks in Savannah. He was challenging the
preachers in Savannah to show where his teachings on the Sabbath
question were unscriptural if his teachings were. And finally he
challenged all the preachers in the state to meet and to debate him
on the Sabbath question. Bedford Beck had previously written a
letter to Goodpasture saying: "We may want you to come down
and answer him. Be ready to come on a moment's notice."

In two or three days a telephone call came from Beck advising
him to come to Savannah at once. B. C. Goodpasture and Reece
Rogers boarded a train for Savannah. When they got off the
train, Beck asked Goodpasture, "Do you think we ought to go over
and see the Adventist preacher?"

And he said, "No, we will not go over to see him now. We'll
see him tonight in the presence of his audience so everybody will
know what happened. If we talk to him in private, he can get up
and tell anything he wants to, and the audience won't know any
better." So that night Goodpasture and his brethren went over to
the tent. There were around five or six hundred people present
under a large tent.

Shuler got up before the audience and announced, "We are
going to sing a song or two, and then we are going to take up a

collection. If anybody has an announcement to make, he is at liberty to do so." Goodpasture was on the front seat and he arose and said, "I would like to make an announcement."

Shuler asked, "Does your announcement have any bearing on the literature we are distributing?"

Goodpasture answered, "Yes, not directly, but indirectly it does."

He consented, "All right, go ahead and make your announcement."

Goodpasture stood and turned to look at the audience and said, "Now for five or six weeks, Mr. Shuler has been challenging the preachers of this city to show what he has been preaching is wrong, and so far nobody has answered him. He became emboldened and extended his challenge to the preachers of the state. Well, I am not a preacher of the city, but I am of the state. And I am here to expose his teaching on the Sabbath question. I am ready to begin tomorrow night. I am wondering if he is ready?" Then Goodpasture turned to face Shuler, "Mr. Shuler, are you ready to begin this thing tomorrow night?"

Shuler responded with a show of emotions, "No, I wouldn't debate with any little 'Dick, Tom, or Harry.'"

Goodpasture never at a loss for just the right words said, "Well, that's the way Goliath felt about David!"

Shuler came back, "I know who you are." Presumably he meant that he knew Goodpasture was a member of the church of Christ.

Goodpasture replied, "That may be the reason why you don't want to debate."

Then Goodpasture turned to address the audience again, "This has taken Mr. Shuler rather suddenly, but maybe on second thought he will screw up his courage to the sticking point. I am going to challenge him to defend his teaching on the Sabbath question."

Again Goodpasture turned to Shuler, "Are you willing to have this debate?"

Shuler emphatically said, "No!"

Goodpasture faced the audience again, "Now you know his challenges did not mean anything. They were just a big bluff. Tomorrow night I am going to review Mr. Shuler at the Knight's Hall." Oscar Rawlings left the meeting that night and arranged at his own expense for a quarter-page advertisement in the morning paper. The ad was headlined "Shuler Backs Down."

Early the next morning Jasper Copeland, who preached for many years in Alachua, Florida, was on hand as the newsboys left with their papers. He urged them, mischievously, to hawk the paper with the cry, "Shuler backs down!" In those pre-radio and pre-television days, their cries had quite an effect on downtown Savannah. The Knight's Hall was jammed with people on Thursday and Friday nights to hear Goodpasture.

The extent of the Shuler fiasco can be evaluated by the failure to make good the often repeated announcement that at least one hundred people would be baptized at the end of his meeting. When the time came, there were less than twenty baptized by the Adventist preacher. Actually, the Seventh Day Adventist meeting died on the night Shuler backed down. In later years, Goodpasture regretfully said that a golden opportunity was missed when they failed to conduct a gospel meeting at the Knights Hall location in Savannah while the interest was running high. When Dan Harless came to Savannah, Georgia, twenty years later, there were many in the area for whom the incident remained a vivid memory.

Later Shuler rather lamely said that he had refused to debate because "Goodpasture was not endorsed by the ministerial association."

Goodpasture promptly replied that "Shuler did not have the association's endorsement either."

B. C. Goodpasture said recently, "I never had a religious debate and I never sought one. But I never ran from one." And he described the Savannah episode as "just a little squabble."

The West End members were happy with B. C. and Cleveland in their midst. As they prepared to leave for the Christmas holidays, the church presented them with a gift of aluminum kitchen ware and other gifts from their respective Bible classes. The following January, the churches of Christ in Atlanta, and there were only three then—South Pryor, East Point, and West End Avenue—planned to conduct a series of union services. The first service was conducted January 9 at East Point, the following Sunday at South Pryor, with the concluding service at West End the next Sunday.

Goodpasture owned his first automobile in February of this year. The church bought him a 1918 Buick. He had a choice between a new Ford and the Buick. The Buick had a self-starter and that was the reason he chose it. Two of his cousins in Nashville suffered a broken arm about the same time cranking their Fords. Over the years, Goodpasture has owned a Willys Knight, Cadillac, and Oakland. He traded the Oakland for a Hudson. He drove Hudson cars twenty-five years until the car disappeared from the market. Then he changed to a Chrysler Imperial. He drives the same car for several years because a good serviced car will give carefree performance for about one hundred thousand miles.

There were several other matters of interest in 1921. He announced in the *Advocate* that the Savannah church had purchased their meetinghouse, but were still pressed for money. F. B. Srygley came to hold a meeting for the West End Avenue church in June. Goodpasture informed the *Advocate* readers that Don Hockaday then preaching for the South Pryor church was married to Anna Lee Baxter, Director of Music in Harper College in Harper, Kansas. They were married in the residence of Batsell Baxter, brother of Anna Lee, at his home in Abilene, Texas. The wedding ceremony was performed June 30 with Batsell Baxter officiating.

But the finest experience of that year appeared in the form of an announcement in the *Advocate:* "Arrived in Atlanta, Georgia on May 28, B. C. Goodpasture, Jr. 'A babe in the house is a wellspring of pleasure.' "

The following year was another banner year. Goodpasture was doing what he could to push the work in Georgia. He encouraged the churches and preachers in Georgia and kept a running account of the Georgia work in the *Advocate* about their work. The men of the *Gospel Advocate* were solidly behind him. A note was run in the November 16 issue of the paper: "B. C. Goodpasture was a welcome caller at this office recently."

The West End church engaged Hugh E. Garrett to work in the field. In September, Goodpasture conducted a sixteen day meeting in Norcross, Georgia. Six members from the West End church who had moved there encouraged Goodpasture to come for a meeting. There were twenty-six baptisms. Twelve came from the Baptist and four from the Christian church. Four Methodists and the son of a Baptist preacher were baptized. When people heard B. C. Goodpasture, they heard the gospel preached and they

knew there was a difference from what they usually heard. The
six members and the new converts started worship services in
Norcross the next Sunday. O. D. Bearden who conducted the
song service began preaching for them.

A memorable year for all Christians especially in Nashville,
Tennessee, was 1922. This was the year N. B. Hardeman conducted the famed Ryman Auditorium meeting in Nashville, Tennessee, with C. M. Pullias conducting the song service. In 1922,
the church census counted 317,937 members of the churches of
Christ, and 63,521 were in Tennessee. N. B. Hardeman who was
forty-seven years old started the meeting March 28 on a Sunday
afternoon. The kind of crowds that had flocked to the Ryman
Auditorium to hear Gypsy Smith and Billy Sunday came to hear
Hardeman in a three weeks' meeting. The whole city was excited.
The Nashville newspapers carried the full text of his sermons, and
the members of the church were jubilant. During the meetings,
the church of Christ came into prominent and favorable attention
all over Middle Tennessee. David Lipscomb and his associates
had won the battle against digression. The masterful Hardeman
called the starting signals for the beginning of phenomenal
growth among the churches of Christ in Middle Tennessee and
elsewhere.

Goodpasture took notice of the meeting in a note he wrote to
the *Advocate:* "Will the Nashville brethren secure excursion
rates for us fellows who live so far from Nashville? We may
not be able to attend if they do not."

Almost from the time, he started preaching, B. C. Goodpasture's name appeared in the *Gospel Advocate* under articles he had
written and reports of his church activities. He seldom went outside Georgia to preach. With the exception of a meeting or two,
he held all of his meetings in Georgia. And there was never a
time he was not securing subscribers for the *Advocate*. In March
of 1923, he sent in a list of sixty subscribers for just that one
month. His oldest sister Ethel passed away on June 8, 1923, and
he went to Flat Creek to attend her funeral.

The pattern of work that B. C. Goodpasture set in the first two
years in Atlanta expanded year by year. In January of 1924, R.
R. Brooks came to the East Point church and James H. McBroom
went to the South Pryor congregation. Goodpasture welcomed
each co-laborer and became a loyal friend to each preacher who

came to work in the Georgia field. The following May, Goodpasture preached the commencement sermon for the David Lipscomb College graduating class.

The church lost J. C. McQuiddy this year. He suddenly died, August 3, 1924, at the age of sixty-five. In the memorial issue honoring the life of J. C. McQuiddy, Goodpasture wrote one of the eulogies of his friend and benefactor. Over the years, Goodpasture has been the close friend of Leon and David McQuiddy, sons of J. C. McQuiddy, and David McQuiddy, Jr., the grandson of J. C. McQuiddy. For thirty-two years, B. C. Goodpasture has edited the *Gospel Advocate* with the complete confidence of the McQuiddy family. The year of 1924 marked the birth of the middle child of B. C. and Cleveland. On April 18, 1924, their middle child, Eleanor Pauline, was born.

The church in Atlanta, Georgia, won every foot of ground it gained. The West End Avenue church was located among the working people of Atlanta. West End Avenue was a short street that headed into Welborn Street which ended at the city dump. It was not the best place for a meetinghouse; but when the church started in Atlanta, the members did not have much to do with at the time.

Judge Hathcock, a member of the Christian Church and a city judge, had a chance meeting with B. C. Goodpasture. The judge was also one of the founders of the Atlanta Christian College. Judge Hathcock upon meeting the young preacher said, "Goodpasture, yes, I've heard that name. Oh yes, you preach for a little church over on Welborn Street." The judge was rubbing it in a little by saying Welborn Street instead of West End Avenue because it ran down to the city dump. This exchange of words took place the early summer of 1924 between the two men.

The young man reacted, "I just thought, old boy, I'll just fix you so you will not have any trouble remembering my name." So two or three weeks later, Goodpasture and some of his brethren eased over into the Capitol View section of the city and put up a tent on a Saturday afternoon and scattered circulars all over that part of town. It was too late for the preachers who did not want them there to do anything about it. The meeting ran for four weeks beginning the last of July and closing August 18. And what a meeting! There were thirty-nine additions—sixteen came out of Judge Hathcock's Christian Church where he served as an

B.C. and Cleveland

B.C. and Cleveland,   Eleanor and Cordell
Cordell and Eleanor

elder. One of the sixteen was the organist. He also baptized the
organist of the Presbyterian Church and her mother whose husband was an elder in the Presbyterian Church. The judge did not
have any trouble remembering the Goodpasture name after that.

In March of 1925, N. B. Hardeman came to the West End Avenue church for a meeting. N. B. Hardeman had the year before
met Ira M. Boswell, a Christian Church preacher, in a religious debate in the Ryman Auditorium. The Nashville church was just as
well satisfied with Hardeman's management of the debate as they
had been with Hardeman's Tabernacle meetings in the Ryman Auditorium. Those who were informed knew the churches of Christ
in Middle Tennessee were on the move and the Christian Church
was not. Goodpasture had briefly met Hardeman in Henderson in
1920 and had spoken to him briefly the evening he led the prayer
in the Ryman Auditorium meeting. Record breaking audiences
came out to hear N. B. Hardeman in Atlanta and were impressed
with his clear, convincing, and masterful way of preaching.
Goodpasture was then thirty years old and Hardeman had reached
his fiftieth year. The two men spent a day together walking over
Stone Mountain and talking. Hardeman invited the young man to
come to Freed-Hardeman College to teach, but he declined.

The last two years of Goodpasture's work with the West End
Avenue congregation were filled with endless church work. The
Goodpastures moved into their own brick-veneer home in the early
part of 1926 located at 654 Holderness Street. The membership
was largely scattered. There were the sick to be visited and funerals and weddings to be conducted. All of this was in addition
to a heavy preaching schedule. His services were in constant demand.

The following year had its enjoyable experiences. The statement appeared in the *Advocate* from time to time that a gospel
meeting was conducted in the West End Avenue church by the
"home forces." That meant Goodpasture was preaching and he
was being assisted by the members. He held one of his great
meetings at West End in May of 1927, with one hundred and four
additions. The meeting ran over four weeks with audiences larger
than any of the previous years. On one of the Sundays, the over-
flow audience spilled out to the front steps of the building and on
to the sidewalks. There were sixty-six baptisms—fifteen came
from the Baptist Church, five from the Christian Church, six were

Methodists and three were Presbyterians. This was the fourth such meeting he had conducted for the West End Avenue church. He had held twenty other meetings in and around Atlanta where the church was not established.

Then suddenly the *Advocate* carried the announcement that B. C. Goodpasture was changing his address to Florence, Alabama, where he would preach for the Poplar Street church. His work with the West End congregation was ended the last week in August with an audience too large to be seated. Twelve were added to the membership that day, and more than one hundred and fifty members had been added since the first of the year.

Why a preacher leaves for a new work in the upswing of a great work may be puzzling, but Goodpasture had his reasons. The work had reached what he perhaps thought was a climax to his labors, and he perhaps thought that it would be better for another preacher to come as most often is the best judgement in such cases. He was tired and worn out with meeting work coupled with his other church responsibilities. And there were personal reasons. His family lived east of Nashville and his wife's family lived south of Nashville. Florence, Alabama, was midway between Livingston and Childersburg; and he was closer to Nashville where many of the activities of the church were centered. No preacher wants to leave a work that is falling away.

The Atlanta congregation was reluctant to see B. C., Cleveland Goodpasture, and their small son and daughter leave Atlanta. They presented him with a Hamilton Railroad Special pocket watch with the inscription inside the case: "Presented to B. C. Goodpasture by the West End Avenue Church of Christ in August, 1927." He still wears the watch.

B. C. Goodpasture preached only one year for the Poplar Street church in Florence, Alabama. The year was not marked by anything of unusual interest. The Florence church was an old established congregation without the excitement that usually attends a new growing church in a mission field. His work was appreciated by the Florence church, and he held his usual number of gospel meetings that summer.

The Atlanta brethren were not to let B. C. Goodpasture be. Not long after he went to Florence, some of the church members set to work organizing a church in the "North Side" section of Atlanta near Ponce de Leon Avenue, one of the main thoroughfares in Atlanta. The new church grew out of the membership of the West End, East Point, and South Pryor churches. The members lived mainly in the "North Side" section. The "North Side" Christians meant business when they started the only church of Christ in that section of Atlanta. The new church was called the Seminole Avenue church. The new meetinghouse was a brick-veneer structure with a seating capacity of four hundred. The main auditorium and the class rooms seated eight classes.

Among those responsible for the new work were Dr. C. H. Paine, N. A. Hunter, F. P. Morris, George J. Morris, Ed Venable, J. C. West, W. D. Kerby, J. H. Timmie, J. J. Klaitz, A. M. Holty, E. B. Casey, J. T. Harrison, F. J. Turner, C. E. Cox, H. H. Jones, T. J. Cleibron, and others. B. C. Goodpasture was called to Atlanta to preach the third Sunday in February for the new church. The Seminole Avenue congregation numbered seventy-six when it started. Goodpasture preached three sermons that day. The afternoon service was attended by the other churches and they came out in good numbers.

As it turned out, Goodpasture's year in Florence, Alabama, was an interruption in the Georgia mission field. He left the Poplar Street Church with the complete good will of the members. Their need for his services were not as crucial in Alabama as in Georgia; at least, this was the thinking of the Georgia brethren. Nothing would do them but for the Goodpastures to move back to Atlanta. And until he became editor of the *Gospel Advocate* in 1939, Goodpasture never thought about leaving, and the Seminole congregation never entertained for a moment the need for a change in preachers.

Why did the people in Atlanta come out to hear B. C. Goodpasture preach? He made an imposing appearance in the pulpit. He was easy to look at and listen to and he used wonderful English. His illustrations were always apt and he had something to say worth listening to. Perhaps no person is better qualified to make the analysis than Gus Nichols. And there has not been another preacher in this century held in higher esteem by the entire brotherhood of the churches of Christ than Gus Nichols of Jasper, Alabama. He described B. C. Goodpasture as he is known by the people who have known him the longest. Gus Nichols wrote what follows as an eulogy of B. C. Goodpasture, but that makes it nonetheless reliable:

Personally I consider B. C. Goodpasture in my thinking as the greatest and best gospel preacher whom I have ever had the privilege of hearing. I doubt that any living preacher could excel several of his great masterpieces which I have heard under varying circumstances. He is truly a master of assemblies. His presence commands attention. His voice was rich and mellow which at times plucked the heart strings of those who heard. His delivery was warm and fervent with interest in his audience whom he loved and admired. He always spoke deliberately and with ease—yes, and without notes. His vocabulary was always ready to lend him the right word, or phrase, or the right quotation, at the right time. His illustrative material makes one think of the parables of Jesus. His power of exhortation and persuasion made his discourse and the invitation almost irresistable. But, as I view B. C. Goodpasture, he cannot be put into the molds and confines of a book. It will take the divine picture of his whole life of loving and sacrificial service in the Kingdom of God, both as a great preacher and editor of the *Gospel Advocate*, to portray the greatness of this man whom I love and admire for his work's sake.

B. C. Goodpasture has not questioned his course in life as a preacher of the gospel. He is confident that the "gospel is God's power" to work out his will in the lives of men. When Paul was on his way to Rome, his ship was caught up in a great wind, and Luke wrote, "And when the ship was caught, and could not bear up into the wind, we let her drive." Paul was confident no harm could come to him until God had accomplished his purpose in him. This has been the courage of B. C. Goodpasture who too has passed through many of life's stormy passages. The story of B. C. Goodpasture's life however, does not approach a climax at this time in his life. What had gone before in his life were preparations for the best that was yet to be. He won all the early skirmishes; the big battles were ahead.

IX

The Hook and the Staff

Jesus commissioned his disciples to go out and win men by "hook or by crook"—the shepherd's staff and the fisherman's hook. For more than half a century, B. C. Goodpasture has been shepherding men into the church. He has become truly a great fisher of men. When Goodpasture returned to Atlanta in the late summer of 1928, he took up where he had left off a year ago. His work with the Seminole church duplicated his work with the West End Avenue church only in another part of the city.

H. Clyde Hale began work with the West End Avenue church at the time Goodpasture went to Florence, Alabama. Clyde Hale was a promising young preacher who came to West End through the recommendations of S. H. Hall. The West End congregation and Hale were somewhat apprehensive Goodpasture would draw away a part of the membership from West End Avenue church because of his close personal ties with them. That did not happen. The Seminole Christians were simply using good logic in starting a church in a section of Atlanta where one did not exist and where one was needed.

H. Clyde Hale is now living in Nashville, Tennessee, where he has resided for many years. S. H. Hall and H. Clyde Hale had close ties with each other since the early twenties. Their close relationship grew out of the fact that Hale was baptized by S. H. Hall in 1922 at the Russell Street church of Christ. Clyde Hale said the first time he saw B. C. Goodpasture was in 1923 when he preached the commencement sermon at David Lipscomb College. Hale was impressed by his eloquence of speech, his personal demeanor, and his coal-black hair. He stood so straight and behaved like a perfect gentleman. Hale went up and introduced himself and Goodpasture was very cordial and friendly.

Clyde Hale said when he moved to Atlanta to preach at West End that he was filled with fear and trembling because he knew he was to follow B. C. Goodpasture. And when Goodpasture returned to Atlanta to preach for the Seminole church, it put a strain on the members at West End. Clyde Hale said Goodpasture was exceptionally courteous and helpful to all the churches. Hale summed up his feelings about Goodpasture in recent times:

> I have never known him to say a harmful word about anybody. His sermons were challenging. I never knew anybody to say a harmful thing about him. His character and reputation were far above reproach. Nothing could be said in a critical way about his mannerism, his preaching, his life, or even his return to Atlanta. The church needed to be established on the North Side and it was very fortunate for the Atlanta churches that he returned to Atlanta.

H. Clyde Hale moved to Nashville in 1944 to preach for the West End church and afterwards for the University church. He and B. C. Goodpasture grew to be closest of friends. They have enjoyed many hours together reminiscing over their years in Georgia. Clyde Hale said that he regretted now that he had not taken better advantage of Goodpasture's scholarship, spirituality, and influence. This was the first important work H. Clyde Hale had done and he was young in the work.

In less than a year the membership in the Seminole church doubled. Despite the apprehensions of the other churches of Christ in Atlanta, the Seminole church was not growing at their expense. Instead, the other churches of Christ in Atlanta were experiencing a growth in membership. H. Clyde Hale proved to be a valuable asset at the West End church. In the early part of 1928, the West End members purchased a lot and moved into their new building February of 1929 about a year later. The meetinghouse was an attractive two-story brick structure. The auditorium had a seating capacity of five hundred and a balcony with another one hundred seats. On February 10, the congregation met for the first time in their new quarters. The afternoon service was attended by the other Atlanta churches. S. H. Hall had been invited to speak for the occasion, but other commitments precluded his acceptance.

B. C. Goodpasture

J. Roy Vaughan and
B. C. Goodpasture

Goodpasture home in Atlanta

H. Clyde Hale

Nineteen and twenty-nine was a typical preaching year for Goodpasture in Atlanta following about the same patterns that he had set in the years before. He started his summer meetings the first Sunday of April in Valdosta, Georgia. A. B. Lipscomb was working then with the Valdosta congregation. Goodpasture performed also his home work with the Seminole church between meetings. He conducted a meeting at Seminole in October with the "home forces" which meant no outside preacher or evangelist was brought in. There were seventeen additions. This was his thirty-second meeting in the Atlanta district.

B. C. Goodpasture was also a popular commencement speaker for high school graduations. Such opportunities, however, were limited since the public schools dismissed the same time.

Goodpasture went in January of 1930 to St. Petersburg, Florida, for a gospel meeting. J. Roy Vaughan was preaching there at that time. This was the first time Goodpasture and Vaughan worked together in a meeting. They had been students together in the Nashville Bible School. Their friendship then was the usual friendly relations of students. Goodpasture had manifested a spirit of friendliness toward the younger boy which he appreciated and remembered. That occasion provided an opportunity for the two men to become better acquainted. Goodpasture was with Vaughan in other places in later years for meetings. After Goodpasture became editor of the *Gospel Advocate,* he invited J. Roy Vaughan to edit the "News and Notes" section of the *Advocate.*

During the St. Petersburg meeting, they went one day to fish in the Gulf. J. Roy Vaughan borrowed a rod and reel from an old man for Goodpasture. They were fishing at a place where the sea was running roughly. Goodpasture had laid the rod and line down with a fish for bait on the hook. A pelican flew in for the fish on the hook and dragged rod and reel out to sea. They were not able to retrieve the borrowed gear. They sadly informed the old man what had happened, and he sadly informed them that he too had borrowed the rod and reel.

At one time or another such honors that his brethren could bestow upon Goodpasture, they have done so. During the school year of 1930 and 1931, he served as the president of the David Lipscomb College Alumni Association. The Great Depression of the 1930's had settled in deep gloom over the nation. Goodpasture recalled in the eleven years while he preached for the Seminole church that his salary was not raised.   His salary, however, was reduced in the "hard times" of the Depression.

The summer of 1931 was especially significant for Goodpasture.   Marshall Keeble was holding a gospel meeting in Valdosta, Georgia, which started in July and ended August 9.   The meeting was one of the most memorable events in both the lifetimes of B. C. Goodpasture and Marshall Keeble.   Goodpasture first heard Keeble preach in a meeting in Sheffield, Alabama, where Keeble was holding a meeting.   Goodpasture was then living in Florence, Alabama, preaching for the Poplar Street church.   He went over one night to attend a meeting.   Goodpasture and Keeble saw each other for the first time on that occasion.

The fame of Marshall Keeble who became a legend in his lifetime was rapidly growing at this time.   The meeting of the two men that night in Sheffield started a friendship that lasted until Keeble's death.   There was a growing demand at that time for some of Keeble's sermons to be put in print.   After Goodpasture heard him, he knew why.   Goodpasture after the first Valdosta meeting corresponded with Keeble about publishing some of his sermons.   The two men decided Valdosta would be a good place when Keeble returned for another meeting.   The story of that meeting which was conducted in the summer of 1931 will be told in another place.

Goodpasture and Keeble met another time that summer.   After the Valdosta meeting, Keeble came at the invitation of the West End Avenue church to hold a meeting beginning August 10 in Atlanta for the black people of Atlanta. What a meeting it was! As many as twenty-five hundred people came to hear Keeble some of the nights, and there was never less than a thousand people present.   Goodpasture attended the meeting every time he could.   S. H. Hall was there and he said, "I had to stand, but I could stand flatfooted and listen to Keeble preach three hours and never grow tired."   H. Clyde Hale at a loss for words could just say, "It was the most wonderful meeting I ever witnessed."   This story will be more fully detailed in a later chapter.   N. B. Hardeman also expressed his admiration at that time for Keeble:

> I have known Brother M. Keeble since 1922, and have followed him with interest and appreciation all along the years since.   I have said many times privately and publicly, that I consider Brother Keeble one of the very best preachers in

the church of Christ, and that he is possibly doing more good than any man among us.

Keeble teamed up with some great men in his time. The two men that meant the most to Marshall Keeble in a personal way were A. M. Burton and B. C. Goodpasture. A. M. Burton founder of the Life and Casualty Insurance Company, in Nashville, Tennessee, was the first among the outstanding church leaders to recognize the worth of Marshall Keeble to the church. Beginning in the early twenties, A. M. Burton supported and encouraged Keeble in his preaching. A. M. Burton had supported Joe McPherson, a white mail carrier, who held a meeting for the Jackson Street church in 1914 where Keeble was a member. A. M. Burton became aware of Keeble during that meeting. Keeble said three people helped him more than any other persons—A. M. Burton, N. B. Hardeman, and B. C. Goodpasture. Whatever doors needed to be opened for Keeble in the church, they could open them for Keeble and they did.

B. C. Goodpasture reached his thirty-seventh year in 1932. He had suffered no reverses in life. From the time he first entered the Nashville Bible School, his older contemporaries were aware of him. Each had been profoundly inpressed with the young man and said so publicly from the pulpits and the religious papers. No one person knows the worth of B. C. Goodpasture because no man knows the story of his full life. These early years were not marked by spectaculars, nor have the years since. Every year has found him in the high country and climbing higher. The Cumberland "mountain man" has found the mountain trail to his liking.

In the issue of the *Advocate* for May 12, 1932, Goodpasture announced the publication of Keeble's sermons which contained a brief biography of Keeble with pictures of Keeble's first wife and the Valdosta meetings.

B. C. Goodpasture started writing for the *Gospel Advocate* when he was circulation manager in 1920. From time to time articles from his pen appeared in the *Gospel Advocate*. He was made a staff writer for the *Advocate* in 1931. He started writing under the caption—"Pioneer Pulpit." The materials printed in the department were mostly taken from early Restoration literature.

The friends who have known Goodpasture the longest associate him with books and with good reason. He has always loved books. The first book he ever bought with his own money was *Natural Law in the Spiritual World* by Henry Drummond. He paid fifty cents for the book and worked an entire day for the money. The second book that he purchased was a first year Greek grammar. He first mastered the alphabet. After a while he could read a good many sentences in Greek, look up words in a Greek lexicon, and read some simple sentences in the New Testament. Goodpasture has the knowledge of an expert in buying books. He started collecting books when he was a student in David Lipscomb College. The Methodist Publishing Company had a sale disposing of some eight or ten titles. He asked the sales lady what kind of price she would make him if he bought all the books. She set a price and he bought about fifty books. He carried them out to the school and sold enough of them to get his money back and keep the ones he wanted. That was more or less the beginning of his book collecting.

From that time he continued to purchase books. Afterwards he would buy private collections and sometimes he bought book collections of preachers who had died. Most of the book collections were small. He would sell some books and keep others, and he gradually accumulated a private collection of some ten thousand volumes. Most of the books he purchased were religious. He frequently imported books from Europe.

The *Atlanta Journal* featured B. C. Goodpasture in the summer of 1932, as a book collector. Among the rare documents in his possession at that time were the correspondence of a "carpetbag" governor of Georgia to his successor in office, state papers signed by President James Madison during the War of 1812, papers signed by James Monroe who was Secretary of State during the same period. He owned other documents from the hands of Ulysses S. Grant and Rutherford B. Hayes. And he possessed a rare book written by William Penn published in 1797.

Gooodpasture has an interest in certain types of Americana. At one time he built up a valuable collection of books on the American Indian, some rare Tennessee histories and other state histories. He sold at one time his book collection on the American Indian to the University of Tennessee, but he has since built the collection back up. He has given sizable collections of books to David Lipscomb College, Freed-Hardeman College, and Alabama

Christian College. At the present time he owns about fifteen thousand volumes.

Goodpasture's knowledge of books is not a haphazard thing. He subscribes to the *Antiquarian Bookman* which is published for new and used book dealers. The publication contains advertisement for books wanted and books to be sold. The publication is published by the Boker Company of New York. The company also publishes annually *Book Prices Current* which contains a list of the books that sold for five dollars or more at auction the previous year. He knows where to go to find books—second hand bookstores and furniture stores, Salvation Army, private and public sales. His encyclopedic mind is like a steel trap. What he learns he remembers. When he looks over a book there is no doubt of his knowledge about that book.

Whoever has marvelled at the repertory of Goodpasture anecdotes and quotations running the entire gamut of classical and modern literature has also wondered how he learned and retained so much. He said, "I just picked them up here and there." His power of memory is phenomenal. Goodpasture could take up printed material, read it two or three times and have it committed to memory. He memorized one thousand lines of Tennyson while he was in college. His teacher asked for only five hundred.

The people in Atlanta remember another side of B. C, Goodpasture—he enjoyed hunting while he was growing up around Flat Creek. He occasionally would bring down a quail, but that was not his favorite game. After he moved to Georgia, he took up bird hunting. There was a lot of quail in Southern Georgia then. He never shot ten birds straight without missing. Ten was the limit, but he had fired nine times without missing. He killed three birds on the wing with one shot several times.

Flavil Hall Smith who was a young man lived in Atlanta at that time. Smith attended the Seminole church. He went hunting with Goodpasture and in explaining the superior marksmanship of Goodpasture, for want of a better expression, he said, "He was quite a woodsman." What startled Smith the most was Goodpasture's ability to bring down a flying bat. Goodpasture has enjoyed most of the outdoor sports. He has enjoyed fishing and brought down his first deer near San Antonio, Texas.

Not in this lifetime has B. C. Goodpasture allowed his diver-

Eleanor, Cleveland, Cordell

Cliett and Cleveland   Eleanor, Cliett, Cordell

sions to interfere with his church work. The Atlanta churches were on the move in 1932. The West End church had grown to a membership of eight hundred and were meeting in their new church home on Hopkins and Gordon Street. The Seminole church was steadily growing and in the early part of 1933 had reached a membership of almost four hundred.

While B. C. Goodpasture was holding a meeting for the Union Avenue church in Memphis, his second son, John Cliett was born, March 30, 1933. Batsell Baxter who had succeeded H. Leo Boles as President of David Lipscomb in 1933 invited Goodpasture to deliver the baccalaureate sermon on Sunday evening, May 23, 1933, at Central church of Christ. The service was carried over WLAC radio station.

B. C. Goodpasture was not widely known as a preacher during the years he stayed in Atlanta outside the pages of the *Advocate*. He reported the results of his meetings in the *Advocate*. And from time to time he wrote in news items about the Seminole church. But there were other preachers doing similar good work and they contributed to the *Advocate* from time to time. There were not many in the church who knew of his rare talents. H. Leo Boles was one who did and that would make all the difference in the future of B. C. Goodpasture.

Goodpasture came in the summer of 1934 to preach in a meeting in Jasper, Alabama. Gus Nichols was the preacher there. The Jasper church learned about Goodpasture who delivered the commencement sermon at Fayette, Alabama, several years back. The meeting started on a Sunday morning. None of the members had ever heard Goodpasture or seen him. After a brief introduction, Goodpasture arose to speak. The auditorium was so crowded that Gus Nichols had to sit on the rostrum. The congregation was tense with expectation. They could hardly believe that the speaker was as talented as they had been led to believe in the introduction given to the strange but handsome young man. Within sixty seconds, the congregation was completely relaxed and at ease with this unusual personality who had come to them as a friend and brother.

After the meeting that Sunday morning, visitors from Haleyville and Birmingham said, "That is the best preaching and the best preacher we ever heard." That evening, the service was moved outside the building with enough seats to accommodate a

thousand people.   The attendance grew during the meeting with a
large number of responses.   Something came out of that Jasper
meeting that never happened to Goodpasture anywhere before or
since.   When he returned later for a second meeting, on the first
Sunday of the meeting, Gus Nichols told Goodpasture the elders
would like to meet him in a Sunday school room.   So he went into
the room where the elders were.   They asked him if he still had
the sermons that he preached in the previous meeting.   And he
told the elders that he thought he had the sermons.   Then they
said, "We want you to preach those same sermons in this meeting."   Several years later, Goodpasture returned for a third meeting in their new meetinghouse, and they asked him to preach the
identical sermons again and he did.

The Seminole church was steadily growing, and in 1934 the
church was pressing its accommodations.   Goodpasture continued
holding his usual number of summer meetings and concentrated his
work mostly in Georgia.   There was another matter of special interest in this year.   Marshall Keeble's first wife died on December
11, 1932.   When Keeble began to think seriously about marrying
the second time, he told Percy Ricks, a close friend, "Some of you
boys ought to find me a good wife.   I can't live single the rest of
my life as young as I am."   Percy had just the right person in
mind, Laura Catherine Johnson.   He told Keeble, "You get her,
and you are going to get the best girl in the Johnson family."
Percy Ricks had married Laura's sister.

The courtship of Marshall Keeble and Laura Johnson blossomed.   Keeble approached Goodpasture about performing the
ceremony.   Goodpasture told Keeble, "I'll perform the ceremony
anywhere east of the Mississippi and south of the Ohio."
Goodpasture said he did not want to travel so far, but that still
covered a wide territory.

Keeble responded, "I can marry in lots less territory than
that."   Goodpasture went to Corinth, Mississippi, April 3, 1934, to
perform the wedding ceremony.   Keeble would tease Percy Ricks
his brother-in-law, "You told me I would get the finest rose in the
Johnson garden, and I believe I did."   Sometimes Ricks would get
a little peeved with Keeble when he teased a little too hard.

H. Leo Boles came to Atlanta in April of 1935 to preach in a
meeting with the Seminole church.   This was the first meeting for
Boles in the Seminole church.   Although H. Leo Boles and B. C.

Goodpasture had not often crossed paths in their preaching work, their friendship had grown over the years. Whenever Goodpasture came to Nashville, he would spend the night in the Boles' home, and Brother Boles' feelings would have been hurt if he had not. They would talk over old times in the Cumberlands and matters of interest to the church. Goodpasture was still thought of as a young man in 1935. He was then forty with everything promising for the future. The words from the Houston Space Center reporting the moon shots fitted this gospel preacher—"All systems go and you are looking good."

During his last three years in Atlanta, B. C. Goodpasture did whatever a preacher is supposed to do. His performances were pleasing and appreciated by both church members and non-church members. He preached funeral services and performed wedding ceremonies. In 1938 the Seminole membership had increased three hundred and fifty percent. Then all of a sudden his work with the Seminole church came to an end. Leon McQuiddy invited B. C. Goodpasture to become editor of the *Gospel Advocate*.

B. C. Goodpasture accepted the editorship of the *Gospel Advocate* to begin his work March 1, 1939. J. P. Sanders who was then preaching for the Hillsboro church of Christ in Nashville was leaving for Los Angeles to work on his Ph.D. degree in the University of Southern California. Several of the Hillsboro members had known Goodpasture in Atlanta. And because of their recommendation, the Hillsboro elders invited Goodpasture to preach for the Hillsboro church for one year. He had never seen the Hillsboro church or preached for them before beginning regular work with them. The one year was extended into twelve years at Hillsboro church and now he serves as an elder of the church.

X

The Helm of the Advocate

The *Gospel Advocate* is now rounding out one hundred and sixteen years of publication counting from the time Tolbert Fanning and William Lipscomb issued the first copy in July of 1855. More than five hundred religious papers have been started by members of the churches of Christ since the publication of Alexander Campbell's *Millennial Harbinger,* and each journal ceased publication for one reason or another. The official religious journal of the ultra liberal wing of the Disciples of Christ now, if it is proper to designate the paper in this fashion, is the *Christian Evangelist,* published in St. Louis, Missouri. The *Christian Standard* is the publication of the conservative wing of the Christian Church who label themselves Churches of Christ. Neither of the two churches and their publications sound anymore the Restoration plea "to speak where the Bible speaks" as its keynote, and both groups are now swept into the mainstream of liberal protestantism.

On the other hand, the *Gospel Advocate* enjoys a confidence among the membership of the churches of Christ unparalleled in any period of its publication. This is due in no small measure to B. C. Goodpasture who has steered the *Gospel Advocate* now thirty-two years. The *Advocate* has been edited by several editors over the years. The editors were capable men, but they were all short-term editors with the exception of David Lipscomb. J. C. McQuiddy, H. Leo Boles, James Allen, Foy E. Wallace, and John T. Hinds served the *Gospel Advocate* in the best sense of its tradition.

The giant stature of the influence of David Lipscomb, editor of the *Advocate,* towers over the church to this day and the journal is still referred to as David Lipscomb's paper. E. G. Sewell was an exceptionally talented preacher and helper of David Lipscomb. But it was in a supporting role to David Lipscomb that Sewell performed his splended services.

B. C. Goodpasture has measured in stature with the incomparable David Lipscomb who won the battle against digression after the Civil War almost to the time of his death. If David Lipscomb made the *Gospel Advocate* the "Old Reliable" among the members of the churches of Christ, B. C. Goodpasture has increased and enhanced the meaning of that expression. Such words are easily spoken, but there is not enough room in this book to document the accuracy of the assertion.

During the eighteen years Goodpasture lived in Atlanta, Georgia, it never occurred to him he would in future time edit the most influential religious journal among the churches of Christ. As a matter of fact, he had never entertained the thought that he would like to do so.

The opportunity for Goodpasture to edit the *Gospel Advocate* came about in a wholly unexpected fashion. John T. Hinds became editor of the *Advocate* on April 2, 1934. John T. Hinds died January 1, 1938 unexpectedly. Leon McQuiddy had to find a successor to John T. Hinds. He did not have an easy job. Unlike his father, Leon McQuiddy was not a writer or a preacher. But he fully understood the mission of the *Gospel Advocate* and chose staff writers for the *Advocate* of unquestioned integrity whose first loyalty was to the Bible and the church. It was Leon McQuiddy who set up the Gospel Advocate Company so the church could have a reliable supply of teaching and instructional materials from the pens of brethren who were sound in the faith.

It would be difficult to assess the subtle qualities and qualifications for an editor of the *Gospel Advocate.* In the first place, no shadow of any kind can be tolerated. The editor must enjoy the unbounded respect of his preaching brethren which is almost impossible. The personal influence of preachers is incalculable in the church. And each member of the church is subject to no authority other than the Bible. The editor must possess sound biblical scholarship. He must command an articulate use of the spoken and written word. His ability to appraise the issues confronting the brotherhood must be sound and accurate. Finally, whatever

B. C. Goodpasture

H. A. Dixon

Guy N. Woods

the editor allows to go into the paper can greatly help or hurt and only he is responsible.

Leon McQuiddy was in no hurry to appoint a new editor. That would be easy. To make the right choice was another matter. Several men were considered for the important and influential post. There were some pressures and persistent appeals. Leon McQuiddy who was president of both the McQuiddy Printing Company and the Gospel Advocate Company had the final say in the matter, and he consulted a great many leading men in the brotherhood. L. O. Sanderson talked the matter over frequently with McQuiddy. The two men made the three-day trip together to Fayetteville, Texas, for the funeral rites of John T. Hinds; and they discussed the matter then at great lengths.

During the interim before the selection of a new editor, L. O. Sanderson and W. E. Brightwell were responsible for the contents of the *Advocate*. The name of B. C. Goodpasture came out of the discussions and made good sense to those who were best informed and responsible. Leon McQuiddy enjoyed the confidence and counsel of the best church leaders, and he respected their judgment. H. Leo Boles was one of those men. In the late 1930's, Leon McQuiddy relied on the judgment of Boles when it came to the Bible and what it taught, and the church and its problems; and no man knew the history of the church, the Restoration movement, and the *Gospel Advocate* as well as Boles. N. B. Hardeman and other outstanding men in the church too were coming more and more to rely on the judgment of H. Leo Boles.

H. Leo Boles first approached B. C. Goodpasture about becoming editor of the *Gospel Advocate*. He was visiting in Boles' home at the time. Boles asked him if he would be interested in considering to become the editor of the *Advocate*. Goodpasture told him he had not thought about it and was not especially interested in it; however, he promised to think about it. Later Boles wrote to him in Atlanta a letter of insistence. Then Leon McQuiddy asked him to come to Nashville for an interview. Finally Goodpasture agreed to accept the position after he and Leon McQuiddy talked it through. The Atlanta church put pressure of their own on him and Goodpasture decided to remain in Atlanta. But Leon McQuiddy and H. Leo Boles were not easily put off. They applied such pressure on B. C. Goodpasture that he committed himself to the new job. Marshall Keeble claimed a part of the credit for Goodpasture's selection. Keeble and McQuiddy were great friends. Keeble often came by the *Advocate* office to enjoy a talk session with McQuiddy. He discussed McQuiddy's trying to find just the right man for the *Advocate;* and Keeble told McQuiddy, "B. C. Goodpasture is the man you need." Keeble learned that Leon McQuiddy was also thinking the same way.

At the time B. C. Goodpasture accepted the position, a succession of editors had followed each other in rapid order. Actually the *Gospel Advocate* had lacked the stability of a firm guiding hand for any long period of time after the passing of David Lipscomb. In the late thirties, the *Gospel Advocate* offices and sales room were pushed over to one side of the McQuiddy Printing Company building located on Seventh Avenue in downtown Nashville. A more unpretentious setting could hardly be imagined.

This, however, was not an index to the importance of the *Advocate* at that time to the brotherhood. The political slogan several years back said, "As Maine goes, so goes the nation." It would be saying too much to say that "as goes the *Gospel Advocate* so goes the church." But for a century and more, members of the churches have trusted the "men of the *Gospel Advocate*" who have helped advance and strengthen the church everywhere and helped the church to understand the Bible. It is a chilling thought to anticipate the future of the church without a continuation of *Advocate* policy in the hands of men like David Lipscomb who have been reliable "watchmen on the wall."

B. C. Goodpasture explained his reluctance to accept the new challenge. His hesitancy grew out of the eighteen pleasant years he had spent in Atlanta doing a great work. In the second place, he had little experience in editing articles with no experience at all in editing a paper. The whole proposition was more or less new to him. And he never thought about becoming an editor. The whole thing came as a surprise. In looking back thirty years, he commented about that decision: "If I had my time to go over again, I would accept the position."

H. Leo Boles announced the selection of B. C. Goodpasture as the new editor of the *Gospel Advocate* in the March 2, 1939, issue of the paper. Boles wrote a brief biographical history of B. C. Goodpasture. He prefaced this with the following paragraph:

This is not written as a compliment, commendation, or a eulogy of B. C. Goodpasture, the new editor of the *Gospel*

Advocate. Neither is it written to introduce him to the brotherhood. He is already very favorably known to all the readers of this religious journal. The purpose of this brief article is to call attention to some of the characteristics which are outstanding that caused him to be considered for this very responsible position. The public is interested in the details of a man's life who has achieved success and who has led many to a higher and better life. The more that is known of some people the better will they be appreciated. He has not sought this high position of honor and trust, but the responsibilities of the editorship have been thrust upon him. It was thought that he was competent and efficient in every way to fill this position; hence, he was sought and prevailed upon to occupy the editorial chair of the *Gospel Advocate.*

The following business statement had appeared February 2, 1939, in the *Advocate.*

B. C. Goodpasture, Atlanta, Georgia, has been selected to be editor of the *Gospel Advocate.* He plans to assume his duties about March 1. He will have the cooperation of an editorial Committee that will control the editorial policies of the *Advocate.* The personnel and functions of this committee and details about Brother Goodpasture will be given in full in a later issue.

A committee of twelve reliable men were chosen to advise B. C. Goodpasture in pursuance of his new duties as editor. Leon McQuiddy was the kind of man who would stand by the editor of the *Advocate* and help him in any way he could. The policy statement stated that Goodpasture was to enjoy:

. . . full and unreserved right to use his own judgment as to what is to be published in the *Gospel Advocate.* No staff writer, no contributor or manager has the right to go over the 'head of the editor.' The editor will be exercising his own judgment in rejecting articles that may be submitted. There is a group of three brethren of the committee with whom the editor will advise should he receive a request to publish an article about what he may have doubts as to its publication.

No mention is made again in the *Advocate* about the committee, after Goodpasture became editor of the *Advocate.* H. Leo Boles made a daily morning trip downtown to the *Advocate* office. The two men talked about personal things, but mainly they talked about the state of the church. H. Leo Boles by then had joined N.

B. Hardeman in the Freed-Hardeman College lectureship program
in Henderson. Boles had become the trusted spokesman among
his brethren without portfolio when it came to their confidence in
his biblical scholarship and judgment. He was their champion in
public religious debates and discussions. He was a matchless
preacher of the gospel. For seven years he studied the Bible
under the venerable David Lipscomb. David Lipscomb personally
chose H. Leo Boles to become president of the Nashville Bible
School. Yes, B. C. Goodpasture was the understudy of a master
teacher. H. Leo Boles said not long before his death, "B. C. has
now gone far beyond me."

In 1939, B. C. Goodpasture was standing on the threshold of
an influence in the church through the *Gospel Advocate* that would
extend over a period of time surpassed only by that of David Lipscomb. The accomplishments of David Lipscomb are solid facts in
church history. The great worth of B. C. Goodpasture to the
church in helping to stop the erosion of the forces threatening the
church coming into sharp focus when he became *Advocate* editor is
now a matter of record.

Goodpasture entered the *Advocate* office on March 1, 1939.
But he did not move his family to Nashville until the Atlanta
schools were out in June. He traveled back and forth between Atlanta and Nashville each weekend. He would leave Nashville on
Friday for Atlanta and return the following Monday. He
preached for the Seminole church until June.

When some of the members of the Hillsboro church in Nashville learned Goodpasture was coming to the *Advocate,* they
brought up the possibility of his preaching for the Hillsboro church
with the elders. So he had a meeting with the Hillsboro elders
and arrangements were made for him to preach for the church before he had met the congregation, and only a few of them had ever
heard him preach.

B. C. Goodpasture preached for the Hillsboro church for
twelve years. Cleveland Goodpasture was equal to the measure of
her husband in assuming her responsibilities. Success in life never
spoiled Cleveland Goodpasture. She had a fine instinctive feeling
for her role as the wife of a distinguished preacher and editor ; and
like her husband, she was accustomed to excelling. She visited
among the members of the Hillsboro church while her husband
worked in the *Advocate* office. Cleveland studied the Bible and

knew it. She taught a class of young girls for several years. No person from the Hillsboro church went to the hospital whom she did not visit. She liked to be with people. Young people loved her.

Bill Ruhl said when he was a student in David Lipscomb College that he and some of the college boys would wait around after church service hoping for an invitation to go home with the Goodpastures for dinner. And often they were invited. A long dining table that would seat twenty-four people was in the Goodpasture home. Cleveland Goodpasture was a grand cook and a gracious hostess. The number of guests entertained at the Goodpasture table would tax the imagination. The guests were family, friends of their children, preachers, dignitaries of one kind and other, and just people. All who came were impressed by the open-hearted kindness and warmth of the Goodpasture home.

At the time Goodpasture became editor, the church was beset with problems. It should be pointed out that beginning with Ananias and Sapphira, the church has been troubled with this and that ever since. Granting the proposition that the church is a divine institution and the inerrancy of the Bible as the inspired word of God, whatever threatens either or questions both should be closely examined.

One church trouble that long had been smoldering was "premillennialism." A handful of preachers led by R. H. Boll advanced the belief that Jesus the Christ failed to establish his kingdom because his enemies nailed him to a cross. The theory held that Jesus' body was raised without "flesh and blood" and that his "second coming is imminent." The universal battle of Armageddon will be waged between the legions of Satan and the army of the saints led by Christ. The battle will be won by the "King of kings" who will afterwards sit on an earthly throne in Jerusalem and rule a thousand years. During the "messianic reign," Satan will be bound in the one thousand year interim. After this, the end of time will come and all men shall stand before God in judgment.

Another matter was facing the brotherhood. James DeForest Murch of the *Christian Standard* and Claude F. Witty, a highly respected preacher among the churches of Christ in the Detroit area, were leading a movement to re-unite the churches of Christ and the Disciples of Christ. Goodpasture more than any other outstanding leader among the churches of Christ acted as the moderator for the discussions through the *Gospel Advocate.* Goodpasture had little to say during the forties when both issues came to a head and were finally resolved. The policy of the *Advocate* to both positions was clear and unequivocal. In both cases, Goodpasture had the last say. Recently B. C. Goodpasture commented with the words of Nehemiah about the unity movement of the 1940's: "It was like meeting the folks down in the plains of Ono."

The most unpleasant church controversy for some brethren centered in World War II about the right of a Christian to bear arms. Feelings were intense and some of the brethren were militant. Goodpasture took no extreme stand and refused to allow the *Advocate* to become a battle ground over the issue.

There were those who thought Goodpasture was not the man to edit the *Advocate.* Some said so, but not very loudly. When he came to the *Advocate,* he was not as forward in meeting the opposition as some of the former editors had been. Occasionally some one took a "pot shot" at him. It took his brethren a while to learn the lesson the boys knew that grew up with Goodpasture on Flat Creek. The elder Goodpasture had taught his boy, "Don't ever pick a fight with anybody, but give a good account of yourself if you are attacked." What some may have judged as indecision or weakness in Goodpasture was neither. He simply waited until he was convinced of the right course of action. Truth even then was the standard of his judgment. Some of his early critics admire him today as much as they do any man.

Rex Turner described Goodpasture in recent years on one of the occasions honoring the *Advocate* editor. What he said was an accurate description of Goodpasture in 1939 and now in 1971:

> He is not a man who can be prodded into hasty and rash editorials, regardless of the attendant irritating and aggravating circumstances. He calculates the results as well as the certainty of both his writings and the writings of his staff. He has demonstrated time after time that he purposes to carry in columns of the *Advocate* only those writings that will serve a good cause.

J. Roy Vaughan recalled that there were those who believed that the *Gospel Advocate* was going under at the time Goodpasture became editor. After he became editor of the paper, however, the

Advocate took a turn and has been going strong ever since. Vaughan attributed this to the fact that Goodpasture has a good business head, and he exercised good judgment both as editor and manager of the business side of the Gospel Advocate Company.

The key to understanding B. C. Goodpasture was provided by John Allen Hudson, a long-time staff member of the *Gospel Advocate,* who resigned from the *Advocate* staff in 1952 because of other writing chores. After working under Goodpasture for thirteen years, he knew the man. He first heard him during a David Lipscomb College lectureship. Hudson wrote at the time of his resignation a description of the editor, "Here is a high type gentleman of the famed old time—a gentleman born, and nothing has happened since to mar the picture."

B. C. Goodpasture steered the *Gospel Advocate* through many stormy passages during the 1940's and early fifties. After these worst of times were over, the best of times began for the man at the helm. H. Leo Boles was dead. N. B. Hardeman was advancing in years. All of the old champions were gone or superannuated. In the fifties, there were only a few who anymore questioned the ability of B. C. Goodpasture. One reason why Goodpasture's abilities were questioned earlier may have been in the man himself. He looked too good to be true; he spoke as few men could. The wait was worth it. Hardly another leader of this century in the church promised so much, and gave so much more than what was expected of him.

The role that Goodpasture played as editor of the *Gospel Advocate* becomes crystal clear with an understanding of *Advocate* policy. Tolbert Fanning and William Lipscomb who established the *Gospel Advocate* accepted the Bible as the inspired word of God. They accepted the inerrancy of the Scriptures. David Lipscomb joined Tolbert Fanning in 1866 to re-publish the *Gospel Advocate* after the Civil War. The writers in the *Advocate* were controlled with one purpose—to investigate the Scriptures as they related to the faith and practices of Christians. They accepted the church as the "blood-bought" institution established on Pentecost in 33 A.D. Since 1855, the "men of the *Advocate*" have resisted every move to secularize the church and to introduce unscriptural innovations into the church such as the missionary society, instrumental music in worship, premillennialism, anti-isms, and every form of theological liberalism both past and present.

Not once has B. C. Goodpasture complimented the *Gospel Advocate* because it has been non-polemical. The dubious praise that a person can pick up a copy of a religious paper without having his tender feelings disturbed has never been said about the *Advocate*. David Lipscomb would have been ashamed for this to have been the strongest commendation of his paper. David Lipscomb never thought in this vein, nor has B. C. Goodpasture. Whatever the church may be today is largely due to the credit of such great-souled men. Just as a carpenter is known by his chips, a man of character and conviction is best judged for what he will stand up and fight for.

In the first place, the *Advocate* has not, since its founding, been an open forum for the discussion of current issues. H. Leo Boles commenting about this wrote:

> There is such a confusion in society today that the *Gospel Advocate* has not felt that it should add its voice to the confusion that already exists on these questions. It feels a weighty responsibility to maintain its policy of teaching the truth that saves the souls of men.

This had been the thinking of David Lipscomb, and H. Leo Boles was closer to David Lipscomb the last fifteen years of his life than any other church leader. B. C. Goodpasture bore the same relationship to H. Leo Boles. David Lipscomb was interested in the truth revealed in the New Testament. This meant most to David Lipscomb. Beginning with Tolbert Fanning and David Lipscomb, the *Advocate* has been a constant and reliable medium for discussing timely issues of a biblical nature of vital interest to the church.

David Lipscomb wrote clearly and simply. He did not write to be ambiguous. No staff writer who worked with Lipscomb was allowed to be. Goodpasture is such a man and he explained the policy of the paper: "The *Gospel Advocate* doesn't give an uncertain sound. It is our purpose that the people know where we stand and what we stand for."

Goodpasture has been a matchless pilot for the *Gospel Advocate* because he knew his cargo and the seas he had to sail. G. K. Wallace wrote: "It has always amazed me how he knew every argument, true or false being made by the brethren and just who was making them." No truer statement could be made about Goodpasture than he has humbly exercised his position as editor in keeping with what he sincerely believed to be to the best interest and welfare of the church. He has refused to become involved in personality quarrels and to use the *Advocate* for vindictive ends. Goodpasture stated his thinking in this respect:

> We want the *Advocate* to support only what is right and good and oppose only what is evil. We want to maintain its reputation as being the 'Old Reliable.' We want our readers to feel that when they read anything in the *Advocate* it is true.

Goodpasture has found that the most plaguing problem in editing the *Advocate* is deciding what should go into the paper and what should be kept out. Some articles coming to the editor's desk were of doubtful propriety since they dealt with problems on the margin that could stir up old animosities and do more harm than good. Guy N. Woods summed up this trait in the editor:

> B. C. Goodpasture has, through the years, demonstrated his ability to discharge this function in the most widely read periodicals as well as the most influential journal published among us; he has adhered faithfully to the truth and the best traditions among the people of the Lord, avoiding radicalism and hobbyism on the one hand, and contending for a pure faith and faultless practice in all matters religious on the other hand.

Goodpasture set up specific standards for articles to be published in the paper. The author must be in good standing, and the articles must be scriptural and timely. Sometimes an article is not published because the author does not deserve recognition, or because the article is not timely. Then there are times when there is simply no room.

The charge has been made that the *Advocate* does not publish both sides of an issue and this is true. David Lipscomb refused even to mention the name of Daniel Sommer, the anti-Christian college spokesman, after he was convinced that Sommer was showing duplicity in refusing to answer certain issues in order to raise others in the *Advocate* to get them before the brotherhood. Goodpasture said in this connection that "a man in one short article can present enough error to keep a writer busy for a whole year just answering it."

When the "anti-college" and "anti-orphan home," and the "anti-*Herald of Truth*" crowd mounted their attack in the late 1940's charging that the autonomony of the local churches was being violated, their spokesman accused the editor for refusing to print both sides of the question. The editor explained his position in the April 16, 1959 issue of the *Advocate*:

> It is not the policy of the *Gospel Advocate* to print everything that is sent to its offices for publication. It is quite true that some papers may print what 'other papers will not print.' On scanning some papers we wonder what, if anything, their editors kept out.
>
> Nor do we profess to publish both sides of everything that may be a subject of discussion. We do not feel that we are obligated to furnish a medium for radicals and hobbyists to ventilate their hobbies, nor are we obligated to become an agency for the dissemination of error. It is not our remotest intention to give brotherhood publicity to every hobby rider and his fancies. *This does not mean, however, that there are not times and questions which merit full and free discussion. We are not disposed to profess to publish both sides of everything that comes up for attention, and then publish both sides only of those things that suit our peculiar purpose.*
>
> When the farmer gets ready to sow a bushel of wheat, it is not necessary for him to sow a bushel of weeds in order to be fair; neither is it necessary for the editor, when he gives space to truth, to give equal space to error. It would be downright silly for the farmer to sow weeds which would impose additional toil on himself or some other and do great damage to the wheat.

The last thirty years of the church have been the most propitious of times, and at the same time, the most threatening because of the "isms," hobbies, and heresies aimed at the church. Not since the "digressive erosions" of the Disciples of Christ at the turn of the century has the church been so sorely tried from within. One of the most subtle dangers has arisen through the liberal theologies imported from the liberal theological schools of religion. L. R. Wilson summed up the whole matter:

> We may be thankful that through all of this period of growth the editor of the *Gospel Advocate* kept a level head, and encouraged every good work among us, while adhering to the same principles that have characterized our work since the beginning of the Restoration Movement. We are somewhat fearful of what might have happened to our cause if the *Gospel Advocate* had taken off on a tangent during this crucial period.

B. C. Goodpasture

B. C. Goodpasture and
J. Cliett Goodpasture

Ruth Collins and Willard Collins

Cleveland Goodpasture

The people who know B. C. Goodpasture best are those who have worked closest with him. The loyalty of his friends to him is not hard to understand when once his nature is known.

Fawning or obsequious behavior will get a person nowhere with Goodpasture. Burton Coffman in addressing a group of friends who celebrated his birthday at the B. C. Goodpasture Christian School described him as "an undeceived man" meaning that he is an uncanny judge of human nature.

One of the *Advocate* secretaries, Virginia Phillips, said, "Working with B. C. Goodpasture is not like working under a boss. The office help feels completely free and the editor keeps it that way." But everyone has the deepest respect for him. No visitor is ever unwelcome—no matter how poor or rich, poorly or beautifully dressed. He especially enjoys having the men enrolled in the Nashville School of Preaching to stop by his office for a chat. Carl McKelvey, Dean of Students in David Lipscomb College, was in the editor's office a few years back. A distinguished looking man came into the outer office to see Goodpasture. Carl excused himself and left to accommodate the important visitor. Later the editor told McKelvey, "Carl, the next time you come by for a visit, it makes no difference who is out there, let's have our talk first."

Violet DeVaney came as Goodpasture's secretary in March of 1946. Miss DeVaney had been the secretary for H. Leo Boles the last years of his life. Boles was well-organized and systematic in his work habits. He lived on a well-planned seven-day week. After Boles' death, Violet moved to the *Advocate* to help with the completion of the *Gospel Advocate Adult Quarterly* that Boles had not finished. Since Violet knew about the arranging and typing of the manuscript, she performed an invaluable service in this respect; and she stayed on with Goodpasture until 1962. Goodpasture had not had such a trained secretary before. She had begun work with the incomparable Boles in 1927. She was knowledgeable of the ways of the brotherhood.

Violet described B. C. Goodpasture's way of working with his office help:

B. C. tried to be fair with all employees—even the mailing room girls. When he used to buy ice cream for all the first floor girls, he would also buy some for the mailing room girls. At Christmas time, he gave all the girls a box of candy. He would give everyone the same size.

B. C. Goodpasture has been the despair of his secretaries. His desk is piled with correspondence and publications of all kinds. What he needs, he knows where to find it. Violet, who had worked with Boles for so many years, understood how to manage his correspondence that needed to be answered, keep all the loose ends tied, and generally handle the mechanics of the office. Virginia Phillips, when she was asked about taking dictation from the editor, remarked that she rarely does. She said that Brother Goodpasture would type a few letters daily with his index fingers on his typewriter. This is just about the limit of his personal correspondence. However, he opens and reads every piece of his mail. When any correspondence should be answered, it is.

It was not all smooth sailing when Goodpasture first became editor of the *Advocate*. To be sure he had his detractors. Some thought of him as being relatively unknown and untried. Some thought he should have come out of the corner with his fists doubled at the first sound of the gong to fight the battles of the brotherhood as a champion should.

The issue over a Christian going to War was a volatile issue in World War II. A great deal was said and written. But Goodpasture said little and wrote less because he knew the *Advocate* could not settle the question and the church would be divided. He did not wholly take the uncompromising views of David Lipscomb and H. Leo Boles. He accepted the biblical injunction that civil rulers were appointed of God to keep the peace.

Goodpasture gave H. Leo Boles the task to answer the Disciples of Christ and Christian Church people who were calling for unity. He turned over the pages of the *Advocate* for the airing of the premillennial controversy that was steaming. He patiently watched the gathering storm over the rights of Christian colleges and orphan homes to exist and the methods for their organization and support. The *Gospel Advocate* was in good hands. H. Leo Boles, the "old master," and the young editor watched the rising and falling of the tides. They carefully discussed and analyzed every issue and decided what to do.

Leon McQuiddy too had the ears of the brotherhood. He heard all the sides, and, he too was an undeceived man when it came to brotherhood issues. Violet DeVaney described the relation between McQuiddy and Goodpasture:

> B. C. was a 'good boss man,' almost too good for his own good. With Leon McQuiddy, B. C. was the 'last word' with anything pertaining to the *Gospel Advocate*. Leon had confidence in B. C. and very few times would he object to anything B. C. said as far as printing a new book, a new manuscript, or anything like that.

L. O. Sanderson, who has been music editor for the *Gospel Advocate* since 1933, evaluated B. C. Goodpasture as editor of the *Gospel Advocate* several years after he became editor:

> Some, ineptly, referred to B. C. as a scissor and paste editor —true, he did not have an article in every issue, and some which he placed there were reprints of worthy dissertations; however, he held not to the view that an editorial is always necessary, nor that he must needs be given prominence, and he humbly reckoned that some previous treatises were pertinent, well written, and calculated to have great influence, even beyond what he might write. In the realm of scriptural reasoning, Brother Goodpasture ranks with the best; in the capacity of selection of what to print, he has few peers; in public relations with his corps of writers, he is excellent; at the forum, from the pulpit, or in fireside chats, he is a master; in presenting pungent, relevant wit, he has no superior; in every walk of life, where I have been witness, there has never been a sign of pretense or recoil.

If ever a man was a lover of a good men, it is B. C. Goodpasture. He hated to perform any unpleasant task such as calling some employee on the carpet. Violet DeVaney who worked for both Boles and Goodpasture remembered their working relationship:

> They worked together as a good team. Brother Boles was a 'good fighter,' but B. C. loved peace. He would never pick a fight; but once somebody took the first 'shot' he would let him have it. I have seen him so indignant that fire would shoot out of those black eyes.

The work of B. C. Goodpasture as editor of the *Gospel Advocate* will be related in other chapters. His disappointments have been few. The major disappointments of his work as editor grew out of the duplicity of some of his personal friends and the opposition of those whose support he reasonably expected. By duplicity he meant the persons who professed friendship in order to get some favor and who had been secretly hostile all the time. (But Judas and Diotrephes appear in every generation.) He quoted David Lipscomb as once having said that if a man could be editor of the *Gospel Advocate* for ten years without becoming an infidel, he was an unusual person. Goodpasture said that gave him some comfort.

At the time Goodpasture became editor of the *Advocate,* N. B. Hardeman, president of Freed-Hardeman College, thought of the appointment as a favorable omen for the church. Twenty years later Hardeman said about the *Advocate* editor:

> Many are the very fine articles, written by friends, expressing appreciation of the life, character, and work of B. C. Goodpasture. Thousands there are who endorse such sentiments. I am not a whit behind the chiefest of them in my esteem and high regard for him. I have known Brother Goodpasture for about forty years and to know him is but to be grateful that such a man lives in our day and in our midst. He is among the best informed men in the church of Christ. He has ever been a good student and has lived among his collection of the best books of the ages. He well knows the origin, doctrine, and practice of the body of our Lord.

> When the time came, it was most fortunate that he consented to become editor of the *Gospel Advocate.* Under his guidance, for twenty years, the paper has had a remarkable growth and its influence has spread far beyond former boundaries. By a vast majority of Christians, it is considered the most dependable and the most reliable journal published. Brother Goodpasture is in the best period of life. Many years may be his in which his greatest work can be done.

> There is not a cloud impending over him but the rainbow of promise can shine through the gloom. When the time comes for him to lay aside his armour and to sheathe his sword, it is my sincere prayer that he may come to realize fully all of his hallowed hopes and fondest desires.

But there is no end to this kind of appraisal of B. C. Goodpasture, and a chapter must stop at some place.

XI

Watchman on the Wall

The Bible stands the Rock of Ages as the uncertain lives of men can not. As no other body of writing has been able, the Bible has weathered the slow passage of the centuries. The *Dialogues* of Plato occupy mainly the interest of the scholars, but the Bible has persisted in human hearts almost as long as time itself. The writings of Aristotle are of little interest except to the curious mind eager to explore the wisdom of the greatest thinker of Ancient Greece, but the "Sermon on the Mount" has been etched in the hearts of countless millions of both the humble and the great of the earth.

Tolbert Fanning is entitled to the credit—not Alexander Campbell—with elevating the Bible to its proper perspective as essential to the existence and continuity of the New Testament church. The church historian can honestly do no less than credit David Lipscomb with victory in winning the running battle that lasted a century to restore the pattern of New Testament Christianity. And Isaac Errett, the successor to Alexander Campbell, and his associates, must share the blame for leading the Disciples of Christ clearly into the fold of Protestant denominational Christianity in the years of the Disciples' greatest triumphs in the closing years of the nineteenth century. This is not an accusation, but a patent fact of church history.

Other than David Lipscomb, no person's name has been more closely identified with the *Gospel Advocate* than that of B. C. Goodpasture. And for more than thirty years Goodpasture has kept the *Gospel Advocate* on its charted course. The reason the

J. Cliett Goodpasture and Sarah Lou Traughber Goodpasture.
Children: Amy Lou, Sara Gay, Nancy Lynn

Rebecca and Cordell Goodpasture

Myron Lyzon King, Eleanor Pauline Goodpasture King, Myron, Jr., and Emily Catherine

Advocate is still regarded as the "Old Reliable" of the brotherhood is because Goodpasture has kept it so. The critics of the *Gospel Advocate* include those who clearly understand the policy of the paper and fear it because of their lack of sympathy for the principles of New Testament Christianity.

The primary concern of B. C. Goodpasture is the New Testament church—not the *Gospel Advocate* nor the Christian colleges. Goodpasture is aware of the enormous potentials for promulgating New Testament Christianity through the instruments of the religious journals and Christian schools. Too often the occasional student of the Bible and church history labels the *Advocate* as being argumentative and charges the *Advocate* writers with creating issues for the sake of religious debate. Tolbert Fanning and David Lipscomb meant for the *Gospel Advocate* to be polemical, and there has not been a time in more than a hundred years when the writers of the *Advocate* have not been willing to stand on the "firing line" in both the defense of the gospel and its teaching as the inspired Word of God.

Goodpasture became the leading "Watchman on the Wall" following the passing of his older contemporaries including men such as H. Leo Boles, Batsell Baxter, G. C. Brewer, and N. B. Hardeman. Goodpasture has passed through the crucibles of time. The church members with the greatest knowledge of the Bible and the most excellent of academic training generously acknowledge his superior character and ability among his peers. And he is implicitly trusted by the "rank and file" of the church.

This chapter will concentrate on the major problems facing the church in this century that B. C. Goodpasture had a hand in resolving through the *Gospel Advocate*. At the turn of this century, the Disciples of Christ had made their deepest inroads in liberalizing the church; however, not until the 1920's was it clear that the churches of Christ were no longer their "happy hunting ground" to promote the "society," and the "organ," and numerous other liberal innovations that cropped up in the intervening years.

The first major conflict in the brotherhood was over the teaching of Bible prophecy. The name for the doctrine "premillennialism," and the teaching was centered in Revelation 20 that Christ would rule from a literal throne in Jerusalem for one thousand years in the near future. However, the movement was not at first labeled "premillennialism."

The record of millennial doctrine is almost as old as Christianity. In the Ancient World the expectation of the millennial reign is designated as *chiliasm* by the church historian. The Catholic church discounted the teaching of *chiliasm* in the fourth century and forbade its teaching. However, *chiliasm* continues to crop up from time to time; the Seventh Day Adventists and Jehovah's Witnesses base their existences upon their own peculiar interpretations of Bible prophecy.

The seed bed for the premillennial controversy was first centered in staff writers of the *Gospel Advocate*. The problem surfaced about the time of World War I and persisted for more than twenty-five years. B. C. Goodpasture was at first an observer of the developing controversy. As editor of the *Gospel Advocate,* he performed the last rites over premillennialism as a church problem in the 1940's. The whole story may now be told and needs to be.

The reason for the opposition to premillennialism became crystal clear in the perspective of time. Such church stalwarts as J. C. McQuiddy, G. Dallas Smith, M. C. Kurfees, and H. Leo Boles were convinced that tolerant acceptance of the doctrine would cut away all biblical opposition to the missionary society, instrumental music in worship, open fellowship with protestant churches, or any religious view however vulnerable in its relation to the Scriptures.

The average church member was never clear in his mind about the meaning of the doctrine. And in the 1940's when premillennialism became a divisive issue, some who were implicated in the embroilment pleaded a lack of knowledge about premillennial teachings.

The remaining interest in premillennialism is now mainly academic. The disturbance over premillennialism in the late 1930's grew to a serious magnitude. The casual reader of religious journals may receive the impression that the church is endlessly passing through new and different crises; however, it is common place for the daily newspapers to report endless crises threatening even the existence of mankind.

The premillennial teaching that troubled the church was advocated by R. H. Boll. He was one of the early graduates of the Nashville Bible School around the turn of the century. There were few preachers in the church who could preach as effectively as R. H. Boll, or who were as dearly beloved by their friends.

The readers of the *Gospel Advocate* first learned about the mil-

Angela Odum Goodpasture, B. C. Goodpasture III,
Ginger, B.C. IV, Angela

Alvin Goins, Sherry Anna Goodpasture Goins, Shawn

lennial views of R. H. Boll through F. W. Smith, a staff writer for the *Gospel Advocate*. Smith wrote an article titled "Interpreters of Divine Prophecy" for the April 15, 1915 issue of the *Advocate*:

> There are two brethren for whom I have always had the highest regard who are pursuing a course which I shall take the privilege to criticize in a friendly and brotherly way. I refer to R. H. Boll and H. L. Olmstead, who are using their precious time and spendid intellects in speculative theories concerning unfulfilled prophecy . . . at present they are both engaged in trying to tell the readers of religious papers things about which they know nothing. They are both trying to wade through the book of Revelation, and, like all others who have attempted to enlighten the world on the contents of that book, are doing some tall guessing.

The *Advocate* readers were advised in the May 6, 1915 issue: "In connection with above statement, it is proper to state that the publishers of the *Gospel Advocate* have requested F. W. Smith to write a friendly criticism of Brother Boll's teachings along the lines of prophetic interpretations and to point out in a brotherly way what we consider to be a wise and safe course in regard to unrevealed things."

The editors of the *Gospel Advocate* in 1915 were David Lipscomb, E. G. Sewell, E. A. Elam, M. C. Kurfees, and R. H. Boll, the "First page Editor." J. C. McQuiddy and A. B. Lipscomb were the "Managing Editors." David Lipscomb was then advanced in years and in very poor health. He wrote an article on the "Second Coming of Christ and Prophetic Study" for the May 6, 1915 issue of the *Advocate*. R. H. Boll was called upon by the editors of the *Advocate* to endorse the article. It would not be amiss here to state that the story was circulated in later years that the premillennial controversy grew out of personal differences between M. C. Kurfees and R. H. Boll. Both men were living and preaching in Louisville, Kentucky, at the same time. Actually all of the transactions from 1915 to the demise of premillennialism is a matter of record in the *Gospel Advocate*.

In the May 13, 1915 issue of the *Gospel Advocate*, F. W. Smith enumerated the millennial teachings of R. H. Boll. And he wrote in substance: that Christ's body after the resurrection possessed no animal life; that this inanimate body of flesh and bones without blood went to heaven; that Christ will return in a bloodless body to sit on the literal throne of David and to rule Israel with a rod or iron; and that the church is only a phase of the kingdom such as the relation of a vestibule to a house. R. H. Boll was dropped from the *Advocate* staff.

Boll challenged Smith for a debate and wrote: "I challenge him to a full, fair, friendly discussion of any differences between him and myself, time, place, manner, and propositions to be arranged and agreed upon in private correspondence." The debate never came off. In the passage of the summer and fall months, the publishers of the *Gospel Advocate* reached an amicable resolving of the controversy; and Boll was put back on the *Advocate* staff.

Boll wrote in the *Advocate,* May 4, 1915: "Relative to my teachings on unfulfilled prophecy, I have arrived at an amicable understanding with my former associates on the *Gospel Advocate* and resume my work with the paper with all personal differences eliminated and with the feelings of most cordial friendship toward all." However, this was not the end of the matter. There had not been any real meeting of minds. And the *Advocate* publishers made the announcement December 9, 1915: ". . . I have written Brother Boll that we will drop his name from our editorial staff. . . ." R. H. Boll replied to the announcement December 30, 1915: "I must beg of you to remove my name from the honored place which you have accorded it for the past several years."

The whole premillennial controversy ought to have been laid to rest, but it was not. R. H. Boll and sympathetic friends were convinced he had not been treated fairly by the *Gospel Advocate*. R. H. Boll felt that he should have been allowed to give reply to the whole matter in the *Advocate*. The issue hung on and smoldered for several years.

In order to put an end to the matter once and for all, S. H. Hall initiated the proposal that R. H. Boll should have his say in the *Gospel Advocate* about his "millennial" views.

H. Leo Boles was chosen to reply to R. H. Boll in a series of written discussions which were run in the *Advocate* from May 19, 1927, to November 3, 1927. The theses of Boll's millennial views were in essence the views of Boll described by F. W. Smith in 1917. No unpleasantness marred the discussion and neither was willing at the time to disfellowship the other. And once again the conclusions of the whole matter should have been summed up in the debate; but again it was not. And the church was sorely troubled in the years ahead.

There was a mounting opposition to premillennialism in the 1930's which reached its climax in the early 1940's. J. N. Armstrong, president of Harding College, was charged with being a premillennialist. The persons closest to Dr. Armstrong felt strongly that he was being persecuted and said so. Dr. L. C. Sears knows the facts best as he was a faculty member in Harding College. Dr. Sears relates this dimension of premillennialism in his scholarly work, *For Freedom: The Biography of J. Nelson Armstrong,* published in 1969 by the Gospel Advocate Company. The facts are that the contemporary associates of Dr. Armstrong in Harding College and the faculty have not supported premillennialism in any fashion.

The intention to disfellowship the premillennialists and their sympathizers was running at full tide at the close of the 1930's. N. B. Hardeman, Foy E. Wallace, Jr., H. Leo Boles, and other outstanding men were convinced that premillennialism was not only divisive, but a clear repudiation of the New Testament teaching relating to the establishment of the kingdom. The leaders in the church were persuaded that if the passage of premillennialism was not challenged that the flood gate would be opened to introduce into the church whatever doctrines that suited some church members with little concern or understanding of the implications to the church membership as a whole.

Unfortunately the premillennial controversy rumbled on long after the conclusion of the Boles-Boll debate. The controversy that was generated grew out of the persuasion that R. H. Boll had both the right and liberty to advance his views. In the closing 1930's, any preacher who declined to take a stand was branded as a "premillennialist or a sympathizing fellow traveller." Others attempted to side step the issue by pleading ignorance of the doctrine; however, the Boles-Boll debate had been published in a book by the Gospel Advocate Company.

The grave implications of the doctrine are pointed up in a plea made by L. L. Brigance, late beloved and trusted teacher in Freed-Hardeman College, who urged the presidents of the Christian colleges to declare themselves on the issue, and one by one each did in the *Gospel Advocate.* Preachers throughout the brotherhood followed suit. Just a handful were outspoken exponents of premillennialism. There were those indeed who were passionately persuaded that it was a question of Christian liberty to believe in this ancient theory simply as a matter of conscience.

B. C. Goodpasture who came to the *Advocate* in 1939 was caught up in the controversy. Goodpasture commented about his role in the running battle: "Well of course I had no patience with the theory of premillennialism. I assisted some of the brethren with their arguments. But because a man was a premillennialist, I did not shun him. I considered him an erring brother." In this connection, it may be said that B. C. Goodpasture has never played the role of a belligerent antagonist. He is always respectful toward others and wishes to be treated in such a way. Goodpasture was crystal clear in raising his voice against the doctrine. The pages of the *Advocate* were opened to the militant spokesmen such as G. C. Brewer and H. Leo Boles who were unrelenting.

The premillennial storm was slowly subsiding in the early 1940's, but it was still volatile. Dr. George S. Benson who became president of Harding College in 1936 gradually de-fused the charges implying the connection of the teaching of premillennialism with any of the Harding College faculty.

The passing of the 1930's witnessed other matters of little and great importance to the church. The world was stunned when the German Nazis invaded Poland in September of 1939 precipitating a global war. America's entry into World War II came on with the bombing of Pearl Harbor. In the dark war years, the right of Christians to go to war or to stand upon his Christian convictions as a conscientious objector was debated. Goodpasture allowed discussions about the Christian attitude toward the war, but he wisely steered the issue to keep it from becoming a divisive issue in the church. And in this, he was successful.

The "Unity Movement" created a stir in the 1930's among the members of the church second only to premillennialism. Fortunately, no brotherhood issue grew out of the movement. The so called "Unity Movement" was initiated by James DeForest Murch who returned to rejoin the staff of the Disciples' publication, the *Christian Standard,* as Literary Editor. One reason Murch returned to the *Christian Standard* grew out of his interest of uniting the divergent forces among the Disciples of Christ.

In the course of his work, Murch was invited to Gorouto, Canada, to address a rally in the Old Central Church. At the conclusion of an evening message, an elder of a non-instrumental congregation approached Murch and remarked that such a spirit as that expressed in the present meeting might well be the means of promoting understanding and eventual unity among the Disciples of Christ and the churches of Christ.

Through the offices of this elder, a meeting was arranged between James DeForest Murch and Claude F. Witty of the West-Side Church of Christ in Detroit, Michigan. Murch and Witty became warm friends and set in motion the machinery to bring about discussions between members of the churches of Christ and the Disciples of Christ.

Murch wrote "that it took about seventy years to divide us, and it may take us that long to unite." And Murch commented about his joint unity effort with Witty: "There was no up-rising of the rank and file demanding it. We—Brother Witty and I—were persuaded that unity ought to be. We, as a people, had preached it; we ought to practice it." The unity movement was initiated in 1936.

Murch and Witty first set out to discover who among each group would be interested in such a re-approachment. Each contacted a coterie of friends. Murch said about two hundred men went on record as being friendly to the movement. The first unity meeting was held in the Central Y.M.C.A. in Cincinnati, February 23, 1937. Similar unity meetings followed in Indianapolis, Indiana; Akron, Ohio; Los Angeles, California; and Columbus, Indiana.

Two courses of actions developed out of the meetings: first, a five point "Approach to Unity" was widely publicized; second, a proposal to hold a national gathering of interested brethren in which unity would be the central theme.

The first "National Unity Meeting" was held in Detroit, Michigan, on May 3, 4, 1938, at the invitation of Witty and the elders of the West Side Church. More than a thousand persons assembled to hear a representative message from men of both groups. The major addresses in the assembly were delivered by George Benson, H. H. Adamson, and J. N. Armstrong who represented the churches of Christ; and W. R. Walker, P. H. Welshimer, and O. A. Trinkle were the speakers from the Disciples of Christ. Before the meeting adjourned, a telegram from O. J. Trinkle of the

Englewood Christian Church of Indianapolis, Indiana, was read inviting a similar group during the same week in 1939.

Murch and Witty launched the *Christian Unity Quarterly* to be a medium of free expression and promotion. Murch wrote about the journalistic attitudes expressed by members of the church in the leading papers of the time:

> such papers as the *Christian Leader,* the *People's Bible Advocate,* the *Apostolic Review,* the *Word and Work* have been reservedly courteous. The *Gospel Advocate* was at first violent in its opposition, but now seems to have joined the ranks of the *Firm Foundation* in studiously ignoring and minimizing the effort. The *Bible Banner* leads in outspoken, vitriolic opposition. The *Advocate* and the *Firm Foundation* are perhaps the most widely circulated and influential of these journals.

The "Unity Movement" was short lived. Still fresh in the memories of N. B. Hardeman, H. Leo Boles, and others were the inroads that the "organ and missionary" advocates had made into the church taking over church property throughout the region north of the Ohio River and with not as much success south of the Mason-Dixon Line. N. B. Hardeman and H. Leo Boles had convinced the champion debaters of the Christian Church that they could hope for little success in a free and open exchange of the meaning of the Scriptures before large audiences.

Claude F. Witty's sincerity was never questioned; however, few were convinced that James DeForest Murch and his associates planned for a compromise acceptance of the issues that separated the church at the turn of the century.

The "Unity Movement" came to an abrupt end during the next annual meeting. B. C. Goodpasture was invited to deliver the major address. Goodpasture stated that he supposed this choice was made since he had only a short time before become editor of the *Gospel Advocate.* Goodpasture declined and recommended H. Leo Boles to do the honors because he was convinced that an older and more experienced man should represent the thinking of the members of the church.

A good many leading preachers in the church thought little of the "Unity Movement" and said so. W. W. Otey said what was being generally thought "that little good could come from such meetings, since these so called 'representative' men from the

churches of Christ could not speak in behalf of other members."
This and other matters of significance to the church are detailed in
Cecil Willis' biography—*W. W. Otey: Contender for the Faith.*

The "Unity Movement" had been marked by "sweetness and
light" until Boles spoke to the assembly on May 2, 1939, in Indianapolis, Indiana; what Boles said on that occasion came as no
surprise to those who knew the man, nor has anyone attempted
since to discount the logic of what he said that day.

If some of the leaders thought they were about to come up on
the blind side of some in the churches of Christ, they reckoned
without giving due respect to past memories. Boles dispelled all
illusions that a compromise with the Disciples of Christ was in the
offing. A. T. DeGroot in the *Christian Evangelist* wrote in the
May 11 issue of the journal: "The strongest language employed at
the conference, other than the expected warmth of some exchanges
came in the speech of H. Leo Boles." What Boles said on that
occasion can never become untimely as long as men believe the
Bible to be the inspired Word of God.

In the prepared paper presented by Boles, he stated:

> I am not a delegate to this conference or "unity meeting";
> neither am I a "representative" of the Churches of Christ; I
> have not been sent here by any church or group of
> churches; I am not clothed with any 'official authority.' I
> am here at the invitations of Brother Claude Witty; so I
> alone am responsible for what I say.

Boles told the assembly that both the churches of Christ and the
Disciples of Christ subscribed to the same fundamentals of the
New Testament. Boles charged in the speech that unity was first
destroyed when David S. Burnet introduced in 1849 the missionary society into the church; a second, the introduction of instrumental music into worship about 1859 was an additional divisive
force. Boles added another reason that further aggravated the division: "A Third departure is that the 'Christian Church' has
now become a denomination. It affiliates with the denominations
and has taken its place in the religious world as a 'sister denomination.'"

In the course of his written speech, Boles said what his brethren thought he should say:

> You know where you left the churches of Christ; hence you
> know where to find them; come back and unity is the inevi-

table result. There will be no compromise or surrender on this point. The churches of Christ, as long as they are loyal to the New Testament, cannot compromise on this or any other point so clearly taught in the New Testament.

W. L. Totty was present for the meeting and he described the proceedings:

> The meeting reached the zenith the afternoon of the second day when H. Leo Boles spoke for an hour thirty minutes. He told them in no uncertain terms what had caused the division and what it would take to bring about unity—that if they expected compromise *they were mistaken*.

Claude F. Witty said that the speech of H. Leo Boles meant that the "Unity Movement" would fail. Witty commented that H. Leo Boles resembled his great grandfather "Raccoon" John Smith in one respect that he spoke about as long. The transactions of the "Unity meetings" are recorded in the *Gospel Advocate*. The *Christian Standard* carried accounts of the meeting in the June 3, 10, 17, 1939 issues of the religious journal; and A. T. DeGroot wrote about the "Unity meeting in the May 11, 1939, issue of the *Christian Evangelist*. James DeForest Murch gives his version in his history of the Disciples movement in *Christians Only*.

Just a short time back, W. L. Totty recalled that eventful Indianapolis meeting:

> I remember very well the unity meeting which was held in Indianapolis, in May, 1939, and recall some of the preachers who were present. Of course, Brother Witty and James DeForest Murch were there. R. H. Boll was also present. Jorgenson and another premillennial preacher from Louisville were present. Jorgenson led the singing. The convention was held in the Englewood Christian Church. No instrumental music was used. The only ones who spoke, as I remember, in opposition to the attempt at compromise were Leo Boles, J. E. Alexander, who preached for the Irvington Church of Christ, in Indianapolis, and I. We all three were adamantly opposed to the idea of compromising. However, Brother Leo Boles was the man who was the main speaker on our side. He spoke for an hour and thirty minutes, and his speech was a masterpiece. I had heard Brother Boles speak when I was a boy, but I never heard him equal the speech which he made at that convention. At the close of his speech, the regular preacher for the Englewood Christian Church was so provoked at Brother Boles that he referred to him in a light manner and

said that they had foregone the use of instrumental music in the meeting because of us but that he would never do it again.

The "Unity Movement" kept a semblance of life for the following two years. B. C. Goodpasture directly addressed the "Unity Movement" in an editorial, April 18, 1940, which appeared in the *Advocate*. He carried an announcement of the next annual meeting in Lexington, Kentucky, on the seventh and eighth of May with the comment:

> The fact that the foregoing program appears in our columns does not mean we give it our unqualified endorsement or that we expect any large amount of good to come from it. As a matter of religious news we give it space. No one should fail to encourage any scriptural effort toward unity among the brethren; but it should be remembered that any unity attained on grounds other than those revealed in the sacred oracles is not worth the time involved in its attainment. Any scheme of union which ignores the cause of division is foredoomed to failure. We cannot get rid of effects without removing causes. . . . Why not get down to business or quit? Desirable as unity is, we cannot surrender principle to have it.

Goodpasture wrote what was clear even to James DeForest Murch: "If the 'Disciples of Christ' wish to be united with the churches of Christ, they will have to give up the innovations which have brought about the division. . . . If they are not willing, why the waste of time?"

A year later, Goodpasture took notice of the annual "Unity meeting" to be conducted May 13, 14, 1941, in the Indianola Church of Christ in Columbus, Ohio. And he said what undoubtedly hastened the demise of the movement:

> So far we have been unable to see any visible results of the unity meetings which would justify their existence. We believe that the same effort and time used in preaching the primitive gospel would be productive of a great deal more good. Besides, it seems likely that those meetings are producing more problems among us than they are solving.

James DeForest Murch saw clearly the handwriting on the wall. In the February 14, 1942 issue of the *Christian Standard,* Murch wrote at length an article titled "Straws in the Wind" which points up what he thought was evident that the "Unity meetings" were producing results. He charged that such opposition that had been voiced came from a "coterie of not more than a hundred self appointed men (who) exercise a power over the rank and file of the ministers which is comparable to the power of the bishops in the Methodist Church."

Goodpasture answered this charge of Murch in the *Advocate* by simply stating what Murch had written about the control of the younger men by the older men. Younger ministers were writing Goodpasture their independent judgments supporting with full agreement the editor and his associates. Whoever is acquainted with B. C. Goodpasture knows that he encourages each person to think for and speak for himself, and he wrote: "It is a settled conviction that the young ministers among us, who are so ably helping to man the ramparts we watch will quit themselves like veterans at the crucial hours." This was said in March of 1942, and the "Unity Movement" was about done.

In the spring of 1942, Murch announced that the annual Unity Meeting would not be held due to travel restrictions and other conditions brought on by the war. The announcement was printed in the *Advocate*. Claude F. Witty did what he could to bring the churches of Christ and the Disciples of Christ together and his sincerity to promote Christian unity was never questioned. The efforts of Murch could not be described as a ploy; but judging from the tactics of the Christian Church for about seventy-five years, Murch and his associates never indicated they were willing to redress the causes that brought about division in the first place. Goodpasture, Boles, and others were convinced that the unity meetings were not serving the church with any scriptural benefit. They had thought so all along and said so when the time came to take an uncompromising stand.

The promised resumption of the Unity Meetings never materialized. Some church members were disappointed and thought that a few prejudiced men had scuttled the movement. Some were even persuaded that the opposition to the Unity Movement and premillennialism centered in a few men who were powerfully positioned in the religious journals and colleges. The *Gospel Advocate, Firm Foundation,* and the *Bible Banner* were singled out as being the worst offenders. Several outstanding church leaders were convinced that the *Advocate* and other religious papers had lost their sense of fairness. S. H. Hall took the lead in suggesting the need for a new religious journal that would be fair in discussing problems related to the church.

A meeting was held in Nashville, Tennessee, with G. C. Brewer, S. H. Hall, E. H. Ijams, President of David Lipscomb College, Ben Harding, a Lipscomb board member, J. N. Armstrong, President of Harding College, E. W. McMillan, Jesse P. Sewell, James F. Cox, President of Abilene Christian College, and Clinton Davidson of New Jersey in attendance. The choice lay between starting a new journal outright or purchasing a paper already in existence. Their final decision was to purchase the *Christian Leader,* edited by F. L. Rowe of Cincinnati, Ohio.

The *Christian Leader* was to be enlarged to twenty-four pages and the paper was designed to be a model of Christian journalism. Clinton Davidson, who was a wealthy insurance executive, agreed to provide the financial backing. E. W. McMillan was named the managing editor; A. B. Lipscomb and I. B. Bradley were selected as the managing editors; Jesse P. Sewell was selected the editor of the Sunday School literature. The new *Christian Leader* started off with high hopes.

However, the success of the *Christian Leader* was doomed from its inception. The articles in the *Christian Leader* were copyrighted to keep the articles from being quoted unfairly out of context. This did not set well with the brotherhood because of the implications of the policy. No one seemed to know Clinton Davidson and his relation to the church. The name of Clinton Davidson in recent months has come up in relation to the "modern day miracle healing and speaking in tongues" movement, and a personal friendship with Pat Boone grew out of their common interest in these practices.

Foy E. Wallace, Jr. led the attack in the *Bible Banner* on the policy of the new *Christian Leader,* and he centered his attention on Clinton Davidson whom he addressed as "Copyright" Davidson. Wallace was unrelenting in his attack, and soon after Davidson withdrew his support from the *Christian Leader.* The journal passed into other hands. The *Christian Leader* had proposed a new high for Christian journalism, and there were a good many knowledgeable persons who were convinced that Tolbert Fanning and David Lipscomb first set such a high standard and that B. C. Goodpasture was faithfully maintaining the tradition.

Two other matters of interest followed in the wake of the tur-

moil of the later 1930's and early 1940's. A few of the outstanding
men in the church were unwittingly drawn into the fray. They
were convinced that such persons as Don Carlos Janes and others
were being pillored by over-zealous caretakers of the church.
Janes was particularly singled out for attack. N. B. Hardeman
and others described him as a "one man missionary society" who
personally solicited funds for the missionary efforts of the church
in China and Japan. Janes was not answerable to any sponsoring
church under the supervision of the local elders for conducting
missionary evangelism in the Far East. A good many of the
church members believed in Janes because he kept his commitments to the missionaries for their support and travel funds.

The critics of Don Carlos Janes were not mistaken in branding
Don Carlos Janes a premillennialist. All of the facts became apparent following the death of Don Carlos Janes when the content
of his will became public knowledge. B. C. Goodpasture published
in the March 23, 1944 issue of the *Advocate* the content of the
will. The Janes' will read in part:

> Being fully assured that the premillennial view of our
> Lord's coming is the scriptural orthodox teaching of the
> church from the days of the apostles, and feeling that the
> propaganda of the *Gospel Advocate, Firm Foundation,
> Apostolic Times, Gospel Guardian, Bible Banner* and some
> other publications have done great injury to the cause of
> our Lord in creating and spreading dissension and in creat-
> ing the impression that the doctrine is heresy, and that the
> teachers of such doctrine are to be disfellowshipped . . . I
> will that the residue of my estate . . . shall be used by my
> executors for the publication and distribution, by sale or
> gift, or by both sales and gifts, of the material, which I have
> gathered on the imminent, personal premillennial coming of
> the Lord Jesus Christ to earth to reign gloriously where he
> once suffered. . . .

Goodpasture pointed up the fact that the residue of the estate came
to $40,244.45, and was to be spent, not for the preaching of the
gospel as originally intended, but for the teaching of premillennialism.

Whatever illusions that some may have entertained for Janes
were now dispelled. As is typical of Goodpasture, he had little to
say. He allowed the facts to speak for themselves. This was the
way that Goodpasture conducted the last rites of the premillennial

controversy. But strangely this was not the conclusion of the whole matter.

In the October 30, 1947, issue of the *Advocate,* Goodpasture informed the readers about a letter that Norman Davidson had sent to the editor requesting its publication in the *Advocate.* Davidson had said that he was prepared to spend fifty thousand dollars to make the teaching of the premillennial doctrine acceptable to the brotherhood. Norman Davidson was the son of W. V. Davidson, a wealthy lumberman and elder of the Russell Street church of Christ. At one time W. V. Davidson had been a board member of David Lipscomb College. Norman Davidson was living in Chicago at the time he sent the letter to Goodpasture in which he defended R. H. Boll. Goodpasture refused to print the letter.

Norman Davidson went to Leon McQuiddy for access to the *Gospel Advocate* mailing list, and he had previously told Goodpasture that he planned to do so. Goodpasture told him that was a matter between Davidson and McQuiddy and remarked, "but as far as I am concerned, it is not going into the *Gospel Advocate.*" Leon McQuiddy promised Goodpasture when he was appointed editor of the *Advocate* that he would be the editor and that he would have a free hand in determining what went into the paper. Goodpasture said in this connection: "I have never been handicapped or caused to deviate from my convictions by anybody since I have been editor of the paper."

In a later *Advocate* issue, Goodpasture reminded Norman Davidson that the "rank and file of brethren could not be bought with fifty thousand dollars or even fifty million dollars, and would not be worth the price if they sold out." Actually this was the last short chapter of the premillennial movement that for so long had been a thorn in the side of the church.

The attention devoted in this chapter to the problems of the church is disproportionate to the every day affairs of the church. The files of the *Gospel Advocate* must be carefully researched for these matters. The war years were dark and troubled. The church members went about their daily lives and the deep tragedy growing out of the global conflict was reflected in the work and worship of the church.

XII

Jacob's Staff

The numerical growth of the churches of Christ in the first fifty years of this century was something less than phenomenal, but it was growing. David Lipscomb, H. Leo Boles, N. B. Hardeman, and many other such great leaders in the church were building a solid foundation better than they knew in their lifetime. World War II suddenly ended in Europe. The free world moved to recover from the deep sickness that had paralyzed the earth for six years. Not in almost two thousand years had the church been provided with such opportunities to preach the gospel in such a world wide scope.

The cannons were hardly stilled before missionaries were laying plans to preach the gospel to every nation on a scale never before attempted. B. C. Goodpasture was solidly established as the editor of the *Advocate* on the eve of World War II; and when all hostilities were at an end, he stood at the threshold of unparalleled opportunities to encourage the carrying of the gospel wherever American boys had gone during the war years.

During his first seven years in the *Advocate* office, Goodpasture was fortunate to have his friend, H. Leo Boles, to think and advise with him. Boles had served the church as a preacher, religious debater, author of religious articles and Bible school literature. Perhaps no other leader in the church enjoyed such confidence that Boles commanded among his brethren. He was their Bible champion who knew error and possessed the courage, ability, and common sense to expose unbiblical teachings.

Practically every day when Boles was at home, he would drive down to the *Advocate* office to talk with Goodpasture. The trip downtown finally became a daily ritual. Boles and Goodpasture would discuss the meaning of a particular troublesome passage of scripture, the current church problems, *Advocate* business, and personal matters. And then almost without warning, the meetings ended.

Boles came home from Dallas, Texas, in November of 1945, in great pain. His illness was diagnosed as phlebitis. He died suddenly February 7, 1946, in midmorning. B. C. Goodpasture and Cleveland were standing by his bed with his wife when Boles passed away. Goodpasture had first seen Boles when he was a small child, stood by his death bed, and preached his funeral along with S. H. Hall. A man can go no further with a friend than to his grave side and Goodpasture went there.

Seven years after Goodpasture went to the *Advocate,* he was not standing alone. Boles was gone, but Goodpasture enjoyed the confidence of his brethren. No doubt, some church members wondered how Goodpasture would make it without the helpful and assuring presence of H. Leo Boles. It took awhile for the *Advocate* watchers to learn the editor had hardly an equal since the days of David Lipscomb.

The 1950's were great years for the church. Churches were growing up in the scattered places around the world; Christian schools were flourishing; and the gospel was being preached. Goodpasture was interested in every good work that his brethren were engaged in and encouraged them through the *Advocate* in every way he could. It has been true of the *Advocate* since its founding that the judgment of the men who wrote for the *Advocate* could be trusted. Goodpasture was aware of the great power of the *Advocate* to hurt or help a man or a cause. As J. Roy Vaughan summed up this fact: "Goodpasture would not waste the ink to do an injury to any man or cause out of spite."

Whatever teachings or practices threaten the scriptural integrity of the church, Goodpasture has stood inflexibly against it without fear of friends or foes. This chapter details some of the major movements in the church that Goodpasture was interested in during the 1950's, and the particular influence he brought to bear through the *Advocate*.

The first missionary work in Europe to excite the brotherhood after World War II was led by Otis Gatewood. Gatewood proposed in June of 1942 to a large group of Christians during the Yosemite, California Camp meeting at the very time this nation was preparing for the most horrible war of all times that if American could send her sons to sacrifice their lives in Germany then the church should be willing to send Christians to Germany to preach the gospel of peace.

In a special business meeting, the elders of the Broadway church of Christ in Lubbock, Texas, decided to support Gatewood on a survey trip to Europe as soon as passports and accommodations could be obtained. This was near the end of World War II. Otis Gatewood and Roy V. Palmer and their families sailed on May 16, 1947, from New York and, arrived in Frankfurt, Germany, June 6, 1947. This was the beginning of Otis Gatewood's missionary work in the post-Nazi Germany which is detailed in Gatewood's *Preaching in the Footsteps of Hitler*. The Broadway church in Lubbock assumed the responsibility to be the "sponsoring" church interested in carrying the gospel to German people. Goodpasture believed in the German work and supported it from the beginning through the *Gospel Advocate*.

Although the church had weathered the premillennial controversy and was not taken in by the "Unity" movement, still another matter arose which greatly troubled the church beginning in the late 1940's and has since. In recent years, a considerable number in the church of Christ have been labeled as "antis" because of their opposition to supporting orphan homes, Christian schools, and cooperative mission work directly from the treasury or common fund of the local congregation under the supervision of local elders. The church has not been as severely divided since the "music" and "society" controversy. Perhaps it would be more accurate to say the church has been splintered over "institutionalism" and that will be discussed in another place.

The "anti-movement" in the church actually started in a personality conflict in the late 1940's. Christian colleges were brought under attack challenging the scriptural right of Christian colleges to accept financial support from local congregations to carry on their operations. That the "orphan homes" were also man-made institutions was crystal clear as were also the brotherhood papers. It seemed at the time that the orphan homes would not be subject to attack, but they were. The attack abruptly shifted away from the "college issue," and centered first in the mission efforts supported by cooperating congregations under the supervision of the elders of a local congregation.

Otis Gatewood and the elders of the Lubbock church were singled out and accused with creating a modern day "missionary society" to carry on the German work. The leaders in the opposition were Roy Cogdill and Yater Tant who mounted their opposition in the *Gospel Guardian*. Florida Christian College under the presidency of James R. Cope became a training control center for the movement at a later time. They were joined later by such outstanding preachers as Franklin Puckett, Homer Hailey, and Curtis Porter who were among the most effective preachers of the gospel.

One of the curious twists of church history is the turn of events. Cogdill, Tant, Cope, and their associates led a sustained campaign against churches supporting orphan homes and Christian colleges from the church treasury because of their institutional organization. Such programs as the "Herald of Truth" were branded as thinly veiled "missionary societies" despite the fact that the same preachers had participated in similar cooperative church activities. Cogdill and Tant and others were branding church members as "liberals" who did not share their views and continue to do so now. Their audiences are largely restricted to their own churches and occasional contacts with members of the church whom they seek to proselyte.

Goodpasture watched the gathering storm with concern. He believed in the Christian school, the usefulness of brotherhood papers, the support of orphan homes, and cooperation among consenting churches to spread the gospel. The editor was concerned that the church would be divided, and he waited and hoped the whole unhappy controversy would end. And when he was convinced the opposition would not fade away, the pages of the *Advocate* were only then opened to discussion of the issues with no holds barred in 1951.

Goodpasture, despite what some misinformed readers may think about the policy of the *Gospel Advocate,* moved slowly to answer the opposition. Goodpasture wants to be on the Bible side of any issue; and he wants peace, but not peace at any price. He said about the "anti-movement": "It was started by disgruntled preachers who did not get the attention they thought they deserved. They thought they could get attention by riding some hobby they couldn't get by preaching the gospel."

Cecil N. Wright wrote a series of significant articles for the *Advocate* under "The Cooperation Controversy." Wright wrote a documented article detailing the decision of the *Gospel Guardian* to declare open season against churches cooperating in mission work. The first of Wright's articles was published June 7, 1951, and was followed by others. In this article he wrote:

> The present assault against sponsored cooperative mission work, instigated and conducted by the *Gospel Guardian,* has raged more than a year now, with little or no abatement. On various occasions the *Guardian* has sung paeans of victory, the last of which was an editorial in the issue of April 19, 1951, entitled 'The Voice of the Turtle.' This was somewhat to commemorate the anniversary of the *Guardian's* big push in the fray. Previously there has been some preliminary encounters and border incidents, such as the 'rock fights' articles. But war was not officially declared, battle lines were not definitely drawn, and an all-out offensive was not launched until then. Since that time, however, an almost constant barrage has been leveled against sponsored cooperation in mission work, its participants, and its defenders, in keeping with the *Guardian's* threat to wage battle 'without restraint.'

Wright brought out that as of April 20, 1950, the *Guardian* had drawn up the battle lines declaring that the "sponsoring" church method was wrong labeling it as the "new disgression" and "apostasy" which must be battled "without restraint" even to the dividing of the church.

Goodpasture personally entered the controversy in 1951 through the *Gospel Advocate.* One of his articles which appeared in the May 10, 1951 *Advocate* was titled "Here and There" in which he defended the scriptural right of churches cooperating to preach the gospel. J. Roy Vaughan thought B. C. Goodpasture waited a little too long before engaging the *Advocate* to answer the charges of the opposition and to defend the "church cooperation." The editor from experience knew it would be no small thing to commit the *Advocate* to a program of action. Once the die was cast, there was no going back.

Goodpasture is a long suffering man and refuses to engage in any form of "below the belt" frays. Goodpasture was taken to task and misquoted by a *Guardian* writer, and he apparently ignored the matter. Later he wrote indirectly about the article and said:

In the *Gospel Guardian* of September 20, the editor and the publisher devote four or five pages to the editor of the *Advocate*. The publisher in particular delivers himself of a bitter and unwarranted diatribe which is characterized by the basest of billingsgate. To this article as a whole reply is unnecessary for two reasons: first, the facts of our article of August 23, stand; second, the tone and content of publisher's article supply the most effective answer possible. It does remind one of the Indian's appraisal of the preacher's sermon—'Much wind! Big thunder! No rain!' Or the story of the little boy who was set upon and belabored by a large and noisy dog. When he came into the house someone asked him if he was hurt. He replied: "No, not a scratch, but I have been slobbered all over.'

Whoever the person was that the editor had in mind never cried "foul" and so ended this "small tempest."

Goodpasture possesses a fine sense of humor including the use of satire which he rarely employs in the *Advocate* or anywhere else. During 1951 when the *Advocate* was first brought under sustained attack for its support of "church cooperation," the age of the publication of the *Advocate* dating from its first publication was questioned. The criticism was in the form of "nit picking." The editor answered his detractors facetiously:

How old is the *Gospel Advocate*? That depends on how you mean it. Its age, however, is not changeable and elastic like that of the little boy who was asked, 'How old are you, Jimmy?' To which he replied, 'That depends on where I am. On the street car, I am five; at school, I am seven; and at home, I am six.'

The *Gospel Advocate* was founded in 1855 by William Lipscomb and Tolbert Fanning. Counting from the time it began, it would be ninety-seven; but due to its suspension during the Civil War, it is now in its ninety-fourth year. It depends, therefore, on the point of view as to how old the *Advocate* is:

But individuals and papers may be old in different senses. Someone asked the little colored boy, 'How old are you, Rastus?' He answered, 'That 'pends on how you means it. If you means how much fun has I had, I'm already an old man.'

But the "anti" campaign was no laughing matter because the unity of the church was at stake. The controversy rumbled on through the 1950's and has not ceased. The *Guardian* charged that the *Advocate* would not print both sides of the controversy. As a matter of fact, the *Advocate* has been an open forum to honestly discuss Bible teachings and the *Advocate* remains so to this day. When David Lipscomb was convinced that a writer was using the *Advocate* for self-serving purposes, he would refuse to print his articles; nor has Goodpasture allowed "hobby riders" to vent their spleen through the *Advocate*.

In the August 14, 1958 issue of the *Advocate,* Goodpasture looked back some seven years at the failure of the "anti group" to dismantle the church:

> Several years ago a young preacher from the 'Deep South,' the very 'Deep South,' informed the editor of the *Gospel Advocate* that a 'group of younger brethren' were going to take over the brotherhood.' The editor observed that a 'group of the younger brethren' were going 'to take over the brotherhood' back in the days of Rehoboam and that they did not do so well. There are many fine young preachers in the brotherhood, but they are not of the taking-over variety. They are not 'brain-trusters.' They are humble young men who understand that true greatness is reflected in unselfish service rather than in ambitious taking-over.

> About this time another served notice on the editor that if the *Gospel Advocate* did not line up with the hobby riders it would soon die. Well the *Advocate* did not line up with them and it is not dead. Its circulation is several times larger than when the prediction was made. The *Advocate* has stood for the truth against all departures and hobby riders. It must not falter or fail.

As a matter of record, the "anti brethren" were beginning to fall away in the closing fifties. They were not talking less, but fewer members of the churches were listening and not a great many of them paid much attention.

However, the pages of the *Advocate* were seldom assigned to articles addressing the controversy. As articles came to the editor's desk from time to time, he printed them if they served a good purpose. Whoever would promote a good work in the church from time to time sought out the counsel of B. C. Goodpasture for two reasons: first, the good judgment of the editor is deeply respected; secondly, whenever the *Advocate* is committed to a cause, the success of the undertaking is greatly enhanced.

Just as the "anti-movement" was building up its head of steam to attack the "cooperation" program among churches, a new radio program, the "Herald of Truth" was started under the supervision of the elders of the Highland church of Christ in Abilene, Texas. The first broadcast originated February 10, 1952, over the ABC radio network of some eighty-five stations with a potential audience of some three million. By 1955 the gospel broadcasts were being carried by two hundred ABC and some foreign stations. The broadcasts were being heard from the artic circle to the equator.

The "Herald of Truth" television program was launched in May of 1954 and was being expanded to reach a potential audience of thirty-seven million people in such cities as New York, Detroit, and Los Angeles; and by 1954, more than a million sermons had been mailed. Batsell Barrett Baxter has now for several years carried the major speaking responsibility of the "Herald of Truth" broadcasts. The editor opened the pages of the *Advocate* to promote the programs and continues to do so. In the December 17, 1959 *Advocate,* the "Herald of Truth" was featured in several articles with the announcement that Baxter was chosen to be featured speaker for the television series. The worth of the "Herald of Truth" in carrying the gospel to almost inaccessible places is patent to every interested observer. The appeal of Batsell Barrett Baxter in finding a common ground to teach the gospel to all people is almost without parallel in our time.

B. C. Goodpasture had a more direct hand in promoting one of the greatest works in the 1950's. The largest concentration of people in America is in the Northeast. The church in New York for several years was just getting along. The first meeting of the church in New York was in July of 1921. Two family groups— the George McKees of Georgia, and the Johnson family from England—composed the first congregation. E. E. Joynes of Philadelphia was largely responsible for getting the New York church started. In 1939, Homer Putnam Reeves began regular work with the New York church. Black people were meeting with white people then, and the church numbered about one hundred and fifty. The Negro families decided later to organize a black church, and in 1940, they moved to Harlem.

Goodpasture preached in the first of three meetings for the New York church in 1949. The West Side location was something less than attractive. Goodpasture recalls at that time he was approached by an interested street urchin who asked him, "Do you ever preach in any first class joints?"

A. M. Burton became interested in building a church in Manhattan and devoted his energies and finances toward that end. A massive campaign was launched in 1955 to acquaint the church all across the nation with the New York work in order to attract support. The issue of December 8, 1955 *Advocate* featured the Manhattan work.

B. C. Goodpasture and Burton Coffman

A. M. Burton gave the major part of the purchase property price for the first Manhattan church location at 48 East Eightieth Street. The campaign to buy additional property and to build a new church structure was launched in 1957. The *Gospel Advocate* joined in the drive. In the February 12, 1959 issue, A. M. Burton wrote in the *Advocate* that the church controlled a million dollar site in the heart of the city at 44 East Eightieth Street adjacent to the Madison Street property which had been previously purchased. It would not be fully accurate to say the Manhattan

B. C. Goodpasture and Virgil Larimore

church would not have become a reality without the interest of A. M. Burton and B. C. Goodpasture; but it is safe to say, it would not have happened as early.

On June 30, 1968, the formal opening of the Manhattan church was a great day for the church. B. C. Goodpasture, George S. Benson, and Reuel Lemmons spoke on the opening day, and B. C. Goodpasture spoke each evening during the rest of the week. At a birthday dinner honoring the *Advocate* editor, Burton Coffman who worked with the Manhattan church through the crucial years recalled that Goodpasture promised him in the early stages, "I'll stay with you until we eat cold bread," which meant there was a possibility of failure. Goodpasture is a winner and he likes a winner. But this is not the key to the man. He would rather go down with the truth than to win on the side of error. He rejoices in the fact that the Hillsboro church in Nashville where he serves as elder gave some $100,000 to the Manhattan work which was the largest sum any church gave to the New York church.

Whoever has wondered at the encyclopedic mind of Goodpasture has cause for increased wonderment at the numerous church activities set forth in the *Gospel Advocate* such as colleges, schools, orphan homes, churches, Bible chairs, and a host of good works which were encouraged by the editor. Each good work was announced and encouraged in the *Advocate,* and the editor has at his command an uncommon amount of knowledge about each project. B. C. Goodpasture has not been found here today on some church issue and then somewhere else tomorrow. His record reads the same today as it did more than thirty years ago.

The Gospel Advocate Company handles the largest volumes of printed materials for the churches of Christ today among the loyal members of the church. Among the varied interests which have engaged the concern of the *Advocate* editor, a major one is his interest in black people. The pages of the *Gospel Advocate* have often been used to support the teaching the gospel to Negroes. David Lipscomb was a staunch ally of Negro Christians and helped them to establish the church in Middle Tennessee through the *Gospel Advocate* and other means of support. This story is told in *Roll Jordan Roll: The Biography of Marshall Keeble,* published by the Gospel Advocate Company. Goodpasture too has supported the preaching of the gospel to black people through the *Advocate*. The *Advocate* published the *Christian Counsellor* for

Seated: Lady Bird Johnson, Annie Hardeman, N. B. Hardeman. *Standing:* Dorsey B. Hardeman, J. M. Powell, Governor Buford Ellington, Mayor Edmund Orgill, B. C. Goodpasture, Lyndon B. Johnson, Senator Albert Gore.

B. C. Goodpasture and J. E. Choate

about five years to be circulated among the Negro members of the church. Marshall Keeble served as the editor. The paper did not go over well because, as Goodpasture remarked, "The black brethren did not support it very well."

B. C. Goodpasture has maintained a strong interest in another publication, the *Voice of Freedom* which started publication in January of 1953. The paper was the brain child of B. C. Goodpasture, George S. Benson, and G. C. Brewer. The Freedom Press, a non-profit organization, was chartered to publish the *Voice of Freedom*. G. C. Brewer served as the first editor. The sixteen-page publication and other tracts and booklets were for free distribution. By 1954, hundreds of thousands of tracts were distributed from coast to coast. The purpose of the paper was to expose Catholicism and communism and to make people aware of the threats from both sources. The Freedom Press is incorporated, and B. C. Goodpasture is the chairman of the board. He paid the original twenty-five dollars for the corporation papers. B. C. Phillips gave the first large contribution of $5,000 at the beginning of the publication and George Pepperdine made a contribution later. Goodpasture wrote specifically about the mission of the publication: "This sixteen page monthly has as its specific purpose telling the truth, the whole truth, and nothing but the truth about the threat to our freedom from Catholicism and communism."

The first editor, G. C. Brewer, recommended L. R. Wilson to succeed him. The present editor who has served since the death of L. R. Wilson is P. D. Wilmeth. The present board of directors includes B. C. Goodpasture, J. M. Powell, Cleon Lyles and Clarence Daley.

Goodpasture was instrumental in starting the *Minister's Monthly*. The monthly publication was first published in September of 1955. It was a twenty-four page periodical filled with information for the preachers, elders, teachers, and Bible students. Frank S. Cox continues to serve as editor of the *Minister's Monthly*.

Goodpasture took notice of the *Firm Foundation* in the year that launched the *Minister's Monthly*. Reuel Lemmons had just become editor of the Texas paper. In the process of complimenting the new editor, Goodpasture recalled the words of Governor Robert L. Taylor, retiring governor of Tennessee, who extended his congratulations to the new governor of Tennessee, with the re-

mark: "And now may the Lord have mercy on your soul."
Goodpasture knew that being the editor of a religious paper has its
"built in" problems.

When just a boy, Goodpasture determined the course he would
pursue the remainder of his life; and he has not since deviated
from the "Old Paths." This is not to say his judgments have been
flawless because they have not. But it would be difficult to assess
his worth to the church as the *Advocate* editor now for more than
thirty years.

Willard Collins, vice president of David Lipscomb College and
a longtime close personal friend of Goodpasture, asked the editor
after twenty years with the *Advocate* what he considered to be his
major accomplishments. Goodpasture said:

> I will mention three: (1) I have been able to encourage
> and help the preaching of the gospel in all the countries of
> the English speaking world through the *Advocate*. (2)
> The editorship has offered me an opportunity to help staball-
> ize a brotherhood torn by hobby riders and factionists. (3)
> I hope that I have made a major contribution in indoctri-
> nating and strengthening churches wherever the *Advocate*
> has been read.

Likewise, the encouragement that Goodpasture has given to
preaching in the non-English speaking world has been equally im-
pressive. Ten years after Otis Gatewood with Russell Artist and
others started and consolidated the preaching of the gospel among
the German speaking people, churches of Christ were in Italy,
France, Belgium, Holland, and in other far flung parts of the
globe.

The growing interests of Goodpasture in the numerous good
works of the church is chronicled in the annual index to the *Gospel
Advocate*. In the content index for the *Advocate* in 1942, one section is labeled "Colleges." In recent years, the caption has been
enlarged to read "Colleges, Orphan Homes, Schools, Encamp-
ments." The articles and announcements in the index for 1959
mirrors both the interest and influence of the paper: Abilene
Christian College, Alabama Christian College, Central Christian
College, Columbia Christian College, Hong Kong Christian College,
and many others over the years are detailed in the index.

In this same year, W. B. Richter, Superintendent of the
Tennessee Orphan Home wrote for *Advocate* printing:

At the sixth annual meeting of the executives of homes for children supported by the churches of Christ, that was held last week at David Lipscomb College, it was unanimously resolved to thank you for the whole hearted and enthusiastic support that you have given our institution through the pages of the *Gospel Advocate.*

Every kind of personal honor that members of the church know to express their appreciation of B. C. Goodpasture, they have done so. After he became editor of the *Gospel Advocate,* he was invited to become a board member of David Lipscomb College; Leon McQuiddy thought it not best for the college and the *Gospel Advocate* to be that closely associated. Goodpasture has been featured on the lectureships of the Christian colleges on occasions too numerous to be mentioned. He has enjoyed many special recognition dinners held in his honor at Freed-Hardeman College, David Lipscomb College, and other Christian schools and colleges. The editor had received honorary degrees from Harding College, George Pepperdine College, and Magic Valley Christian College. Goodpasture has lost count of the baccalaureate sermons and commencement addresses he has delivered at David Lipscomb College. Such calls have come over the years from the other colleges, schools, and orphan homes. His aversion to flying has restricted his personal work between Texas and New York. Thousands of Christians who know about B. C. Goodpasture have never seen him or heard him preach.

Guy N. Woods, trusted friend of B. C. Goodpasture, wrote in the centennial celebration of the *Gospel Advocate*:

The *Gospel Advocate* is at its zenith in the long and eventful period which characterizes its history. For one hundred years it has unswervingly adhered to its calculating course of contending earnestly for the faith once delivered to the saints. From the goal it has moved neither to the right nor to the left, but has pressed steadily onward ever fighting for a pure faith and a fautless practice for the people of God.

Athens Clay Pullias, president of David Lipscomb College wrote at the same time: "David Lipscomb College is David Lipscomb's school as certainly as the *Gospel Advocate* is David Lipscomb's paper." President Pullias added, "The *Advocate* and the college have as their supreme purpose the teaching of the Bible as the inspired word of God."

N. B. Hardeman, then an aged man, surmised that the *"Advocate* had been in the forefront for a hundred years. It had more
influence in staying innovations, the hobbies, and the tendencies to
depart from the 'Ancient Order' than any other, perhaps of all
other papers combined."

In the March 5, 1959 *Advocate*, L. R. Wilson evaluated the
worth of Goodpasture to the brotherhood as the editor of the *Gospel Advocate:*

> We may be thankful that through all of this period of
> growth the editor of the *Gospel Advocate* kept a level head
> and encouraged every good work among us, while adhering
> to the same principles that have characterized our work
> since the beginning of the Restoration Movement. We are
> somewhat fearful of what might have happened to our cause
> if the *Gospel Advocate* had taken off on a tangent during
> this crucial period.

And now after many years since the editor set his Jacob's staff
on the Bible to take his bearings, he has helped through the *Advocate* to stabilize the brotherhood torn by "hobby riders" and "factionists"; and of the greatest importance, he has lent his life and
influence to teaching the Bible. The plea of the Restoration
leaders to restore the patterns of the New Testament has not gone
begging in his hands. The massive and continuous growth of the
church for the past twenty-five years has found and still finds a
staunch ally in B. C. Goodpasture.

XIII

I'll Stand

The 1950's were among the most promising years of the growth of the New Testament church in this century. The gospel was being carried into more than fifty nations around the world. The *Gospel Advocate* was supporting the Bible colleges, orphan homes, radio and television programs, and numerous cooperative efforts among the churches of Christ.

The "anti-movement" was thought to be a blight on the church by leading members of the church. Gus Nichols commending B. C. Goodpasture wrote in this connection in 1959 after the movement began to recede:

> The *Gospel Advocate* again defended the truth, and the church has by such noble teachers and teachings been saved from becoming an anti-sect of third rate dimensions. B. C. Goodpasture has been at the steering wheel of the *Gospel Advocate* during all the smiles and tears, smoke and fog, smears and fears of this campaign. Brethren are more and more seeing that the light of Truth is marching on.

Goodpasture as a boy growing up in the Cumberland high country learned "to shoot without rest" at a great distance with pin point accuracy. And over the years his foresight in matters of religion has been improved by his hindsight. Some of the church leaders along the way did not approve of the direction he was guiding the *Advocate*. But Goodpasture knew the past history of the church and the issues of the day; and his judgment about his future course of action was based upon his knowledge of the Scripture. He has a crystal clear understanding of the Christian religion; and over years

L. R. Wilson, Ira North, Rex Turner, B. C. Goodpasture

J. Roy Vaughan, Gus Nichols, Wanda Baxter, Batsell Barrett Baxter

of dedicated study and writing, he qualified himself to know the difference between truth and error with a fine sense of appropriateness of the articles that should go into the *Advocate*.

George S. Benson who guided Harding College through critical years stood undaunted while Harding College struggled through a period of sustained criticism. In a letter to B. C. Goodpasture dated January 6, 1971, Dr. Benson summed up a life:

> Brother Goodpasture, it has been a thrill to watch your good work over these past 40 years and you came in as editor of the *Gospel Advocate* at a very critical time, You have given it stability and greatly added to its worthwhileness and you have been a real pillar in the church of the Lord all of these years and I want you to know that multitudes of us really appreciate it.

The leading Christian colleges enjoyed a phenomenal growth after World War II. Goodpasture is a product of Christian education and the school men depended upon him and the *Advocate* for sustained support, and they were not disappointed. Abilene Christian College, David Lipscomb College, Freed-Hardeman College, and Harding College grew beyond expectation. George Pepperdine College had entered the picture of Christian education offering so much promise. Other colleges and schools were springing up in different places. A new Christian college was started in Tampa, Florida. The church was growing in one of the great states of the union. The "field was white into harvest" in Florida, and a good Christian college promised great boon for the church in that state. Goodpasture used the *Advocate* pages to the hilt in helping launch the new college; and what happened in the course of time led to the undoing of a good work.

J. Roy Vaughan wrote the announcement for Florida Christian College in the February 1, 1945 issue of the *Advocate*. Vaughan wrote:

> For more than a year brethren in Florida have been working toward establishing a school in this state after the pattern of David Lipscomb and other schools in the brotherhood. The board of directors of Florida Christian College are all members of the church of Christ. The board may consist of not fewer than ten members and not more than fifteen members. It is a self-perpetuating body, with each member elected to serve three years, at the end of which time he may be reelected or a new member placed in his

stead. The board consists of brethren from various parts of the state. This, it is thought, will assure greater interest among the brethren over a wider area. Every precaution possible has been taken in drawing up the charter and by-laws to safeguard the college in years to come from false doctrines, such as premillennialism, modernism, and various forms of infidelity.

The board of directors of Florida Christian chose L. R. Wilson of San Antonio, Texas, to be the first president. As a boy, he had entered Freed-Hardeman College where he completed four years of high school and two years of college. Five of those six years were spent in the home of N. B. Hardeman and his family. His formal education was ended at Birmingham Southern College where he received the M.A. degree.

L. R. Wilson worked with Florida Christian College until July 1, 1949. He tendered his resignation December 23, 1948 to become effective on the July date in 1949. J. Roy Vaughan announced in May of 1949 through the *Advocate* that James R. Cope would be the new president. Cope had been a teacher in Freed-Hardeman College for five years. He had come to Henderson from David Lipscomb College where he had taught in the elementary, high school, and college departments.

The "anti-movement" was then in its infancy and no great alarm had as yet been sounded. James R. Cope had received the appointment to become vice-president of Freed-Hardeman College beginning with the 1949-50 session before the Florida offer came. Cope left Freed-Hardeman College with the full blessings of N. B. Hardeman and his faculty on the eve of his new work. Cope was asked by the chairman of the board of directors and other board members of Florida Christian College about his stand on the incipient issues being raised over the support of Christian colleges and orphan homes. Cope's reply then was that he was still studying the question. Over the next few years, it was clear that Cope was leading Florida Christian College into the "anti" camp.

Year after year, president Cope had been using the pages of the *Gospel Advocate* to promote the school. The last advertisement which the *Advocate* carried for the school described Abilene Christian College and Harding College as sister institutions of Florida Christian College and appeared in 1958.

A deluge of letters came into the *Advocate* protesting the advertisement. The editor said he had been "raked over the coals" by letters of protest from different sections. They were saying what was generally known that President Cope and his associates were promoting anti-orphan home propaganda and insisting that it was scripturally wrong for churches to support Christian colleges. They were going wherever they could to hold protracted meetings where their views were not known and were not welcome "to win friends and influence people."

Goodpasture's response was typical of his method of handling such a position. He waited until enough of the facts were in, and he responded in the August 21, 1958 issue of the *Advocate:*

> When this advertisement came in, I knew it posed a dilemma if the *Advocate* did not carry it, then there are those who would likely say that we had drawn the line of fellowship; and if we did carry it there would be those who would question, if not condemn our action in so doing. We prefer to make a mistake on the side of charity rather than on the side of severity. The position of Florida Christian College on the orphan home and *Herald of Truth* is not that of the *Advocate*. But as long as there is reasonable hope of rescuing a college from its unsound teaching, it has been our policy to carry its advertisements.

This statement from the pen of B. C. Goodpasture marked the end of an era in the *Advocate's* support of Florida Christian College which afterwards became one of the rallying points for the "anti" leaders. Athens Clay Pullias who steered the fortunes of David Lipscomb College through this stormy passage wrote afterwards:

> For a quarter of a century, Brother Goodpasture has held the helm of the *Gospel Advocate,* holding a steady course amid the rough seas of religious controversy. Raging around him have been the storms, on the radical right the hobby riders, those opposing orphan homes, those opposing Christian colleges and schools, and other extremists—and on the modernist left, the destructive forces of modernism, in a hundred different hues. In these troubled waters, unmoved and unshaken he has steered a steady and straight course of loyalty to the word of God and to the principles of New Testament Christianity.

The first line of Goodpasture's loyalty is to the church and whatever serves the church is bound to win his unflagging loyalty and support. The Christian colleges and their leaders and faculties never had a stronger champion for their right and need to exist

Seated: Otis Gatewood, J. D. Thomas, L. R. Wilson, P. D. Wilmeth. *Standing:* Thomas B. Warren, L. O. Sanderson, E. Claude Gardner, Dan Harless.

Clifton Loyd Ganus, Jr., B. C. Goodpasture, George S. Benson

B. C. Goodpasture, J. M. Powell, Dr. Perry E. Gresham, President of Bethany College

than in B. C. Goodpasture as long as each remained loyal to the Bible; and the orphans never had a more compassionate friend.

Goodpasture wrote in the *Advocate,* November 19, 1959, an article which sets the record straight:

> Brethren have the same right to establish and operate Christian colleges that they have to establish and operate gospel papers. They stand or fall together. It may be argued that colleges have been instrumental in introducing departures from the faith. Grant it. The same is true of religious papers and preachers. If we are going to close our Christian colleges because colleges have introduced departures from the faith, on the same ground we shall have to discontinue our religious papers and silence the preachers. They, too, have led in apostasies from the ancient order of things. As a rule, those who promote cults, heresies, and hobbies, start papers before they establish colleges . . . yes put this editor down on the side of Christian education.

The editor has never allowed the *Advocate* to introduce divisive issues over non-essentials. Some Christians have been persuaded that a cottage home with a husband and wife is a better method for taking care of orphans than a larger home such as the Tennessee Orphan Home. Some church members do not agree that a church should give from the church treasury to support the Christian school. The editor has not allowed the *Gospel Advocate* to force issues of this kind either to the right or to the left.

The church continued to be troubled by the "anti" brethren in the 1960's. Their efforts were spent in endless polemics in their writings and debates. Cecil N. Wright who wrote a series of articles explaining the tactics of the "anti" brethren, described the movement for what it was in the *Gospel Advocate* for December 9, 1954—a new form of revived "Sommerism." Daniel Sommer was a younger contemporary of David Lipscomb who led the opposition to the right of a Christian college even to exist. Sommer objected to the name "Bible College" because the Bible was only one of the many subjects taught. He thought the name "Christian" was too sacred to be applied to an institution. He thought it was wrong for such schools to call on the churches for donations.

Near the end of his life, Daniel Sommer appeared in the late 1930's on the lectureships of David Lipscomb College and Freed-

Hardeman College; and he said on those occasions that he had no
objection to the schools and their management as the schools then
existed. However, Sommer still disallowed the right of churches—
not Christians—to support the Christian colleges.

In the December article which was published under the title
"Revived Sommerism," Wright said what was apparent that the
writers for the *Gospel Guardian* were anti-college (Florida Christian College was euchred from its founders by the "antis"), anti-
orphan home and old folks' home, anti-cooperation, and such like.
In turn they would with growing vehemence brand the Christians
as liberals who did not agree with their views.

Twenty-five years have now passed. The "anti-movement" has
settled and hardened. Their proselyting efforts are generally un-
productive and their preachers move now only among the sister
anti-churches. Their voices are seldom heard outside their ranks,
and they are often not in agreement with each other. Some of the
finest preachers of this century joined forces with the "antis," and
more than a few have left them. The incalculable services they
could have rendered in preaching the gospel never materialized because they chose instead "hobbyism." They partially succeeded
where Daniel Sommer failed. The church was not split, but it was
"splintered." Serious doubts were raised in the minds of well in-
tentioned Christians to question cooperative work supported by
churches under the sponsorship of local church supervised by its
elders. The specious logic of the "antis" that one Christian could
support a Christian college with his money but that a church composed of two or three could not do so is still a great mystery yet
unexplained. Many good and useful Christians have been led into
misgivings about supporting the Christian schools.

The "antis" are now consigned to the "purgatory" of their own
devising—with that "great crowd" of "anti-Sunday school, anti-
two cuppers" and other such like who have now gone on. And to
respect the "shades of Daniel Sommer," the persons responsible
for Florida Christian College have dropped "Christian" and call
the institution "Florida College." But it has not been difficult to
restore the full name to suit a temporary convenience.

B. C. Goodpasture is a lover of good men and he is willing to
stand by them in a good cause. Too often controversy occupies
the center of attention while the peaceful day by day affairs of the

church often go unnoticed.   There is another story in the life of B. C. Goodpasture that needs to be told.   Marshall Keeble, the famed Negro evangelist, and B. C. Goodpasture enjoyed a friendship that lasted for more than thirty years.   Marshall Keeble never had a friend he loved and honored more than he did B. C. Goodpasture.

B. C. Goodpasture attended a Keeble meeting in Sheffield, Alabama, the year Goodpasture preached for the church in Florence, Alabama.   Goodpasture had never seen or heard Keeble before. Goodpasture remembers the night well and remarked that it was a typical Keeble meeting with a large audience in attendance. Goodpasture noticed several black men with pencils and tablets sitting down front.   He asked Keeble who they were; and he said, "Preachers, they have come to take notes and answer me." Keeble always invited any preacher to share equal time with him during the service and to show his side of the question. Goodpasture noticed that after awhile the preachers closed their tablets and pocketed their pencils.   Keeble then said, "Now if what I was saying wasn't so, they would have exposed me.   I would be in a bad shape if I did not have the Bible to support me." Whoever accepted Keeble's challenges in such a meeting showed poor judgment.   Whoever heard Keeble in one of those impromptu debates never thought Keeble lost; and no preacher ever came back for a second round.   The word finally got around to the black preachers all over the country: "When Keeble comes. to town—don't debate him.   It will just make his audiences grow."

Marshall Keeble was enjoying a growing reputation as an effective evangelist in the twenties.   Keeble conducted a meeting in Valdosta, Georgia, in 1930.   The white people arranged for the meeting and supported it with their money and presence.   The meeting was attended by large audiences and a great deal of excitement.   Keeble baptized a total of one hundred and sixty-three persons during the meeting.

Goodpasture kept up with the Georgia mission work.   After the first Valdosta meeting, there was a growing demand for Keeble's services and for his sermons to be put in print for the present and later generations.   Keeble and Goodpasture corresponded, and they agreed Valdosta would be a good place to take down the sermons.

The first Keeble meeting that Goodpasture attended in Valdosta stuck in his mind.   Goodpasture was impressed that Keeble was a master of ceremonies and equal to any occasion. Keeble possessed a native intelligence and tact which enabled him to judge the feelings and reactions of an audience.

Keeble returned to Valdosta, Georgia, for a second meeting. The meeting was to be one of the most memorable of his life. Goodpasture sat each evening on the stage. He had employed a Valdosta court stenographer to take down Keeble's sermons in shorthand. The lady stenographer had trouble the first evening with Keeble's rapid flow of words and terminology and suffered a badly swollen hand. The next morning she phoned Goodpasture and said she couldn't go on with it. A doctor examined her hand and told her that it did not amount to anything—just muscular fatigue.

She continued to take down the sermons by night and to make a transcription the next morning. In the afternoon Goodpasture and Keeble would go over the sermons to make whatever changes they thought were necessary. In that way they kept everything up to date while the sermons were still fresh on their minds.

Marshall Keeble was furnished published copies of the sermons at cost. He sold them in his meetings and helped with his expenses. The books of sermons were published under the title *Biography and Sermons of Marshall Keeble*. A. M. Burton and N. B. Hardeman opened doors for Marshall Keeble; the men of the *Advocate* from around the time of World War I helped Keeble every way they could. But Keeble never had a better friend to stand with him than B. C. Goodpasture who helped more than anybody else and he knew it.

Goodpasture said in talking about the life of Marshall Keeble that Keeble dealt with conditions like they were rather than how they ought to be. "Brother Keeble had enough sense and foresight to realize that some things couldn't be forced and would come naturally as a matter of education and understanding." Marshall Keeble got along with his work in a fine way, and white and black people were able to work together in a Keeble meeting. No trouble was ever started in a Keeble meeting between the races; however, outside agitators tried and failed from time to time.

Keeble was suddenly catapulted into fame in the summer of 1931. Keeble went to Atlanta, Georgia, for his renowned Atlanta meeting which continued for one month. Clyde Hale was preaching for the West End Avenue church in Atlanta at that time. The

West End church was responsible for the financing and all of the other arrangements necessary to conduct a gospel meeting.

It would be safe to say that no preacher of any faith—that includes Billy Sunday and Gypsy Smith—attracted such great audiences as Marshall Keeble did for more than fifty years in the pulpit with the simple announcement that Marshall Keeble will speak here.

One of the first visitors to the Keeble meeting on Simpson Street in Atlanta, Georgia, was B. C. Goodpasture. He too had held great meetings in Atlanta, Georgia, and baptized sixty-seven with thirty-seven other responses in one meeting. But Keeble walked away in that meeting with a larger number of responses. Keeble baptized one hundred and sixty-six persons.

Goodpasture and Keeble formed a friendship that lasted until Keeble's passing. Goodpasture gave Keeble a new suit of clothes during the Atlanta meeting and each Christmas for the rest of Keeble's life. The giving of the suit came to be a kind of ritual. Keeble would drop into the *Advocate* office to see his friend around Christmas. They talked about church affairs, personal matters, laughed, and joked. Goodpasture would act like he did not know why Keeble had come around other than just to visit. Finally Keeble would get up to leave and he would say, "Now, I've come for my suit." Then Goodpasture would get up and he would reach for his billfold for the check which had been written beforehand and tucked away just for the occasion.

During the Christmas of 1966, Keeble did not come around. At first Goodpasture did not know why. Then he learned Keeble was in Vanderbilt Hospital. But he recovered and lived a little longer than a year.

Marshall Keeble asked Goodpasture to preach his funeral in case he went first. Keeble would sometimes tell this when his friend would be in the audience: "Some of these days I'm going to leave here, and I want Brother Goodpasture to preach my funeral. And I don't want you boys going around crying. I want you to know Brother Keeble has gone where he wants to be."

Marshall Keeble died in the spring of 1968. Keeble's "wake" was held in the Jackson Street church, his home congregation, on a Wednesday evening. After an hour of reading from the Bible, the singing of hymns, and a few brief eulogies, the prayer meeting service ended. Afterwards whoever wished to speak, to lead a song, or a prayer could do so.

Ira North arranged for the funeral of Marshall Keeble to be preached in the auditorium of the Madison church building. B. C. Goodpasture preached the funeral sermon. There was no weeping. The audience was sad because the "Happy Soldier" of the Cross had gone on and not in this world would they see him again.

Goodpasture was honored to claim the incomparable N. B. Hardeman as his friend. What a formidable pair they were! They lost no skirmishes and no battles as they stood together "contending earnestly for the faith." And their brethren were never puzzled to know where they stood on a church issue. Hardeman and Goodpasture knew the difference between the "broad side" of the Bible sword and its "narrow cutting edge."

Goodpasture said he did not know just how he and Hardeman came to be such close friends. But they were and mainly because two great uncommon men shared a great common cause. In the later years of his life, N. B. Hardeman requested Goodpasture to preach his funeral.

In the biography of N. B. Hardeman titled *N. B. H.* by J. M. Powell and Mary Nelle Powers, the great friends of Hardeman are named: B. B. James, L. R. Wilson, Douglas Perkins, J. M. Powell, Stoy Pate, Guy N. Woods, E. J. Estes, and B. C. Goodpasture.

The climax of N. B. Hardeman's life came on the evening of May 18, 1959, in the Peabody Hotel in Memphis, Tennessee, on the celebration of Hardeman's eighty-fifth birthday. The dignitaries surrounding Hardeman on that occasion included Governor Buford Ellington, Senator Albert Gore, and a future president of the United States, Lyndon B. Johnson. B. C. Goodpasture was the main speaker on that eventful evening. He said on that occasion that "had Diogenes lived in our time, he would have stopped with Brother Hardeman in his search for a man."

At the age of ninety-one, N. B. Hardeman died on November 5, 1965, in Memphis, Tennessee. B. C. Goodpasture conducted his funeral in the Highland church. J. M. Powell spoke on the occasion; Stoy Pate and W. B. West led the prayers. The graveside service was conducted by B. B. James in Henderson, Tennessee.

A great many persons have counted B. C. Goodpasture as a good friend. And it should be mentioned Goodpasture has his own favorite friends, and Guy N Woods is singularly honored in this fashion. Roy Vaughan remarked: "Goodpasture highly respects Guy N. Woods' ability to handle a controversy." Woods has demonstrated that rare talent as he appears on the Freed-Hardeman College Lectureship forum year after year with the complete confidence of his brethren.

Guy N. Woods has been a staff writer of the *Advocate* a long time. He travels constantly holding meetings throughout the brotherhood; and he knows the brotherhood and he knows what is going on. From time to time Goodpasture and Woods talk about the church and the brotherhood issues. Woods appraised Goodpasture in this manner:

> Long ago, I learned to trust him implicity, and he has never failed me. In a relationship which has involved matters ranging all the way from things spiritual to those material and financial, in not one instance have we had occasion to be disappointed, dissatisfied, or distrustful of his decisions and actions. In calm, deliberate fashion, he has ever exhibited the knack of getting to the root of a matter in moments, and of viewing it in proper perspective. Among the most magnificent characteristics of this great man are his balanced judgment, 'sweet reasonableness,' and calm appraisal of the problems which pile up in mountainous detail before a man in his position. Those who are closely associated with him soon come to know and to appreciate highly these outstanding personal features. There is an utter absence of peevishness in his dealings with difficult people, and I have again and again seen him exhibit amusement at the antics of others which would have been a source of much irritation and anger to others not thus constituted.

Whoever works with B. C. Goodpasture never has to learn or even to suspect at a later time that he has been used as a pawn in some kind of ploy. To out maneuver a man just to beat him as in a game of chess is repugnant to his nature. He is not the man to let a friend down because he is no longer useful to him. Goodpasture does not prepare a new face for an occasion. He is the same man at all times. His friends find him an enigma because of his extreme self-reserve in personal contacts, but duplicity is foreign to his nature.

There have been times when men were accused of things they weren't guilty of who were on the *Advocate* staff. Goodpasture would make his investigation; and when he was convinced of their

innocence, he did everything he could to vindicate them. Several
years ago, the influence of Leslie G. Thomas would have probably
been compromised had it not been for Goodpasture. The matter
had arisen over Thomas' teachings on the Holy Spirit.
Goodpasture saw it as a matter of terminology. To express his
personal confidence in him, Goodpasture made Leslie G. Thomas an
Advocate staff writer and editor of the *Gospel Advocate, Teachers
Annual Lesson Commentary.* This is just one case where Goodpasture saved a useful man for the church. Goodpasture said, "I
think it is as necessary to defend a good man as it is to condemn
a bad one."

Was it G. K. Chesterton who remarked: "All reputations, except those of utter imbeciles, dwindle and rise again; capable men
are praised twice, first for the wrong reasons and then, after a
cycle of obloquy, for the right reasons."

Perhaps B. C. Goodpasture will wear well in the hands of
church historians in future if we may judge from the approval he
has enjoyed in his lifetime. Perhaps no single group of men have
made themselves better known to Goodpasture than the leaders in
the Christian colleges. Beginning with H. Leo Boles, N. B.
Hardeman, and including Athens Clay Pullias, George S. Benson,
H. A. Dixon, Rex Turner, L. R. Wilson, M. Norvel Young, and
others, each in turn has his own story to tell of Goodpasture's loyalty to their causes and that would require a book to do justice to
their story.

L. R. Wilson out of his own deep and profound knowledge of
church matters wrote: "It is doubtful if the financial contributions
of any one man have meant as much to all Christian schools as have
the combined contributions received by them as a result of the encouragement given by the present editor of the *Gospel Advocate.*"

B. C. Goodpasture is a man who stands by his friends and detractors alike when they stand for the right. Just a while ago, he
commented: "If I have any personal enemies, I don't know it."
And to manage his life in such a manner, he explained, "I have
been trying to go by the 'Golden Rule' and treat the other fellow
like I would have him treat me."

XIV

The Man

The life of a public man is like a book that may be opened and read. A reader is sometimes slowed down by an uncut page here and there which must be opened with a penknife or torn apart. Not a few but could wish that some of the "uncut pages" of his life would never come to light again. The life of B. C. Goodpasture, in spite of the fact that no man knows his full story, is an open record. There is no need to gloss over any part of it. The writer is restrained from turning the biography into an unabashed eulogy of the man.

There is one valid approach to understanding a man—to track him down the years beginning with his family and childhood companions, his peer associates from early to late in life, and his working yokefellows, and detractors if they are around. Goodpasture has lived his entire life in three communities—the first nineteen years around Flat Creek, four years in David Lipscomb College, eighteen years in Atlanta save three, and the years since to the present time in Nashville, Tennessee, on Caldwell Lane.

There is no problem in following his foot prints, and there are no missing gaps. This chapter contains little information that is not somewhere in this study reflected in another context. The content of this chapter may give the impression of an unstructured omnibus, and this is the studied design of its content.

The close acquaintances of B. C. Goodpasture over a long period of time know him well, but he still remains a charming puzzle that they are unable to fully unravel. There is an old folk saying that "still waters run deep." Ships can move over oceans of great depth and mountainous waves may only be churned from such seas. Shallow men are easily gauged, but men of genius may never be. May it be said here that Goodpasture is no ordinary man by any human standard.

Actually, B. C. Goodpasture does not study to be inscrutable. This is partially due to the fact that the Goodpastures are by nature a taciturn people. Any calculated attempt to draw the Goodpastures out in a conversation generally proves to be disappointing. There are, however, a good many persons who know Goodpasture well; and for them, it is no problem at all to portray the man as he deserves to be made known.

In the first place, B. C. Goodpasture is by far the most influential person among the churches of Christ today. This is in nowise intended to underrate a large number of good men of splendid talents who serve in different capacities in the church today. The influence of Goodpasture, however, is not contingent to any particular power base. The *Gospel Advocate* is a tower of strength to promote the spiritual growth of the church and to encourage good men in their work in the church everywhere. To be sure, the *Advocate* has been the leading journal among the churches of Christ for more than a century. Any journal, religious or secular, is dependent for its character and usefulness upon its editor and supporting staff writers. In a similar fashion David Lipscomb gave character to the *Gospel Advocate,* so has B. C. Goodpasture supported the rich heritage of all the past years of its publication.

Editing the *Gospel Advocate* is no small matter because of its great influence in the church, but it is here that the stature of Goodpasture becomes apparent. The pressures are constant and numerous. Goodpasture because of his position has received the most fulsome adulation from both sincere and self-seeking persons, and he has suffered the most caustic attacks from some who have differed with him. Weak men wilt under such assaults, and shallow men frequently yield to vanity. The editor has not bent either to the one or the other. He has followed the course that he thought would most likely advance the church, and in this he has not failed.

As brought out in other places, Goodpasture is not a man that is easily approached; but once his confidence has been won and he is persuaded that a person is not self-seeking, talking with him is a pleasing and memorable experience. To those who come to seek his counsel, he is gracious and willing to listen and to give counsel and guidance.

Batsell Barrett Baxter describing the editor remarked that sometimes he is very severe even to the point of being non-committal. This grows out of the fact that Goodpasture calculates the end results of both his spoken and written words as well as those of his staff writers. He is not the man to be goaded into irrational actions. Fred Mosley who served as assistant to the *Advocate* editor for several years remarked, "When Brother Goodpasture decides to use his influence, every interested person in the brotherhood knows it and not a few feel it." This is especially true when he decides to commit the *Advocate* to a course of action. Occasionally, some brother will react with great feeling about some article that does not please him or serve his personal interest. But after he simmers down, such a person decides it is best not to make an issue of the matter.

J. D. Thomas, Head of the Bible Department of Abilene Christian College and a third cousin of Goodpasture accurately summed up the editor: "As an editor of the *Advocate,* he has of course demonstrated the qualities of a strong character—strong enough to withstand the pressures of such an assignment . . . Brother Goodpasture's tenure as *Advocate* editor has been a great day for the Church, and we all have reason to be grateful for his work."

G. K. Wallace who has contributed many articles to the *Advocate* and continues to write from time to time summed up the man: "He cannot be stampeded. His actions are never based upon emotions, personal preferences, love of prestige, nor the desire for popularity. He has always acted out of a sense of right or wrong."

Athens Clay Pullias has worked closely throughout the years with B. C. Goodpasture and knows him as well as any person in the church. Pullias wrote this interesting description of the man:

> I have had the pleasure of relaxing with him as we hunted the fields together. He is an expert marksman with a gun. I remember one day when we were hunting quail that the dog pointed a covey in a small growth of sumac shrubs higher than a man's head. When the birds rose from the ground, they whipped directly over our heads at a speed that was dazzling. Calmly, Brother Goodpasture, shooting almost straight up, dropped two of them in quick succession. In doing so, his expression hardly changed, and there

was no outward sign of excitement. This brilliant display of shooting skill has seemed to me typical of his life as an editor and as a preacher.

B. C. Goodpasture has an overpowering singular interest in education. He has spent a lifetime improving his mind. Goodpasture has supported all the Christian colleges as they deserved support over the years and continues to do so. The very fact that the *Advocate* will carry the advertisement of a Christian school means that it has the editor's approval. L. R. Wilson was a trusted confidant of Goodpasture. Wilson served as the first presidents of Florida Christian College and Central Christian College; and the *Advocate* served as one of his mighty towers of strength, and he wrote:

> Any time one of our schools has deviated from what he believed to be in keeping with the ideals set forth in the New Testament, Brother Goodpasture has not hesitated to sound the alarm—firm and strong. And he has not used platitudes, generalities, or innuendoes in doing so. He has called names and specified the charges in clarion tones. This he has done with an awareness of the bitter criticism that he was bringing down upon his head. But this has not deterred him from his responsibilities as the editor of a great publication.

Goodpasture has supported all the Christian schools with studied impartiality, but David Lipscomb College (Nashville Bible School) is his first love. Whatever concerns his Alma Mater matters to him. A beautiful room in the Chrisman Memorial Library was dedicated to B. C. Goodpasture in the spring of 1958 during the lectureship honoring at the time preachers with forty or more years of preaching experience. Goodpasture will give a total of five thousand volumes to the library over a period of time.

There is another side to B. C. Goodpasture that needs to be told, and no other person is better qualified to tell it than Batsell Barrett Baxter. In the spring of 1951 Baxter was approached about following Goodpasture as minister of the Hillsboro church. Baxter stated that he had some serious reservations about following Goodpasture who was away at the time the offer was made to him, but he went ahead and accepted the responsibility. Baxter thinking about the occasion a short while ago said: "At first, being relatively young at the time, I felt his presence in the audience knowing of his scholarship and abilities. Yet he went out of the way to minimize that and offered his cooperation in any way that I might need it."

Baxter worked twenty years with the Hillsboro church before resigning to give more time to the Herald of Truth Bible program and his responsibilities as Chairman of the Bible Department in David Lipscomb College. Goodpasture was appointed an elder in the Hillsboro church soon after he gave up the pulpit there. J. W. McDonough acted for the other elders inviting Brother Goodpasture to join them. Baxter said what he appreciated most about him was that he made his work easier. Baxter said, "Through most of those years, I have not felt any sensitivity to his presence. I have just known that he was for me."

As an elder, Goodpasture is most thoughtful for every aspect of the work. He has not wanted to become a leading elder and never a dominating elder. He has leaned over backwards not to become such.

The members of the Hillsboro church know him well. Goodpasture is present for about fifty or sixty percent of the services. Throughout the years, he has been glad to teach the auditorium class. His method of teaching is to take a book and teach it verse by verse which he does in a great way. Sometimes he will spend a whole period on two or three verses.

Since he came to the Hillsboro church in 1939, the Hillsboro members love him in no diminished way. He seldom preaches there, but he looks forward to the opportunity and so does the congregation. They love him with a strong loyalty and they respect him very highly along with the other Hillsboro elders.

In the elders' meetings, he remains as unobtrusive as he possibly can. When they ask him for a judgment, he gives it. Goodpasture never tries to influence a decision; but when he gives his judgment, it is influential. The Hillsboro elders have manila folders with their work assignments in them. Goodpasture's folder is the most ornate with his drawings on the cover. Baxter said his art work was not good—but better than his which was about average.

Baxter who is one of the outstanding preachers in his generation holds his doctorate in speech from the University of Southern California. He thoughtfully evaluated the qualities of B. C. Goodpasture as a preacher. As a young man, Goodpasture had few equals and no superiors. His great dignity, empathy, and ethical persuasion

were unmatched. A handsome man, he stands straight in the pulpit and gives a solid appearance with a pleasing voice.

The message of Goodpasture is strong and is worked out with
great creativity and historical imagination. Ordinarily his sermons are not emotional as such, but marked by a subdued kind of
emotion. He is a polished speaker with superb poise. He is never
off balance, and he has something appropriate to say, no matter
what the occasion, in keeping with what needed to be said about it.

The invitations at the end of the sermons are not strong appeals. He summarizes in a low key and offers the invitation.
Everything Goodpasture says can be depended upon. His scholarship is a great part of his message. The audience is never aware
of his organization. He knows where he is going and when he
gets there he stops. He doesn't preach long sermons.

Baxter stated that he too had heard people remark that Goodpasture was cool and kind of aloof, but that was because they did
not know him. Indeed there are times when Goodpasture is stern
and will hardly respond. Generally that is one of the occasions
when he is called upon to make an important decision without
ample time to think the proposition through.

Goodpasture is a leader in so many ways in the church. He
has been a steadying influence in the church without being a cru-
sader and a name caller and stirring up the brotherhood. He is
just taking a solid stand. He has not allowed the *Advocate* to be
used for hurting anybody or any cause. His influence has been
quiet and unobtrusive. The *Advocate* does not contain an editorial
in every issue from his hand, but his stand is known and that has
quieted many a brotherhood issue.

Baxter commented what others have said that the editor pur-
sues a course that would most likely honor and advance the
church. There are those who have disagreed with Goodpasture
and still respect him as much as they do any man. This is true
because people see in him an absolute honesty. He stands for
what he believes is right and he does not take a stand quickly.
And when he does take a stand, he stands firmly without being belligerent. No other person has a stabilizing influence in the
brotherhood equal to his.

Baxter thoughtfully added that he could think of no person that
B. C. Goodpasture had deliberately hurt, but he could think of a
lot of people he had helped. Goodpasture has a very tender heart

and would go out of his way to right any hurt any person thought
he had received from him.

Sometimes a person wants the editor to do him a favor and he
does not feel that he can. Then sometimes he will be quiet because
he has not been sold on a cause. Goodpasture has from time to
time picked up a man who was in pretty dire straits and helped
him back on his feet again. And the story could go on.
Goodpasture hurries through life slowly in a very calm and delib-
erate way.

The B. C. Goodpasture that his friends know have different
things to say about him to explain his nature. He was unlike others even as a boy. Goodpasture is marked by singular characteristics unchanged by time. Roy Vaughan recalls this about him during the Nashville Bible School days:

> He was a different type from the rest of the students. You
> never heard Goodpasture get into low talk about anybody
> and say things a lot of people would. He kept his part of
> the conversation on a high level when he would talk about
> other folks. If he did say anything critical, it was pretty
> sharp.

Vaughan describes Goodpasture's taciturn nature in the following fashion:

> He's not a gushy kind of fellow. If you talk to him on a
> subject of interest to him, he is very interesting to talk to.
> He doesn't waste time carrying on a lot of foolishness. He
> just doesn't talk like a great many people do. But when
> you get close to him and get him in a conversation down to
> nature, he is very warm hearted.

The name of B. C. Goodpasture gradually found its way into
the brotherhood through the *Gospel Advocate*. Frank Pack, Head
of the Bible Department in George Pepperdine College remembers Goodpasture from the Atlanta years and came to know in
time the warm friendship Goodpasture gives to young men beginning their ministry. Pack describes Goodpasture as so many appreciate him: "He has always been a Christian gentleman of the
highest type; one who is not easily swayed by the emotions of the
hour; and one who does not give up his basic convictions."
Goodpasture has an unflagging loyalty to his friends that the years
do not waste away. The loyalty that Goodpasture commands from
both his friends and detractors is deserved. He will grind no

J. Cliett Goodpasture

Marlin F. Connelly, Jr.

James Lee McDonough

Prentice Meador, Jr.

man's ax and serve at no man's table for a morsel of bread; and for this, those who disagree with him admire him for such courage and conviction. The long years of public service have deepened and tempered his wisdom.

The fact has been brought out that Goodpasture seldom reveals his feelings. But he has a long and good memory. Sometimes he will chastise a particularly talkative fellow out California way when he remembers he once carried the banner for suspected pre-millennialists or some other "off brand" church matter. Goodpasture said that "if I ever tell a person something in confidence and he repeats it, I remember never to tell that fellow anything again." Goodpasture possesses a powerful and trenchant wit, but he is much too wise and decent to engage in ridicule of any form or in personal abuse.

That Goodpasture is a buyer and seller of books was told in another place. But this is only a part of the story. Paul Hunton was baptized when he was just a boy by Goodpasture in Atlanta while Goodpasture was preaching for the West End Avenue church. Hunton remembers trips he would make with Goodpasture to rummage sales and railroad depots to purchase damaged merchandise which he would sell at a profit, and sometimes the profit would be a handsome one. Hunton remembers a kind of "flea market" they would go to—"one place was frightening. It was under the city of Atlanta. Now it has been modernized and is one of Atlanta's show places." And unto this day, this is still an exciting hobby for Brother Goodpasture that he enjoys.

There is another side to B. C. Goodpasture that reads like all the rest, but with a difference. The employees of the Gospel Advocate Company love him and they don't try to conceal the fact. Irvin Wilson, manager of the Advocate Book Store since 1946, said: "You couldn't find a better boss in the world." Wilson said he never remembered seeing Goodpasture angry, or even raising his voice with an employee. He gives all of the help a great deal of freedom, but he expects them to come to him with problems that might reflect on the Gospel Advocate Company. Wilson observed: "He shows more concern than he does emotions."

Goodpasture treats all the Advocate employees alike. When he comes from a trip, he has time to talk to the delivery boy or anyone else who comes to him with a problem or who wants some advice. The editor insists that the work and behavior of each employee to be of such character as to reflect credit on the Gospel Advocate Company.

Mary H. Goolsby shares one of the front office desks as secretary to the editor, and she described a typical day in the Advocate office. Goodpasture comes in around 8:30 each morning and asks for his mail. He enjoys his mail and opens the letters and reads them. Then around 9 o'clock, he will drink his coffee. During the day he spends considerable time looking over articles from staff writers and other articles from brethren around the world. A considerable amount of foreign mail comes to his desk, and he saves the stamps for Mary Goolsby's sixteen year old daughter.

Goodpasture reads every article that goes into the *Advocate* and all of the materials which go into the *Gospel Advocate Quarterlies*. He checks out word by word each Scripture reference to make certain that every article and lesson is letter correct. Mary Goolsby helps proofread the Uniform Bible Lesson Schedule. The writing assignments are mailed to the *Advocate* writers at least fifteen months before they are due. Mary Goolsby also helps in checking each item which is included in the *Advocate* catalogue.

The editor goes to lunch around noon each day and returns around 1:30 p.m. All during the day, he is busy receiving long distance as well as local telephone calls. Visitors come in daily from around the country and throughout the world to tell him how much the *Advocate* has helped them especially in mission fields. The *Advocate* is a reliable source of information about the character of preachers and other workers who deserve help to carry the gospel message at home and abroad. Roy Vaughan said that about the only times he had seen the editor peeved would be when he allowed some individual's name to appear in the "News and Notes" section of the *Advocate* which should not have appeared. And Goodpasture would say: "Now how many more times do I need to mention this?" The office help is always stopping at the office door to ask him how to spell a word or to locate some foreign country where an order is being shipped.

Each Christmas the Goodpastures host a party for all the office help in their home. After being served a full course meal, they exchange gifts. And such stories could go on without end.

B. C. Goodpasture is especially loved and appreciated by his kinfolks. Billie Ruth Bilyeu Hill's memories of B. C. Goodpasture go back to the time when she was a little girl growing up in

the Flat Creek community.   Her maternal grandfather and B. C.'s
father were brothers—Jim and John Goodpasture. When she was
just a child, Billie remembers his crossing the fields in his hunting
clothes with a hunting companion.   On one occasion, she told
someone that B. C. was her uncle, and she was so disappointed
when her mother corrected her and said that he was her cousin.

Billie Hill said that he always seemed to have a special fond-
ness for children.   When he came to Flat Creek on his visits, he
always had his pockets filled with surprise gifts for the children.
This is a special trait of the editor.   A visitor stopping by the
office seldom leaves without a ballpoint pen or something with the
Gospel Advocate name on it. Cliett, his youngest son, said that
the grandchildren could always expect some gift that he would
have in his pockets much to their delight.

Billie Hill wanted to attend David Lipscomb College and could
not because of a lack of finances. Goodpasture gave her a job in the
Advocate office and saw to it that she was financed through school.
She is married to Malcolm Hill, a well known gospel preacher.
What endeared Goodpasture even more to them is the love and
compassion which he shows for their daughter who has been a dia-
betic since she was six months old.   After visiting in their home
and learning how Tammi was susceptible to numerous infections, he
went out and bought the very best dishwasher he could find to help
in preventing infections. Such generous acts have marked the passage of Goodpasture's life.   There is no way to calculate the personal financial helps that he has given to his people including deserving persons who were of no blood kinship.

J. M. Powell who is a widely known Christian evangelist
summed the man as he is known to him over a period of thirty-six
years:

> The man in many respects is a genius.   He possesses more
> knowledge on more subjects than any person I have ever
> known.   He evidently has a photographic mind and never
> forgets anything.   As a pulpiteer, he has no superiors, and
> few if any equals.   When he speaks, one has the impression
> that he knows what he is talking about.   He knows that he
> knows and doesn't want to be second rate at anything
> From the beginning, as editor of the *Gospel Advocate*, he
> has made a determination to be on the right side on every
> question of controversy.   In my judgment, he has suc-
> ceeded with one possible exception.

According to J. M. Powell that gives Brother Goodpasture almost a 1000 batting average, and that is about perfect in anybody's record book. Plato of Athens wrote: "'that the idea of the good is the highest knowledge, and that all other things become useful and advantageous by their use of it." Such is the story of the life of B. C. Goodpasture. It is a joy to meet with the Goodpasture clan in one of their family gatherings in the Flat Creek community. Ray Goodpasture has lived all of his life around Flat Creek. He too helped his father with the younger children while they were growing up, and he is equally endeared to the Goodpasture children for his own worth. And for such likes of the Goodpasture clan, "may their tribe increase."

XV

The Four Anchors

There are decisions that a person makes in life that may neither be changed nor altered. The consequences are as certain as the issues of life. Luke graphically describes the raging storm that caught up the ship that was bearing the apostle Paul to Rome. The storm continued unabated into the fourteenth night, and every person on board the ship was in despair for his own life. On the fourteenth night, the sailors knew the ship was nearing land, and they cast four anchors into the sea to hold the ship from being dashed ashore. After day came, Paul warned every person to stay on the ship or perish in the sea. The sailors cut away the anchors and hoisted the foresail, and the ship was driven ashore without a life lost.

B. C. Goodpasture has learned with the experience of the years when to take hold and when to let go. Now in his seventy-seventh year and as a long-time editor and evangelist, he continues to move forward with confidence in his destiny whatever it may be. His confidence grows out of his conviction that God is working out his purpose in the course of time. Goodpasture accepts the Bible as a revelation from God to man. He believes that the New Testament church is a divinely appointed institution. Whoever has entertained for a moment that Goodpasture would negotiate a compromise with Bible truths never had to wait long to learn that he would not compromise no matter what the enticements seemed to be. At a time when most men are anxious to retire from the pressures of life, Goodpasture continues to serve as editor of the *Advocate* with the confidence of the church in no undiminished way. Few there be who would question the present course of the "Old Reliable," but there are a great many people who are concerned with the direction of the *Advocate* in the years ahead.

In addition to being editor since 1939, Goodpasture has served as president of the Gospel Advocate Company since 1950 with the general oversight of the publications and sale of all books, Sunday and Bible school literature, and the publishing of the *Gospel Advocate*. He also serves as the editor-in-chief of Sunday school and Bible school literature. Along with J. Roy Vaughan, every word is read and tested against the Scriptures to weed out any statement that is not crystal clear in a scriptural context.

The centennial of the founding of the *Gospel Advocate* was celebrated July 14, 1955, in a special issue of the paper. Goodpasture wrote for the occasion:

> It has been one round century since the natal day of the 'Old Reliable.' During that time according to one authority, more than four hundred religious papers have been started and failed among those who sought to restore the New Testament order of things. But the *Gospel Advocate* under the same name and in the same city has weathered the storm for a hundred years.

Since the founding of the *Gospel Advocate* by Tolbert Fanning and William Lipscomb, David Lipscomb and E. G. Sewell, J. C. McQuiddy, A. B. Lipscomb, H. Leo Boles, James A. Allen, Foy E. Wallace, Jr., John T. Hinds, and B. C. Goodpasture have served as editors of the *Advocate* in this order. Only David Lipscomb served over a longer period of time than B. C. Goodpasture.

A new and singular dimension was added to the life of B. C. Goodpasture in the late part of 1965. On November 11, 1965, he was married to Mrs. Freddie Goetz in the home of Mrs. Otis Payne Grant, a daughter of the late A. M. Burton and his wife who is still living. Zell Burton, as the daughter of the Burtons is called, was a student in the David Lipscomb Primary Department when Goodpasture came as a student in 1914, and a mutual friendship started and has grown over the years.

Batsell Barrett Baxter and Willard Collins performed the wedding ceremony. The children of both families were present including Patsy Powell Mitchell and her husband. Patsy is the daughter of J. M. and Mildred Powell. Wanda Baxter and Ruth Collins accompanied their husbands. A reception for the newlyweds was later hosted in the home of J. L. Perry and his wife with the help of Mr. and Mrs. Aubrey Shaub, Mr. and Mrs. Robert Walker, and Mrs. Otis Payne Grant. The marriage of B. C. Goodpasture to Freddie Goetz was a matter of interest to a great many people in Nashville and many other places. Freddie Goetz was a relative newcomer to Nashville. She had been preceded by her lovely daughter who had enrolled in David Lipscomb College in 1960. Almanda Goetz came to Lipscomb because it was a Christian college.

Freddie Goetz was married at that time to J. C. Fremont Goetz, a large land holder and business man in Sikeston, Missouri. Fremont, as he was called by his acquaintances, was highly respected in the Sikeston area and by others who knew him in widely scattered places. Fremont enjoyed hunting; and during the duck and goose season, he counted among the guests in his home a United States ambassador and other dignitaries. Fremont Goetz died suddenly in 1961 on horseback while riding with a patrol at a horseshow in Sikeston. Freddie Goetz was suddenly left with her two daughters Alamanda Sue Goetz and Marky Bess Goetz. Marky was just seven years old at the time. Fremont Goetz had been the kind of man in life that resulted in his being honored in death by a great number of people who came to pay their last respects including two state governors, and the sharecroppers who too had been generously welcomed into the Goetz home.

Freddie Goetz was born August 17, 1918, as Freddie Joan Armstrong. She was the daughter of Mark D. Armstrong who was born November 2, 1886, in Granbury, Texas. His father was William S. Armstrong who was a Civil War veteran. He was a prisoner in New York for two years. He would tell the story that the only dishonest thing he ever did was to copy his discharge papers putting another man's name in who was dying of homesickness so he could go home.

The mother of Mark D. Armstrong was Janie Messer Armstrong. Her grandfather was scalped by the Indians in 1863 at the foot of Commanche Peak in Hood County, Texas. A large monument in Hood County gives the details. He was the first white man to be buried in that area. The grandmother would tell how a lookout was kept to watch for the presence of Indians. If Indians were spotted they would keep absolutely quiet, and the mothers would press their small children close to their breasts to keep them from crying out.

The mother of Freddie Goetz is Cordia Sue Armstrong who was born November 2, 1890, in Granbury, Texas. Her father was William Fred Sue. He was separated from his brothers and twin sisters during the Civil War, and he was sixty-three before they were re-united. The mother of Cordia Sue Armstrong was Amanda Tippitt Sue. Her father was a slave owner; and after the Civil War, the black people requested permission to continue to live with them.

In addition to Freddie, there were seven other children born to Mark and Cordia Armstrong—Opal, V. H., Hettie Lena, Sue, Mark, Jr., C. P., and Mollie Kate. All of them are living in Texas. Mark D. Armstrong died recently. Freddie said that was the first death in the immediate family for sixty-four years. Freddie Goodpasture remembers her parents as open-hearted and generous people who taught their children by example to respond to the needs of others. While she was just a child, there were three families in the neighborhood whose mothers had passed away. Cordia Sue Armstrong would have the children, on their way home from school, sometimes as many as seven each day, to stop by for homemade bread, popcorn, or sweet breads. The Armstrongs were of church of Christ background. And at the recent funeral of Mark D. Armstrong, the minister took as his text James 1: 27 to describe his generous and good life. Mark D. Armstrong and his wife had been married sixty-four years at the time of his death. In addition to their eight children, there are twenty-three grandchildren and twenty-three great-grandchildren.

After the death of Fremont Goetz, Freddie and Marky continued to live in Sikeston while Mandy continued her schooling in David Lipscomb College. Mandy was married in 1963 to Roger D. Meyer of Salem, Indiana, who was also a Lipscomb student. Roger had to serve his stint in the army before he finished his degree. He was sent to Germany. Mandy did not accompany him since she was expecting their first child, Monty Goetz.

Freddie and Marky later accompanied Mandy to Germany, and Monty Goetz was born in Germany. They stayed in Germany eleven months before they returned to the States. Freddie and Marky toured several of the European countries and met several of the church missionaries. Freddie became interested in a Christian youth camp in Bern, Switzerland, and worked there for awhile during the summer. She continued to raise funds and send personal contributions to the camp after returning to this country.

When the families returned from Germany in 1964, Freddie moved to Nashville to put Marky in the David Lipscomb Elementary School. Freddie enrolled as a special student in the college to study German which grew out of her interest to do missionary work at a later time. She also enrolled in a Bible class taught by Willard Collins. Freddie took a special interest in the college students and especially those who were having a difficult time financially. She helped such students with just one request that they would later help other deserving students as they became financially able. Her home was opened to the college students and they enjoyed the gracious generosity of the Goetz home.

Freddie became involved in church work which included several Christian charities. While no public announcements were made anywhere, it is not possible for matters of that kind to go unnoticed. Freddie and Marky made the Hillsboro church their church home; and as would naturally be the case, B. C. Goodpasture was aware of their presence.

Mandy and Roger continued their work in David Lipscomb College; and in the spring of 1966, they graduated from the college. Marky graduated from the David Lipscomb High School in the spring of 1971. She is now a freshman in Freed-Hardeman College. Marky's interest in Freed-Hardeman College came after the death of her father to whom she was deeply devoted. H. A. Dixon had come to hold a meeting in Sikeston, and the young preacher, Jimmy Miller and his wife, invited Freddie and Marky to come over to their home to help entertain the Dixons at the evening meal.

That evening as they were going into the church, H. A. Dixon reached down and took Marky's hand. That night she told her mother, "Brother Dixon held my hand just like Daddy did." Freddie and Marky found a good friend in H. A. Dixon as so many others did in his lifetime. Later Marky suggested to her mother that she be allowed to use some of her money to build a cottage and a bath house for the Mid South Youth Camp in Henderson, Tennessee. President Dixon had earlier persuaded Freddie to send Marky to the camp for a short while. Marky has since spent a part of each summer at the camp and served as a counsellor this past summer. Freddie sent her thirty-second "camper" to the Mid South Youth Camp this summer.

Mandy and Marky are especially talented and intelligent young ladies. Each won her own place among their associates in the school and the church. Mandy and Roger now have another boy who is named Roger D., Jr. They are actively engaged in church work and other useful activities.

The presence of Freddie Goetz and her family naturally elicited interest and comment in the college and particularly in the Hillsboro church. Freddie Goetz's first personal contact with B. C. Goodpasture came in the spring of 1965. Joan Howard, daughter of Jennie Howard who is the youngest sister of B. C. Goodpasture, was thinking of going to Japan as a missionary and she felt that she should first consult her uncle. Joan carried along Freddie as a support for the occasion. He listened but made no comment about what he thought of the proposal at the time.

Later he called Freddie and discussed the matter with her concerning Joan. Following that call, B. C. and Freddie talked almost every evening by phone. After a few weeks, he came over one evening to talk with Freddie and Marky who was eleven at the time. Zell Grant told Freddie a short time later, "If B. C. is in your presence three times, he is interested in marrying you." Freddie's primary concern had all along been for Marky's welfare. The death of her father had left her deeply troubled. B. C. Goodpasture is deeply devoted to his children and children of all ages are attracted to him. It soon became apparent to Freddie that he had won the child's admiration, and Marky approved of the marriage when the plans were far advanced. After the marriage of B. C. and Freddie, the child was concerned that her mother's name was different from hers. B. C. and Freddie Goodpasture had her name legally changed to "Goodpasture." So now she proudly wears the name Marky Goetz Goodpasture. She affectionately addresses her stepfather as "Pop," and so does Mandy and her children.

B. C. Goodpasture has been in good health all of his life and is remarkably strong at the present. But he has long suffered with a chronic asthmatic condition. The only present danger to his health grows out of virus infections which could possibly run into pneumonia. A few years back the doctors despaired for his life in a long period of a respiratory illness. A strong heart and a rugged constitution have kept him going.

A great many advantages have accrued to both since their marriage. A man alone can not carry on numerous multiple responsibilities as does B. C. Goodpasture without constant and reliable help. He has such help in the Advocate editorial offices, and Freddie Goodpasture has become a supporting pillar in their home and in his work as the *Advocate* editor and evangelist. She entered the marriage fully realizing that it was no small matter to be the wife of B. C. Goodpasture, and she meant to assume her responsibilities from the start.

Freddie has been especially solicitous for her husband's health. She accompanies him on all of his preaching appointments Sundays and during gospel meetings. Goodpasture said about his wife in this connection: "She has been willing in the later years of my life to take my hand and walk with me." During the gospel meetings, Freddie writes to their many friends in all sections of the country and especially to the "shut-ins" much to their appreciation. She frequently speaks to ladies' classes and other groups of women on matters of Christian concern.

Only one problem has grown out of the marriage. Freddie must be away from Marky more than she would like to be. Many of the preaching appointments of Goodpasture are around Nashville; however, some are in Texas, Florida, and New York and other states. But his speaking engagements and his responsibilities as editor would tax the time and energy of any man whatever his age. Marky is an alert and self-reliant girl. She never feels neglected because she is constantly assured of her mother's and Pop's love and the home of her sister provides her with all the temporary security she needs. Freddie and her children are accepted and appreciated in the circles where B. C. Goodpasture moves.

Following the marriage of B. C. Goodpasture, and Freddie, they went to Atlanta, Georgia, for a meeting with the Forest Park church of Christ. The meeting had been scheduled for some time. Malcolm Hill was preaching there at the time. On Wednesday evening before the meeting began, Goodpasture phoned Malcolm and told him, "I have a surprise for you."

Malcolm asked, "What is it Brother Goodpasture?"

And he told him, "Malcolm, I am getting married tomorrow, and I am going to bring my wife with me to the meeting."

Mizella Burton Grant, Freddie Goodpasture
B. C. Goodpasture

Batsell Barrett Baxter, Willard Collins, B. C. Goodpasture

J. L. Perry, Ellouise Perry, B. C. Goodpasture,
Freddie Goodpasture

Malcolm almost dropped the phone in surprise. He had no in-
kling of the matter and finally asked, "Who is she, Brother Goodpasture?"

Goodpasture told him, "Freddie Goetz." That meant nothing
to Malcolm Hill since he had never met her.

The forthcoming meeting took a different tone after that. The
Hills could talk of nothing else and the church members in Atlanta
were anxiously awaiting to meet the new wife of B. C. Goodpasture. A great many different descriptions were given to the Hills
about Freddie, but none were like what they found her to be.
Billie Hill said a short time ago: "She was everything that we
hoped she would be for Brother Goodpasture. After being with
her for just a few minutes, it seemed like we had known her all of
our lives."

That was a week that will be long remembered by Freddie. It
was her first meeting with her husband. Eating out each day with
different people and trying to keep up with all that was going on
was especially difficult for her. When the meeting was finished,
the elders of the Forest Park church invited them to return each
year in August for their homecoming Sunday with Goodpasture
filling the pulpit. And they have kept the appointments.

The worth of Freddie Goodpasture to her husband is now fully
realized and appreciated. Her constant care is for his personal
welfare that he may continue with "strength unabated and eye
sight undimmed" in his work with the *Advocate*. Ray Goodpasture and his sisters love and appreciate their sister-in-law, and they
look forward to their visits in the Flat Creek neighborhood. And
in the midst of his family, B. C. Goodpasture enjoys some of his
favorite Cumberland Mountain food—cornbread and sweet milk.

Freddie Goetz Goodpasture is now an inseparable part of the
Goodpasture story. The worth of her role as the wife of B. C.
Goodpasture is generously recognized by all who have come into
their presence in their gracious and hospitable home, in the church,
and in general public life. Freddie soon learned that when her
husband came home, it was just the continuation of a day in the
Advocate editorial offices. Phone calls come in from around town
and all around the whole country from ocean to ocean and border
to border. He picks up the telephone and talks calmly and
thoughtfully with never the slightest indication that an intrusion is
being made on his time in the home. Since the closing weeks of

Roger, Jr., Roger D. Meyer, Almanda Goetz Meyer, Monty Goetz

Freddie Goodpasture

B.C. and Freddie Goodpasture,
Marky Bess Goetz Goodpasture

1965, Goodpasture has preached in eighty churches and conducted fifty-six gospel meetings through 1970. That B. C. Goodpasture has chosen to cast off the anchors and to press on in the mounting years of his life is not only to his honor and credit, but also in a double measure to Freddie Goodpasture who is standing by. It is not a thing surprising that B. C. Goodpasture has found a good wife in Freddie. His personal judgment has throughout his life been unusually good and so has it been also in the case of his second marriage.

The statement was made that life is not a measure to be emptied but to be filled with meaningful experiences. There has been no single crowning climax in the life of B. C. Goodpasture. The 1960's were fruitful years in his life. One of the greatest pleasures in the long and eventful career of Goodpasture is centered in the Nashville School of Preaching. Roy J. Hearn first brought up the matter to start such a school in Nashville. The Nashville School of Preaching was suggested by such schools already in existence in the West.

Roy Hearn first talked the matter over with Roy Vaughan in his Advocate office. Vaughan thought a great deal of the proposal. Hearn and Vaughan then met with H. Clyde Hale and E. Ray Jerkins to explore the possibilities in greater depths. Their next step was to invite Goodpasture to attend one of their meetings. He recognized the need for such a school and gave his endorsement to it. A general meeting of church members was called in the Waverly-Belmont church building for the men over the city to come in and discuss the matter. Their response was immediate and affirmative. Plans began to firm up for organizing the school.

Hearn and his associates asked Goodpasture to serve as chairman of the board and he accepted. J. Roy Vaughan was made vice-chairman; E. Ray Jerkins was named secretary; H. Clyde Hale was appointed treasurer; and Roy J. Hearn was to be director of the school. A central location for the school was sought, and the Waverly-Belmont elders made the church building available.

The Nashville School of Preaching was scheduled to open in the early part of 1966. Charles E. Chumley was added to the permanent faculty. The school opened February 6, 1966, meeting on Monday, Thursday, and Friday nights from seven to ten with no

Left to Right: Freddie Goodpasture, B. C. Goodpasture, Burton Coffman

Nashville School of Preaching: *Front row:* Charles Chumley, Charles R. Brewer, B. C. Goodpasture, Dorris Billingsley, E. Ray Perkins, J. Roy Vaughan.

tuition charge to the students. Such courses as the textual study of Bible, Bible geography, church history, and Greek were among the offerings.

Roy Hearn in the meantime had accepted the offer to start a similar school in Memphis. Charles R. Brewer, who had been added to the faculty, was made the temporary director of the school and later became permanent president of the Nashville School of Preaching and served until his untimely passing due to injuries suffered in a car accident. The original purpose of the school, which has not changed, is to help men to better prepare themselves to teach and preach the Bible and to better qualify them to serve as elders, deacons, and church workers. No academic credit is offered. The school draws men who have not had the opportunity to attend college and can not afford to do so and some men who have attended college. The classes are conducted in the evening enabling the men to work by day and study by night. Some of the students drive for the classes over a hundred miles in distance. Boys just out of high school may not enroll in the school since it is believed they should be encouraged to attend a Christian college to further their education.

The Nashville School of Preaching has prospered from the beginning. J. Roy Vaughan now serves as president of the school and Charles E. Chumley is dean. The latest session of the school started August 30, 1971, in the education building of the Hillsboro church with sixty-three men enrolled and others expected.

B. C. Goodpasture has taught Genesis and Acts since the school started, and his work with the school has afforded him one of the most useful pleasures of his life. Several of the graduates are now full time preachers and others are serving more usefully in the churches where they attend. His office door is especially open to the men of the Nashville School of Preaching. Goodpasture does not keep a time schedule of appointments. All visitors are welcome. Goodpasture's interest in the school is typical of the man. He saw another opportunity to advance the kingdom of God on earth and he took it.

A survey of the life and work of B. C. Goodpasture discovers that a large measure of his attention has been directed to Christian education. The school men have not been unmindful of his help. Harding College, George Pepperdine College, and Magic Valley Christian College bestowed the honorary doctor's degree upon B.

C. Goodpasture. At the present time, he is serving on the Freed-Hardeman Advisory Board. In 1968, the Greater Atlanta Christian School opened its doors; and a year later claimed assets of more than a million dollars. Since the school's founding, Goodpasture has been added to the board of directors. He is also a member of the board of directors of the Potter Orphan Home in Bowling Green, Kentucky.

Two Christian schools in Nashville, Tennessee, are named after the two most illustrous editors of the *Gospel Advocate*—David Lipscomb College and the B. C. Goodpasture Christian School. Sometime in 1964 a group of interested men in East Nashville started talking about launching a Christian elementary school in East Nashville. Their main reason for locating a school in East Nashville was to place a Christian school in reach of their children. One of the largest concentrations of Christians on this earth is east of the Cumberland River in Nashville. And at the same time, there is no place anywhere that the church is more strongly committed to the New Testament order of things than in East Nashville.

At the outset, the interested parties made it clear that the East Nashville school would not be in competition with the David Lipscomb Elementary School. Only three children from East Nashville were in the Lipscomb Elementary School and only four in the high school. The men who were interested in the East Nashville school met once a month in the Morrison Cafeteria for discussions of the matter, and their plans began to firm up. Then a select group of men began to meet on Saturday mornings for breakfast to discuss in depth prospects for the new school.

A board of directors was selected from the group, and a committee was formed to look for available property. Another committee was created to raise funds. The plans materialized and an option was taken on land on Due West Avenue opposite the Nashville Memorial Hospital at the hub of the population in East Nashville. More than twenty-five thousand members of the church live in easy driving distance of the school.

The East Nashville Christian School became a reality in September of 1966 when the school was opened in its beautiful new facilities with an enrollment of 149 pupils in grades one through six. Plans were already in the works to expand the school until all twelve grades were added. William F. Ruhl was appointed presi-

dent of the school. Mrs. Martha Batey Uffelman, one of Nashville's finest school principals, became the principal of the elementary school. A careful selection was made of superior teachers to
staff the school.

H. Philip Sadler became chairman of the board which was
composed of Lewis Gaines, B. C. Goodpasture, Dr. Burton P.
Grant, Ira North, Charles W. Morris, Clifford S. Owens, Dr.
Robert Pettus, W. Doyle Tidwell, Jr., and Dr. Jefferson Penning-
ton. Another group of men serve on the President's Advisory
Board. The group includes: Harold Davis, W. A. Tidwell, Sr.,
Harold Bradley, Dr. George Binkley, Dr. Robert Pilkinton, Dr.
Roy Ezell, Charles Laine, Carney Bell, Don Payne, Boggs Huff
(chairman), George Bivins, Jim Dunn, James Newman, Leo
Greer, Charles Turner, Robert Pennington, and Lester Stone.
This board meets quarterly to study the progress and financing of
the school. The President's Advisory Board represents largely the
community interest in the school and the children who are enrolled
there.

After the school was firmly on its feet, the board members
thought it would be good to name the school in honor of some
great man in the church. And they decided upon the name of B.
C. Goodpasture. Bill Ruhl was asked to go to the Advocate office
to talk with B. C. Goodpasture for his permission to name the
school after him. In this connection, it is needful to say that William F. Ruhl was born in Atlanta, Georgia. His mother and
father attended the Seminole church while Goodpasture preached
there. Goodpasture visited the mother and Bill at the time of his
birth in the hospital. After Goodpasture moved to Nashville, the
Ruhls spent many nights in the Goodpasture home when they were
in the city. Goodpasture recently in commending Ruhl said, "Bill
has enough sense to ask older and more experienced people for
their judgment and advice on matters of serious interest, and he
takes a level and solid stand on things of importance."

William F. Ruhl said that the editor's response was characterized by a humbleness and grateful appreciation for the honor. On
Thursday evening, January 25, 1968, at a dinner celebrating the
new naming of the East Nashville School, B. C. and Freddie were
seated in a position of honor at the head table surrounded by a
great many friends, local and national dignitaries, and several presidents and leaders of the Christian schools and colleges. On that

occasion, the official announcement was made that the school
would henceforth be called the B. C. Goodpasture Christian
School. Freddie Goodpasture takes a great pride in the school,
and portraits of B. C. and Freddie Goodpasture will command a
place of honor in the school. A dinner celebrating the birthday of

B. C. Goodpasture Christian School

Clifford S. Owens, Dr. Burton Grant, Charles W. Morris, W. Tidwell, Jr.,
B. C. Goodpasture, C. A. Scarboro, H. Philip Sadler, W. F. Ruhl, Lewis
Gaines.

B. C. Goodpasture is held each year at the school for a special occasion to honor B. C. and Freddie Goodpasture.

A beautiful and modern high school complex has just been finished. When school opened this year, 690 students were enrolled in grades one through eleven. Grade twelve will be added next year. James Bridgeman, a graduate of Harding College and principal at the DuPont High School for the past three years, is the new principal of the high school. The school will eventually accommodate an enrollment of 750 pupils. The community of East Nashville has a great measure of pride in the B. C. Goodpasture Christian School. The school is flooded with a long waiting list of student applications for nearly all the grades. William F. Ruhl summed up his thinking about his personal friend: "I don't know of any man who has done more for the cause of New Testament Christianity than B. C. Goodpasture." And all who are interested in the school too feel honored that it wears the name of the editor of the *Gospel Advocate*.

Since a last chapter on the life of B. C. Goodpasture must end somewhere at a time when he is as strongly engaged in the work of the church as at any time in his life, the history of the *Gospel Advocate* should be updated. The memory of a large number of the *Advocate* friends will recall that the old Gospel Advocate Company headquarters were pushed over to one side of the McQuiddy Printing Company building located on Seventh Avenue South in Nashville. In November of 1960, the Gospel Advocate Company moved into its own building at 1113 Eighth Avenue South. Then in July of 1966, the McQuiddy Printing Company moved to their modern new plant covering 73,000 square feet, located on Spence Lane just off Interstate 24. In the late part of 1967, the modern facilities for the Gospel Advocate Company were under construction.

The Gospel Advocate Company moved to its new home at 1006 Elm Hill Pike in May of 1968 just a short distance from the McQuiddy Printing Company. The commodious building covers 23,000 square feet with its editorial offices, retail sales, and warehouse facilities. And now after one hundred and sixteen years, the "Old Reliable" is still on course.

Goodpasture serves on the board of directors of the Gospel Advocate Company and the board of directors of the McQuiddy Printing Company. Garnett Landrum, who is the president of the

Freddie Goodpasture, W. F. Ruhl, Annette Ruhl, B. C. Goodpasture, W. Tidwell, Jr.

Ira North, B. C. Goodpasture, Congressman Richard H. Fulton, W. F. Ruhl

McQuiddy Printing Company, said that his only relation to the *Gospel Advocate* is to keep it solvent and meet the printing needs of the Gospel Advocate Company. David McQuiddy, Jr., who is the third generation of the McQuiddy family connected with the *Gospel Advocate,* is the vice-president of the Gospel Advocate Company. He shares the confidence of his grandfather, uncle, and father in B. C. Goodpasture with one difference. David said, "Brother Goodpasture is his own master in managing the *Gospel Advocate* and the company." David McQuiddy, Jr. is fully aware of the worth of B. C. Goodpasture to the *Gospel Advocate* and the worth of the paper to the brotherhood, and he is concerned that the dignity and honor of the *Gospel Advocate's* reputation as the "Old Reliable" will grow undiminished in future years.

An old folk cliche often repeated is that after all we are just human. And so is B. C. Goodpasture who has his own feelings which he pretty well keeps to himself. He has a great capacity for life and personal enjoyment. A man would not be fully human who could not appreciate personal recognition. Sometime back, Goodpasture was talking to Wirt Harlan of Franklin, Tennessee. The name of N. B. Hardeman came up and Goodpasture said, "It has always been a puzzle to me why Brother Hardeman wanted me to preach his funeral. I thought he would want one of his former students or faculty members to preach his funeral."

Wirt Harlan who was also a friend of N. B. Hardeman remarked, "Why didn't you know that Brother Hardeman thought more of you than he did anybody?" Of course, that did not include N. B. Hardeman's family. Wirt Harlan also said, "Brother Hardeman said that you had carried the flag for the church."

Dorsey B. Hardeman, who was the Speaker of the Texas House of Representatives, shared his father's admiration for B. C. Goodpasture. Dorsey B. Hardeman served for a very brief period as Acting Governor of Texas. One thing he did was to appoint B. C. Goodpasture "Honorary Texas Colonel." The document bears the date—the third of December, 1954.

In several respects, the nature of the *Gospel Advocate* is like its editor and could not be otherwise. Goodpasture never allows the paper to be used in a reckless fashion. He is careful to avoid promoting the private ends of any person or cause. Goodpasture, of course, is aware that the *Advocate* has helped some preacher or church in a very special way. He is disappointed that after some

preacher has been helped by the *Advocate* that the church where
he preaches will begin purchasing its hymnals and church supplies
from another publishing house.   The Gospel Advocate Company
does not go begging for business being the largest supplier of religious supplies in the brotherhood.

Goodpasture never forgets his friends, but they sometimes forget him.   The invitations to preach on Sundays and during meetings are endless.   But he especially appreciates being remembered
by the younger preachers that he has encouraged and the number

Batsell Barrett Baxter, B. C. Goodpasture, Freddie Goodpasture, Athens
Clay Pullias, Frances Pullias, David McQuiddy, Jr., Kerri McQuiddy, Malcolm L. Hill, Billie Ruth Hill, Dan Harless, Gus Nichols

B. C. Goodpasture, Freddie Goodpasture, Dr. Burton Grant

Athens Clay Pullias, David L. Mc-
Quiddy, Jr., B. C. Goodpasture

grows annually. This past summer, Goodpasture held a meeting for the Livingston church in Overton County where Stanley McInnery preaches. On Sunday, July 5, Mayor J. R. Needham of Livingston and Judge Elmo Swallows signed official edicts declaring the day to be the official "Goodpasture Day" in Livingston and Overton County.

B. C. Goodpasture has a special love for the membership of the Hillsboro church. His acquaintances now run into the third generation from the grandparents to their grandchildren. Pictures of three of the children who have especially loved B. C. Goodpasture from the time of their birth, along with their parents, appear in this chapter. There are four young men who grew up in the Hillsboro church of whom Goodpasture is especially proud. He baptized each one of them and all are preachers of the gospel. One is his son, J. Cliett Goodpasture, James Lee McDonough, Marlin Connelly, and Prentice Meador.

There is no end of what could be said and told about B. C. Goodpasture. Frank L. Cox has known B. C. Goodpasture for almost as long as he has been editor of the *Advocate*. Frank L. Cox came to Nashville in 1941, to speak on a Sunday in the Central church of Christ. And while he was in the city, he met the new editor of the *Gospel Advocate*. After the passage of several years, Frank L. Cox wrote the following words at a time when the editor received special honors:

> A lot of things have happened since that day. As editor of this powerful paper, you have not drifted with the stream; but you have moved upward against the current. You have been steadfast. I am grateful for you and the *Gospel Advo-*

Mary Alice Shaub   Nancy Elizabeth Hall   Kathy Anita O'Brien

cate. God be gracious unto you, my brother. May he give you strength and a long life in his service.

The pilot of the *Gospel Advocate* continues to stand at the helm. There may be the likes of him around, but he is undiscovered as of now. This book is closed with the comment that surely no church leader has stood longer, in this century, with a clearer understanding of the meaning to restore the patterns of New Testament Christianity than B. C. Goodpasture. We are not persuaded to place B. C. Goodpasture in second position to Alexander Campbell if we judge by the success of a life mission to hold fast to the plea "to speak where the Bible speaks and to remain silent where the Bible is silent."

Index

New Providence meeting, 51-53
New York church, 163-166
Nichols, Gus, 106-107, 117, 172

"Old Guard," 7
"Old Reliable," 121
Otey, W. W., 148-149
Overton County, 19-20

Pack, Frank, 192
Pate, Mrs. Florence, 37
Phillips, Virginia, 135
Pittman, S. P., 79, 81
polemical (*Gospel Advocate*), 130
Poplar Street church, 105, 106
Powell, J. M., 79, 183, 196
Powers, Mary Nelle, 183
Premillennialism, 140-146
Pullias, Athens Clay, 84, 170, 176, 188-189

Rawlings, Oscar, 98
Reeves, Homer Putnam, 163
Restoration Movement, 1-2, 15
"Reverend" Shuler, 97-99
Ricks, Percy, 118
Rocky Mound School, 31-33
Rogers, Reece, 97
Ruhl, William F., 211-214
Ryman Auditorium, 101

Sanderson, L. O., 123, 136
Sadler, Dr. S. Comer, 68
Seminole Avenue church, 106
Sewell, Elisha G., 6-7
Sewell family, 50
Sewell, Jesse P., 153
Shelbyville church, 86
Smith, Barlow, 41, 42
Smith, F. W., 90, 96, 143
Smith, Sarah Ann, 70
Smith, William E., 40, 41
Sommer, Daniel, 131, 178-179
"Sommerism," 178
South Pryor church, 96
Srygley, 7, 8

Standing Stone Park, 25, 33
Stone, Barton W., 1-2
"subscription schools," 44, 45
Sue, Amanda Tippitt, 201
Sue, William Fred, 201

Tant, Yater, 159
Tennessee Orphan Home, 169
Thomas, Leslie G., 185
Thomas, Lydia L., 24
Thomas Uncle Jim, 43
Thompson, Elora Annis, 25, 29
Thompson, Isaiah, 29, 31
Thompson, Jesse Calvin, 29, 31
Thompson, Luther A., 29
Thompson, Martha, 30
Thompson, Tina, 29
Thompson, William, 27
Totty, W. L., 150-151
Tracy City preachers' meeting, 87
Traughber, Sarah Lou, 84
Turner, Rex, 128

"Unity Movement," 146-152
Upton, Tina, 30

Vaughan, J. Roy, 58, 62, 84, 111
Voice of Freedom, 168

Wallace, Foy E., Jr., 120, 145, 153
Wallace, G. K., 130-131
Ward, Christine, 81
Ward, Dr. J. S., 61, 80, 81
Wedding ceremony, 81
West End Avenue church, 93-94
"whirl hole," 42
Willis, W. E., 68
Willow Grove, 50, 64
Wilson, Irvin, 194
Wilson, John, 51
Wilson, Wilma, 51
Wilson, L. R., 132, 171, 185, 189
Witty, Claude F., 127, 147-152
Woods, Guy N., 131, 170, 184
World War II, 128, 135, 146
Wright, Cecil N., 160
Wynn, Emily, 71

92   11941
Goo   Choate, J   E

       The Anchor that holds: a biography
       of Benton Cordell Goodpasture